GUIDEBOOK TRADE DISTRIBUTORS British Isles & General World

CORDEE
3a De Montfort Street, Leicester. LE1 3HD, Great Britain.
Tel: 0116 254 3579   Fax: 0116 247 1176
sales@cordee.co.uk   www.cordee.co.uk

David Atchison-Jones
Chief Editor

Climbing Dyno-mite
Jingo Wobbly – Learning books
First Published in April 2004
By Jingo Wobbly Climbing Books
(An imprint of Vision PC).
Holmwood House, 52 Roxborough Park,
Harrow-on-the-Hill, London. HA1 3AY

Copyright © David Atchison-Jones
Graphics by Botticelli
Image Scanning – Professional Film Company, London
Printing – Fratelli Spada S.p.A, Roma.

ISBN   1-873 665 71-7

Photos:
Front top left: Sunderland climbing wall
(Toby Austin on something hard)
Front top right: The Bowderstone, Lake District, UK
(Caleb Reid on something friggin hard)
Lower left: Chimpanzodrome 7c+, Saussois, France
(Jean Claude André, cranking hard)
Lower right: Via Ferrata, Les Collets, Briançon, France
(Jean Mangharam, waving hello)

Back Cover: Roçadela na Massa 7b, Poios, Portugal
(Jerry Moffat drifing up something easy!)
Back inside flap: Thin Wall Special 4c, Craig Clipiau,
Wales (David Atchison-Jones, solo)
Photo, Gary Morgan

Frontispiece: Bristol Climbing Centre
(Bean Sopwith)

Title page:
Hatfield University Wall
(Joey Bull)

CLIMBING DYNO-MITE

DAVID ATCHISON-JONES

JINGO WOBBLY ▲ EURO-GUIDES

ESSENTIAL INFORMATION

CONSTANTLY UPDATED

LEARNING SERIES

Jingo Wobbly are specialist climbing book producers, making very high quality books that will visually inspire you to visit a vast number of different climbing locations. Our books are always highly illustrative with lots of colour photographs and fun graphics that should appeal to both adults and kids. We have three different series: **Euro guides** are our major information guidebooks, which present an unparalleled level of information in an easy to use format - ideal for planning any climbing day, inside or out, and where to buy equipment. Climbing Dyno-mite is the first book in our **Learning Series**, practical information by climbers who are exceptionally experienced. **Topo guides** are both informative and evocative, in presenting both the precise climbing routes of an area, along with travel and holiday information.

Topo area guidebooks

Sunny holiday climbing

nearest climbing to London

Central France

All of our books are available from good climbing shops.
Trade distribution, UK & World-Cordee, Leicester; D,A,CH-Rother, München; F-Rando diffusion, Paris;
NL-Nilsson & Lamm; CZ,SL,HU-Freytag & Berndt Praha; Japan Pump-climbing, Tokyo
To buy direct online - www.jingowobbly.com - for links to worldwide mail order companies.

HEALTH WARNING
CLIMBING

IS MOVING THE BODY OVER ROCK
YOU CAN INFLICT SERIOUS INJURY TO YOURSELF BY MUSCLE POWER ALONE
THINK BEFORE YOU CLIMB, AND NEVER CLIMB IF YOU ARE INJURED
PHYSICAL INJURIES ARE SELF INFLICTED, DON'T CLIMB IF YOU ARE CONCERNED
HOLDS MAY FALL OFF, SPIN, BREAK, SHATTER; ROCKS AND EVEN THE CLIFF MAY FALL DOWN
CLIMBING IS NOT A SAFE ACTIVITY AND CAN NEVER BE MADE SAFE

The author here accepting the risk at Crookrise, Yorkshire: In climbing, you live purely by your own judgement.

FALLING

IS INCREDIBLY DANGEROUS WITH ENDLESS POSIBILITIES TO DIE
NEVER COPY TECHNIQUES ON THE UNDERSTANDING THAT THEY ARE SAFE
YOU ALWAYS ASSESS YOUR OWN SAFETY AND MAKE YOUR OWN DECISIONS
EVEN THE MOST SENSIBLE ASSESSMENTS CAN BE WRONG AND YOU CAN DIE
ANY TECHNIQUE MAY BE UNSUITABLE AND YOU MAY DIE
YOU ALWAYS CLIMB AT YOUR OWN RISK
YOU PERSONALLY ASSESS ALL EQUIPMENT BEFORE
USING IT - YOU DON'T HAVE TO USE IT
IF YOU DON'T ACCEPT THE RISKS IN CLIMBING - THEN DON'T CLIMB
THIS IS NOT A COMPLETE DESCRIPTION OF ALL THE RISKS INVOLVED IN CLIMBING

! *DYNO-MITE CAUTION* ☠

All the photographs in this book have been taken in real climbing situations, with no known accidents to the climbers at the time. They show techniques chosen at the time by the climbers themselves, for their own personal safety. They do not represent how one should or should not do anything; that can only be ascertained by any person at the actual point and time of climbing.

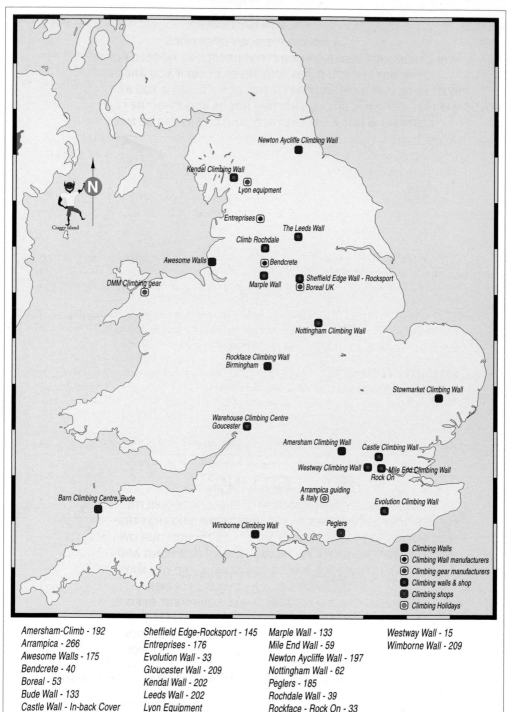

Newton Aycliffe Climbing Wall

Kendal Climbing Wall

Lyon equipment

Entreprises

The Leeds Wall

Climb Rochdale

Awesome Walls

Bendcrete

DMM Climbing gear

Sheffield Edge Wall - Rocksport
Boreal UK

Marple Wall

Craggy Island

Nottingham Climbing Wall

Rockface Climbing Wall
Birmingham

Stowmarket Climbing Wall

Warehouse Climbing Centre
Gloucester

Amersham Climbing Wall

Castle Climbing Wall

Westway Climbing Wall

Mile End Climbing Wall
Rock On

Arrampica guiding
& Italy

Evolution Climbing Wall

Barn Climbing Centre, Bude

Wimborne Climbing Wall

Peglers

Climbing Walls
Climbing Wall manufacturers
Climbing gear manufacturers
Climbing walls & shop
Climbing shops
Climbing Holidays

This book has been designed into sections rather than chapters. It will logically read from start to finish. By spliting the climbing styles into sections, the book can be used again and again, for refining techniques and studying particular areas that you are interested in. We have used edge markers to most of the pages, so that you can qucikly find the different sections; on pages with photos, we have left these clean to give a nicer appeal. Every effort has been made to keep each learning skill to a 2 or 4 page spread, and to contain the relevant photos and diagrams to hand. The flaps at the front and back, enclose useful info such as the index, but are also very handy to use as page markers.

INTRODUCTION - page 8   This illustrates all the different styles of climbing that there are, from indoor walls through to big Himalayan peaks, and emphasises the differences between each style. It also deals with some of the principle risks involved in each style of climbing.

GIVE IT A GO - page 24   If you want to simply give climbing a go, then visit your local indoor climbing wall. We show the type of session that will most probably be offered, what you can learn, and how to get the best from it.

INDOOR BOULDERING - page 34   The simplest form of climbing is bouldering, climbing up a few metres, and then jumping off - usually onto a small protective mat. This physical way of climbing forms the basis for all climbing movement, and it's now an indoor sport in its own right.

OUTDOOR BOULDERING - page 82   To make the transition to outdoor bouldering, we illustrate the techniques that you will have to adapt from your indoor wall to outdoors. Then we help you to get the most out of a visit to an outdoor bouldering area on natural rock.

IMPROVEMENT TECHNIQUES - page 134   Here we examine high standard bouldering techniques, introducing the tips and tricks that you need to master improvement on your bouldering skills. We show top boulderers in action, illustrating all the special toe holds, knee bars etc., The photos also illustrate many of the top European bouldering venues.

INDOOR SPORT CLIMBING - page 172   This section deals with the introduction of equipment, such as ropes and harnesses. Because the reader has learnt to actually climb on rock in the bouldering section, we can concentrate directly on climbing with equipment, and deal with special skills necessary, such as lead falling off the climbing wall in different situations.

OUTDOOR SPORT CLIMBING - page 222   To go from an indoor climbing wall to an outdoor cliff is a big step, and you need to learn a lot more about rope techniques, and how to recognise and evaluate outdoor dangers. We illustrate a lot of development skills for this transition.

MULTI-PITCH SPORT CLIMBING - page 264   This section introduces the bigger cliffs and concepts. It covers the pure sport climbing techniques used in multi-pitch climbing and abseiling.

VIA FERRATA - page 278   This is really an extra section that stands on its own. It covers the alpine climbing technique, where you have permanent steel cables to hold, and clip into for security.

WHERE TO GO - page 284   We include many of the climbing walls in Britain; also a European map to show good beginners areas, alongside the very famous bouldering and climbing spots.

INDEX - page 289 (Inside back cover)   Key words to quickly locate points and topics.

INTRODUCTION | GIVE-IT-A-GO | IND/BOULDERING | OUT/BOULDERING | IMPROVEMENT | IND/OOR SPORT | OUTDOOR SPORT | MULTI-PITCH | VIA FERRATA | WHERE TO GO | INDEX

INTRODUCTION | GIVE-IT-A-GO | IND/BOULDERING | OUT/BOULDERING | IMPROVEMENT | INDOOR SPORT | OUTDOOR SPORT | MULTI-PITCH | VIA FERRATA | WHERE TO GO | INDEX

This is an introduction to all the different types of climbing that there are generally out there, and will illustrate that there's more to climbing than you may think. Sure, you've picked up this book indicating your interest, you may have a friend who has climbed on an indoor wall and recommended you try it out, or maybe you're just intrigued to find out why all the mountains in Switzerland are made of triangular chocolate like Toblerone! Climbing can be anything from simple and easy tree clambering, up to scaling the north face of Mt. Everest in a winter blizzard. It can be fun, explorative, energetic, and happy. It can also be packed full of terror, anguish, pain, danger; and on a bad day - death. What makes it a highly attractive activity, is that it's the same as baking your own personal cake; it can be as simple and straightforward as you want, or it can be hideously fiendish with tremendous complications.

To choose a cake that is just right for you, find all the ingredients available, and generally how they go together. Climbing is subdivided into many different categories apart from indoors and outdoors. You can begin with pure rock climbing which this book covers; separately there is mountain climbing, and eventually you get to ice climbing on the larger, permanently snow covered mountains around the world. Even to do any sort of climbing competently, you need a good general level knowledge of pure rock climbing. When you combine rock climbing with getting up an actual mountain, you get into considerably more dangerous territory. As a beginner, you need to understand all the different climbing styles that there are, so you can understand the associated risks. We give each style of climbing, a numbered value from our risk-insanity scale, which runs from 1-12. (see full explanation on pages 22-23).

INDOOR CLIMBING   [RISK-1/3]

You most probably think that indoor climbing walls are purely a training ground for going onto bigger and better things outside. Well they are. But we now consider 'indoor climbing' to be a fully blown style in its own right. This is due to the sheer size and design of some modern indoor climbing walls, along with the huge amount of people who climb inside for the majority of their climbing time. Certainly in countries like Holland there is no option but to climb on indoor walls. For England, and especially Wales, the rain and inclement weather makes climbing outside in winter completely impractical. There are a huge number of different indoor wall designs that have developed over the past 30 years. Wall designers began by adapting existing walls in chipping out bricks and replacing them with natural stone for handholds and footholds. As popularity grew, architects started to integrate walls of planned sports centres with this design. The major breakthrough came in the early 80's when a French company called Entreprises developed a system of making small handholds from resin, mixed with sand. These were drilled with a 10mm hole so they could be attached with a bolt to

At Wirksworth wall, the bouldering section is a lovely cave of artificial rock, looking and feeling like real rock; plus a good selection of bolt-on plastic holds. Climber; Lucy

Bouldering at Rocher Fin, Fontainebleau, France; Jamie Ogilvie

a wall with a threaded fixing. These holds became known as plastic bolt-ons, and revolutionised the world of indoor climbing forever. It meant that you could take any shaped hold, and place it in any position you wanted to on a wall with these standard mountings. You could for the first time, actually invent a climbing route, and then tailor it exactly to your requirements, simply in minutes. Entreprises also built on this to design, wonderful forms and shapes of walls; you not only had designer routes, but walls that emulated rockfaces. Today there are lots of companies making superb walls, each with their own character and style, but all using the bolt-on technology. Some walls are hydraulically controlled, changing the overall angle of the rockface from a beginners doddle, to an experts nightmare at the touch of a button - such is technology. The ability to change and design climbs, gives centres the chance to run competitions and festivals for everyone. It also allows that wall to adjust the level of climbing difficulty to suit any level of climbers. Ropes can be attached to the top of the wall to give excellent security to the climbers, and safety clipping points can be incorporated in the wall, wherever the designers want to. Indoor climbing will remain popular, because it can be designed to suit a wide variety of requirements.

BOULDERING [RISK-4]

Nothing is simpler than bouldering. You first find a boulder the height of yourself and climb up onto it, and hey presto – you are a boulderer. Welcome to the club and feel proud to wear the badge. After a seaside holiday of skipping around the rocks, we are all boulderers. To some people, even the actual classification of climbing miserable little lumps is ridiculous. The perfect boulder is probably about the size of a small minibus. Each side can be climbed independently, and the different sides will always have different angles and different natural holds. On one boulder alone, you can have 10 different ways of climbing up it; the middle of the face, just left, just right, just using the corner edge, even going round the whole block without touching the top. Immediately you can see, that a whole series of little climbing problems have been initiated. Some sides of boulders are simply too flat, but this is far rarer than you might think.

What makes bouldering attractive, is that you can climb with the minimum of fuss. Indoor climbing walls have excellent boulder sized surfaces, and usually with essential soft crash padding at the bottom. They're just like a kids bouncy play area.

INTRODUCTION

GIVE-IT-A-GO

IND/BOULDERING

OUT/BOULDERING

IMPROVEMENT

INDOOR SPORT

OUTDOOR SPORT

MULTI-PITCH

VIA FERRATA

WHERE TO GO

INDEX

INTRODUCTION

GIVE-IT-A-GO

IND/BOULDERING

OUT/BOULDERING

IMPROVEMENT

INDOOR SPORT

OUTDOOR SPORT

MULTI-PITCH

VIA FERRATA

WHERE TO GO

INDEX

Outside it's different. Falling from only a few feet can be very hazardous, especially if there's a tree root sticking up, or a stray ankle-twisting rock. Sensible boulderers climb with a friend (spotter), who can support their body, if they fall off. Also they use portable little crash pads to cover rocky stones, which also protects the ground from erosion when they fall off repeatedly. But it's the dynamics, which is the large attraction to bouldering. You can leap dynamically from the ground to grab a handhold. If you fail, you shouldn't be in danger. You often expend all the energy in your whole body, on one single climbing move. Bouldering is the shortest and most compact form of climbing. It is where you can climb completely to your physical limit in a few feet. A very real hazard in bouldering is pushing your body too hard, wrenching the muscles and tendons in your arms and fingers. Bouldering though is not just about pure power; there is grace too. Many a boulder can be climbed by delicate means, balancing on tiptoes whilst your fingertips crimp the tiniest of holds to gain the top. It is a very popular form of climbing today, and attracts a huge following worldwide. Climbers will even travel thousands of miles to go and try their skill on a small, little boulder. It's very addictive – beware.

SPORT CLIMBING [RISK-5]

Sport climbing outdoors, generally follows the same rope and climbing techniques as for indoor sport climbing, it's climbing by using only the natural holds on the rock. You climb from the ground up, linking your climbing rope, through permanent attachment points (bolts), on the rockface. If you fall off at any time, you will however take a short fall. You are like a dog on a lead; if you are one metre above a bolt, you will fall to one metre below the bolt. Sounds risky eh! How strong are the ropes! Well, most top sport climbers fall off many, many times each day and don't hurt themselves. The potential to hurt yourself is there for sure, falling off from 30 feet up may to kill you if things go wrong. It's not a sport where you even think of making a mistake with your climbing equipment. You must go on a course to learn how to use your ropes properly, and learn about buying the correct climbing equipment for the job. The attraction is that you can climb to your physical limit, because it's a lot longer that bouldering, it is more about endurance than power. On steep, overhanging climbs, you often climb until you drop off.

High-ball at Baía de Mexilhoeiro, Cascais, Portugal; Mário Albuquerque

Nice, middle grade level - 5a sport climbing at Loubiere, Monte Carlo, France; Laurence Ricco

INTRODUCTION

GIVE-IT-A-GO

IND/BOULDERING

OUT/BOULDERING

IMPROVEMENT

INDOOR SPORT

OUTDOOR SPORT

MULTI-PITCH

VIA FERRATA

WHERE TO GO

INDEX

On an indoor wall, a lot of effort usually goes into making climbing low-risk. The anchor points, called bolts, are usually set at 1 metre intervals, and are meant to be checked and maintained. The wall management will also insist that you use every bolt, which is to keep everything nice and controlled. If you fall off, you may bang a knee or elbow, it's a bit rough on the surface of the wall. Most people opt to voluntarily fall off when they are getting tired, usually just after they pass a bolt and therefore don't fall any distance at all. Indoors - it is something you can make quite comfortable and acceptable.

On an outside cliff, it is a lot more serious. There are no regulations or rules for putting bolts into a cliff. You rely completely, from your own visual inspection of the bolts. It's usually good enough since most bolts are usually very good or very bad, but you do rely on personal judgement for which experience is essential. Also the distance between bolts is far bigger, up to 5 metres or more sometimes. That can mean a fall of double the distance – 10 metres. That is a big fall, and if you hit anything, you are in serious trouble. However, the hard parts of most climbs are usually peppered in bolts, and it is the easy parts where there are no

bolts. When you get to the top of a climb, 10-40 metres-ish, you clip your rope through a ring and lower back down to the ground. A sport climbing cliff may be a lot bigger, but usually only has these bolted, short 20-40 metre climbs at its base.

MULIT-PITCH SPORT [RISK-6]

Instead of lowering off from the top of your typical 30-metre sport climb, you decide to continue upwards. Each section of a climb is called a pitch, and is around half a rope length (ropes are typically 50-80m). Now life starts to get a lot more serious. You need a climbing partner to climb up and join you, so you both need to be of the standard required for the climb. Most sport climbs stop, bang in the middle of a blank piece of rock. Then you have to hang in your harness, sometimes from only a 'single bolt;' something which you have to reliably judge on your own. Additionally, if anything were to fall down the cliff you, might not be able to move out of the way! There is no room for error. A multi pitch climb can have lots of pitches, so after 3 or 4, you could easily be 120 metres up. Any accident at this height is a major problem. To abseil back down from this height would take up to 30

High mountain sport climbing at Crépe de Oucèra, Dolomites, Italy; Jingo

DÉMON 7a+, Verdon Gorge, France; Dyno-mite

INTRODUCTION

GIVE-IT-A-GO

IND/BOULDERING

OUT/BOULDERING

IMPROVEMENT

INDOOR SPORT

OUTDOOR SPORT

MULTI-PITCH

VIA FERRATA

WHERE TO GO

INDEX

mins for you both. In that time, bad weather can come in, rain, or even lightning. A lot of multi-pitch climbing takes place in giant river gorges. Here you abseil in from the top, and then climb back out – hoping that you are good enough. I can promise you, that the sense of freedom in a wild 1000 metre gorge is incredible, but the risk is now definitely cranked up a full notch.

VIA FERRATA   [RISK-4/6]

This is climbing – a la cheating, on a grand scale. Wars have often been fought in the Alps, and getting troops around the mountains was never going to be easy – just try climbing in boots, rucksack, and carrying a rifle. Troops could however, navigate the mountains quickly and efficiently if there were steel cables attached to the rock, and the steep bits had chunky ladders in place. Between the two world wars, everyone else realised that this was a great fun day out, and a easy way to climb a big mountain without carrying

ropes etc. Over the past 30 years there has been a great development of Via Ferrata routes all across the Alps. Additionally, because of the expansion of skiing, there is now an excess capacity of mountain guides who have little to do in the summer. The solution has been to create a whole load of new Via Ferrata climbs - for general public consumption. In Italy and Austria meanwhile, some of the old routes have been improved and go through incredible and startling scenery. To any accomplished climber, the climbing is simple. You also have the safety protection of wearing a harness, and are attached into a special safety device, which in turn clips onto the metal safety wires. The dangers here are more objective, high mountain risks. A climb may be a good 1000 metres long and this commits you to a whole day on a high 3000m mountain. Even in June the routes are often still covered in ice; whilst in August, a warm day will bring huge lightning storms in the afternoon, which are incredibly lethal. A great challenge in good weather, but it can easily be a lot more dangerous than sport climbing.

Punta Anna-Giuseppe Oliveri Via Ferrata, Tofana Mezzo, Dolomites; Wobbly

INTRODUCTION

GIVE-IT-A-GO

IND/BOULDERING

OUT/BOULDERING

IMPROVEMENT

INDOOR SPORT

OUTDOOR SPORT

MULTI-PITCH

VIA FERRATA

WHERE TO GO

INDEX

Trad climbing in Yorkshire. Low gritstone outcrops are particularly suited to mechanical devices - cam protection, where the climber can easily assess the obvious risks involved with each climb, from the ground.

TRAD CLIMBING   [RISK-7]

This is a very quirky style of climbing, and as you may well guess, is very much a British thing. You certainly don't find this style anywhere else in Europe. Trad is short for Traditional, and describes the way the climbing style has evolved. You cannot describe it, because it is not exact. It's a style that is linked directly to historical development, and might change next year anyway. If you think of it as an ideological and particularly British way of climbing, you'll get the drift. The idea came from Stone Age climbing in Britain in the 50's, where you were allowed a chunky hammer, to bash steel pegs into the rock when you came across a hard bit. Then came the European industrial revolution with the drill; sorry, tut, tut – not allowed in Britain; we only use chunky hammers. The principle being, you could drill a bolt anywhere – not cricket: We in Blighty, only hammered pegs into hairline cracks,

that even an ant couldn't crawl into; sense – none really! During the next 30 years, things moved on and engineering came to the rescue. Cunning invention produced some amazing hand-sized, spring-loaded little expanding devices (cams). These you could pop into little crevices in the rock, thereby reducing the hammers and pegs. Even better, they come out too and the following climber collects them. Do they hold if you fall off? – sometimes yes, and sometimes no. Wow - sounds a dodgy game: you place them and they 'just might hold,' also the rock may be blank, so you have no option but to go on without them. It is a highly dangerous game. Suicidally surprising, it is a very popular style in some parts of Britain and the USA. This is mainly on the lower grade climbs where there is plenty of opportunity to place the cams in the crack systems, and where carrying a ton of equipment with you is not going to prevent you from getting up the climb. In most other European countries, there is a popular style called 'Classic.' It is similar, but climbers only carry a few cams for the easier sections; when they get to a hard move or reach the top of a pitch, there's generally a bolt.

BIG WALL CLIMBING   [RISK-8]

Multi-pitch sport climbing is all very well if you are a good climber, and the cliff is a comfortable size; usually around 6-9 pitches long. One hour per pitch is about right for any self respecting climber. There are some walls however that are 'BIG.' Take the Yosemite Valley in California, here there are 3000 ft. cliffs. It takes 3-10 days to climb some of these. Also the granite is often so smooth, that there really isn't anything to get a grip of. The climbs are achieved, by drilling holes for bolts, and bashing metal into every possible crevice. By directly pulling on the equipment in place, you get up the rock. Some of this 'aid' climbing is outrageous as well. We can all happily hang off a 10mm bolt, but I've seen ¼ inch tiny pins used in the desert canyons of Arizona and Utah – they only penetrate ½ inch into soft sandstone. If one pops out, you can literally unzip the whole pitch, falling 300 ft. You also have to carry all your food, hammocks, water and waste during the whole climb. It's pure hardship and suffering, but you get to live in a vertical and crazy world for a week.

Climbers with all the paraphernalia of big wall-aid climbing; El Capitan, Yosemite, U.S.A; Andy Meyers, Pete Cork (Photo Dave Johnson)

INTRODUCTION | GIVE-IT-A-GO | IND/BOULDERING | OUT/BOULDERING | IMPROVEMENT | INDOOR SPORT | OUTDOOR SPORT | MULTI-PITCH | VIA FERRATA | WHERE TO GO | INDEX

ALPINE CLIMBING   [RISK-9/10]

Climbing in the Alps comes in a huge array of forms, from plodding up a snow trail to the top of Mont Blanc, to clawing up the loose rock and ice on the north face of the Eiger. The sheer scale now becomes the principle difficulty. Big alpine peaks are all around 4000 metres and are permanently covered with snow and ice. They are too high to be practically climbed in a single day from the valley floor. There are literally thousands of high mountain huts in the Alps, which are professionally run, basic climbing lodges. You can leave the low valley in the morning or early afternoon, and walk or climb up to their high vantage point of around 2500m. They sell beer and cook meals, and provide a mattress and blankets to sleep on. Overnight, the temperature plunges to the desperately cold, big negative numbers. You then rise at a ridiculously early time in the morning, and start climbing in the dark with ice axes and crampons, across glaciers covered in deep crevasses. The sun then comes out, melting the snow ice and rocks high up. These then cascade down the mountain without warning on top of you. You may even get an avalanche if you are lucky. Of course you need to get up and down the mountain before the afternoon, with killer thunder and lightning storms rolling in. Photographs alone, show why the best days in the Alps are known as 'The Great Days.' You don't want to be involved in a bad day, for sure.

VERTICAL ICE   [RISK-10]

If climbing a big snow peak doesn't drain your adrenaline channels enough, then have a go at climbing vertical frozen waterfalls. Here you turn yourself into a crazed terminator animal, by attaching spikes to your feet, and transforming your hands into cutting and hammering implements. It's certainly got its attractions, because you end up in really spectacular scenery. It does have some huge, inherent risks though. The ice you climb is never totally permanent, so you have to judge if it is going to stay up during your climb for a start. The crampons on your feet, only just claw into the ice, and you need great skill to balance on tiptoes up the vertical ice. Using the ice axes to grip and cut, is another highly skilled operation, especially when you examine the consequences of a mistake. You can put metal screws in the ice to protect you, should you fall off; but again this relies on the solid consistency of the ice. Then there is the miserably cold temperature you are operating in, minus 10 to –40 degrees. It is big on impact, and can be very scary and dangerous. If you then combine this with a giant north face on a mountain, such as the Eiger or the Matterhorn, you have all of the mountain dangers piled on top. A highly serious pastime!

EXPEDITIONS [RISK-11/12]

Even in the Alps, the mountains are generally accessible. However, there are a lot of high mountains around the world that are inaccessible and necessitate an expedition to reach, and then scale them. This sort of climbing can often mean lengthy planning, and the need to get permissions to climb in certain countries or areas. I've even had friends kidnapped in the Himalayas, getting mixed up in civil wars etc. You may think that the climbing then becomes the easy bit. Unfortunately not; no matter how difficult the approach to a climb may be, you still are left facing the objective dangers of the greater ranges. The sheer time you spend on a mountain in an isolated position is longer, and leaves you crucially exposed to bad storms and problems 'when' things don't go according to plan. Because the whole aspect of climbing in these areas is so demanding, very few climbers even think of attempting anything other than very simple technical climbing. The only time this happens, is when a massively talented and skilled climber visits an area, the weather is good, and they grab a very quick and difficult ascent. The major challenge of a big peak is more logistical, stamina over several weeks, coping with the cold, low level of oxygen, disagreeable and awful food, and the general boredom of a big plod.

Denali summit, 6194 metres, Alaska; David Landman, Ray Eckerman (Photo Sandy Ogilvie)

Water ice grade 6, Pont Rouge, Quebec, Canada; Mark Braithwaithe (Photo Sandy Ogilvie)

INTRODUCTION

GIVE-IT-A-GO

IND/BOULDERING

OUT/BOULDERING

IMPROVEMENT

INDOOR SPORT

OUTDOOR SPORT

MULTI-PITCH

VIA FERRATA

WHERE TO GO

INDEX

DANGER, SAFETY and CLIMBING NOUS

There are a couple of words that I try not to use in climbing, those are safe and safety. The reason is very simple, there is no such thing as safe climbing – not even remotely. If you use the word safe, you imply to others around you, that there is this 'safe karma' in existence, a safe state of affairs - chosen of not. In climbing there is always danger, you can either fall off, or something can fall onto you. I certainly approach climbing, believing that you are never in a safe position. Even when I am belayed securely to the rock, I simply say belay on, or good belay - never safe, it's psychological. It gives you that necessary edge to always keep thinking about what is going on around you. Certainly there is always danger around, but that does not mean you are going to die, far from it. I have been climbing for over 30 years, and looked consistently at danger in the eye for 30 years. By knowing that I have never been safe, and appreciating danger for every second of those years, I have always keep that edge of awareness, which is fundamentally essential.

If you want a single phrase, to sum up the techniques that you use to stay alive whilst climbing, then you are well off with CLIMBING NOUS. The word nous itself means common intelligence, which is a pretty good starter for an accident free, climbing life. Climbing nous alone would leave you saying 'I'm not going up there without a bloody rope – not likely.' And of course, you live a lot longer when you are cautious. But the question you should ask; is where do you pick up, all that good climbing nous?

We get accustomed to learning sport at school in a set environment, like a football pitch or tennis court with set rules and regulations to follow, and for the most part – everyone plays by the same rules. In climbing, you strike out into the wild, vertical environment. There is no pitch, no boundary lines, no 'safe' areas. At times, whole cliffs can collapse without warning. Sometimes you want to be attached to the cliff; and at other times, you certainly don't want to be attached. This book is well packed with good climbing nous of course, but you must understand, that any tips or tricks to keep you alive in one situation, might kill you in another. There are no 'safe' procedures.

MINIMISING RISK

Climbing nous says, I accept that it is highly dangerous, but at least let's minimise the risk. This is the backbone to common sense in climbing. You always look to minimise the risk. The first part of good nous, is to read and study as much as you can about climbing; all the different techniques of movement, ropework, abseiling, and even geology. The more you know, then the better your information level will be to assess ways of minimising risks during climbing. The less you know, the fewer options you have for choosing the lowest level of risk. It makes pure common sense to be well read and educated, your life does depend on it.

INSTRUCTION

You can read and study until you are blue in the face, but the urge to get your hands on some equipment and grapple with the rock, is a strong force that will be luring you towards danger all the time. You are exceptionally well advised to find a climbing instructor. There are a few important points to look for. They need great knowledge, and must have an encouraging ability to communicate. But above all, they need a third quality that not all teachers for less dangerous subjects need; and that is extensive basic experience. You should choose your instructor on these qualities. There are of course, different certificates and qualifications that instructors can obtain. This whole certification world is confusing, since there are different levels, for different types of climbing; none of which are familiar or mean anything to you as a beginner. I would recommend that you first find a properly managed climbing wall with a cross section of different courses. As a beginner, you also should have read enough, to have enough climbing nous, to quickly assess how experienced your instructor is. If you are at all unhappy with their level of experience, or any other issue, then do not continue with them, it's your life at risk. Your instructor is your guardian. A book cannot read your eyes, or understand your body movements; an instructor can pick up very easily when you don't understand something correctly. A book cannot see if you have tied your harness incorrectly, a book cannot shout to warn you of something falling from above. Personal instruction however, doesn't stop at the end of your beginners course, intermediates can learn tremendously about techniques and cute skills (over months instead of years). Even world standard climbers sometimes can benefit from teaching.

EQUIPMENT

When you buy most specialist climbing equipment it often comes with a European governing body stamp, to say it has certain EEC standards. There are a lot of climbing companies that work to agreed set of standards and regulations, which are all for the "health and safety" of a climber. It takes a huge amount of technical knowledge to understand any of these, and as technology improves, the standards go up. Something you bought 10 years ago, might not even get a safety stamp today. The most important issue that many climbers forget, is to simply visually check everything for yourself. There may be one chance in a trillion billion, that you have ended up with an unintended piece of equipment. If it fails, you die. You can't sue anyone from a coffin. Check, check, check, check, check. Even if it's brand new.

LIABILITIES

It is pretty obvious in climbing, that whenever your feet leave the ground you are liable and responsible for your own safety. Nearly all climbing walls you will visit, will require that you sign a disclaimer to say this, in case you or your dependents try to blame them for an accident in court. But responsibility and liability go further than that. What happens if you fall off, but land on an innocent walker below and cause them harm? Who is then at fault? There are a wide range of insurance companies that offer both personal, and or third party liability; with emergency medical, personal and effects, as an extra add on.

When you actually start climbing and buying your own equipment such as a rope, you effectively have become a climber. Things to check are the small print on any life insurance or health insurance policies you may have. I would definitely get notification in writing from companies that they have it on record that you go rock climbing.

If you are climbing in the UK and have an accident, you are likely to be rescued by local volunteers or the RAF. This is usually cost-free, so insurance is not necessary. It is very different in the rest of Europe. There, climbing and mountains are taken very seriously. If you have an accident, the local rescue will almost always call in a helicopter to get you off the cliff to the road, then another helicopter to take you instantly to the best hospital. You need a comprehensive insurance policy. Our Climber's Handbook includes an up to date list of insurance companies. Many will quote with a wide variety of different insurance schemes, some for plain rock climbing, others for European rescue etc.

There are a lot of guidelines directed at responsibility, these are the main four;

1). THE INDIVIDUAL CLIMBER IS RESPONSIBLE FOR THEIR OWN SECURITY.
2). THEY MUST PERSONALLY CHECK ALL SAFETY CONDITIONS WHEREVER THEY CLIMB, EITHER BY VISUAL OBSERVATION, OR BY MEANS OF DOCUMENTATION OR INFORMATION BY OTHER CLIMBERS, WHOSE RELIABILITY THEY MUST PERSONALLY ASSESS.
3). THEY MUST BE ABLE TO RECOGNISE UNRELIABLE OR INAPPROPRIATE EQUIPMENT.
4). THEY MUST EVALUATE THE RISKS, AND DECIDE THEMSELVES TO WITHDRAW IF NECESSARY.

Point 1 is a self-statement . The second point says you should be aware of 'safety conditions', but doesn't say you have to follow the conditions if they clash with your own thinking. Point 3 makes the user responsible for using any bolts or insitu equipment in place. Point 4 re-enforces point 3, and firmly puts all judgement in the climbers court.

Some extra CLIMBING NOUS that I use :-

THE LEADER IS RESPONSIBLE AT ALL TIMES FOR THEMSELVES, do not rely on your belayer to make decisions or judgements for you,
ALWAYS KEEP A SCREWGATE KARABINER ON BOTH ENDS OF THE ROPE IN THE ROPE BAG.
ALWAYS REMAIN TIED INTO THE SYSTEM WHEN THREADING A TOP BELAY.
NO ONE IS IMMUNE FROM MAKING MISTAKES;
NEVER STOP CHECKING EVERYTHING FOR YOURSELF AND THOSE AROUND YOU.

INTRODUCTION
GIVE-IT-A-GO
IND/BOULDERING
OUT/BOULDERING
IMPROVEMENT
INDOOR SPORT
OUTDOOR SPORT
MULTI-PITCH
VIA FERRATA
WHERE TO GO
INDEX

CLIMBER'S INSANITY SCALE

	CLIMBING ACTIVITY	RISK INVOLVEMENT	COMPARISON
1	*Induction day at an indoor climbing wall*	*Instructor supervised climbing at a well organised wall*	*1st lesson in gymnastics*
2	*Indoor bouldering*	*A climbing wall with deep and soft crash pads*	*Judo*
3	*Indoor Sport climbing Outdoor top rope climbing*	*Climbing to a controlled height with reliable safety facilities*	*Sailing*
4	*Outdoor bouldering*	*Climbing and assessing as you go on unknown rock*	*Horse riding*
5	*Outdoor single pitch sport routes - Via Ferrata*	*Bolt equipped climbing, with in-situ climbing equipment*	*Horse jumping*
6	*Outdoor multi pitch sport routes*	*Big routes in European river gorges - bolt equipped*	*Round the world Yachting*
7	*Traditional - classic style climbing with protection*	*Free climbing but placing your own protection on lead*	*Motorbike racing*
8	*Traditional climbing on loose rock*	*Climbing where even the protection you place can fail*	*Isle of Man TT racing*
9	*Alpine rock climbing*	*Trad-climbing, at high altitude and 7 hours plus on a route*	*Cave diving*
10	*Alpine North Faces*	*Very steep and committing rock and ice climbing*	*Solo round the world yachting*
11	*Himalayan glaciers and remote mountain rangers*	*Navigating giant glaciers and seracs, severe storms, altitude*	*Rowing the Atlantic*
12	*8000 metre peaks*	*Entering the oxygen free - death zone*	*Swimming outside the shark netting*
13	*8000 metre peaks with no experience!!!!!*	*Killing other climbers in rescue attempts*	*Trying to outswim a shark*

This Jingo Wobbly scale of climbing Insanity, is intended to illustrate the level of objective danger that is associated with each different discipline of climbing. Inexperience or foolhardiness at any level - is the equivalent of grade 13; but good knowledge and training, should make the lower levels more interesting and appealing to the majority of beginners. (This book covers levels 1-6)

CASUALTY PROBABILITIES

1 *Climbing for the first time is going to be tough on the fingers and hands. Glossy fingernails can take a bashing, knuckles can get bruised. You may twist your ankle stepping off the traversing wall. Mostly you are likely to suffer sore arms and stomach the day after.*

2 *Indoor bouldering is a real workout, so really expect a bruising the day or two after. Jumping down a lot onto crash matting is soft, but thumpy. The biggest comedy is inhaling the chalk dust on the soft mats (light magnesium carbonate) - a well known laxative! No curries!*

3 *Indoor sport climbing involves falling off, and accelerating over 2-3 metres. You should be OK, but can really bash your knees & body. Taking a pendulum in a fall is nasty too; as in sailing, where a swishing boom can devastate your head, the potential danger is there.*

4 *Outdoor bouldering can be really safe, but torn muscles are a big hazard. You can easily try some highball problems up to 7 metres high, if you fall off this, you can very easily kill yourself. With a good spotter and a portable crash pad, the rating drops to level 3.*

5 *Outdoor sport routes have bolts up to 4 metres apart, so you could fall 8 metres plus. Also the bolting is not designed for a fall anywhere, just usually on the hard moves. Certainly falling off can be fatal if you get it wrong. With caution, you can avoid most danger points*

6 *Multi pitch sports routes are quite wild, and are often equipped by climbers seeking a big adrenalin rush. Monster falls are possible, and inherent dangers are ever present. You can abseil off the end of the rope into a 1000m gorge; and belays are untested for years!*

7 *Trad climbing is risky; your own gear can easily fail in the event of a good fall - hence death! Falling off period - is not an option. Your gear can protect you but should not be relied upon. Easier angled climbs are hazardous since you are very likely to bash yourself in a fall.*

8 *Trad on loose rock is really serious. Being lightweight is a positive advantage. A fall from anywhere above halfway up the climb will result in certain death, maybe to both climbers.*

9 *Here the time above 2000 metres involves getting struck by lightning, routes are very committing and getting hit by loose falling rock adds to new risks outside your control.*

10 *Alpine N.F. Incredibly serious; getting struck by avalanches, violent storms can easily entomb you on the face - not being able to move; waiting only to freeze to death!*

11 *Himalayan glaciers move very quickly and collapse without warning - risky and lethal. The climbing seasons are brief, with dangerously short weather windows allowing climbing.*

12 *Above 8000 metres there is not enough oxygen to live, a lethal addition. Storms can last for several weeks, dying options are freezing, exhaustion, dehydration, lack of oxygen.*

13 *If the weather changes and you're not very experienced - you're dead - simple.*

INTRODUCTION

GIVE-IT-A-GO

IND/BOULDERING

OUT/BOULDERING

IMPROVEMENT

INDOOR SPORT

OUTDOOR SPORT

MULTI-PITCH

VIA FERRATA

WHERE TO GO

INDEX

Have you ever thought about going climbing? Maybe, but do you need to join a club, is it expensive, I don't know any climbers etc. Well it's easy, cheap and no hassle. Go to your local climbing wall and ask to go on a give-it-a-go session. This will typically be 1-2 hours on the indoor climbing wall, which is supervised completely by a trained climbing instructor, and run very much as a taster session where you experience! - rather than learn anything. A lot of indoor walls include climbing as a special event like a birthday party for kids, so that they can have a go and see what being up high is like. It's fun to do all sorts of clambering on an indoor wall, and a lot more cool than endless hours of Maths and Biology homework. Adults can also flop out, cast off that weekday grime or stiffened suit, and turn up to grapple with brightly coloured plastic holds that soon explode your forearms. Sure enough, a give-it-a-go session at an indoor wall is fun, thrilling and an excellent way to find out if climbing is something that is either enticing – or simply too terrifying for words.

The sensible part of the session is that you don't have to buy any equipment or sink huge sums of money in expensive joining fees and annual subscriptions. Climbing can be scary and it's not everyone's cup of tea, climbing centres realise this and offer the solution of giving them a taste in a nice, safe environment. The whole idea is to have a go and see what you get out of it. Nobody at the wall is going to make an idiot of you, climbing is too dangerous for that. You listen to the instructors very carefully, they are there to look after you and try their hardest to give you a good day out and help you edge softly into the world of climbing. To go onto any indoor wall you don't need any specific type of equipment or clothing, but there are a few tips that are very useful to know about if you are a first timer. Here goes – you might have to reach out quite wide with the feet, so shorts or tracksters are best. Trainers are fine to grip the beginner's footholds, but a tip is to use tight fitting ones, instead of loose fitting. To grip the wall with your hands, you are best off with your skin touching

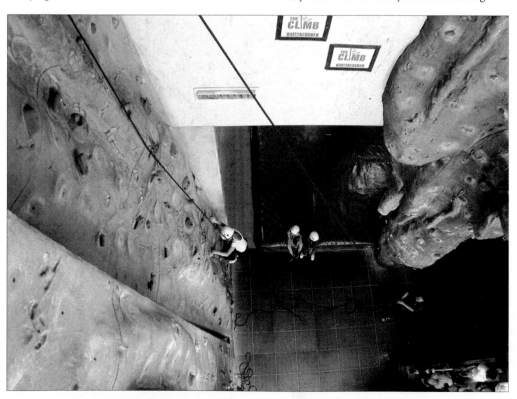

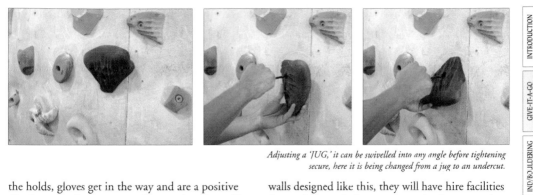

Adjusting a 'JUG,' it can be swivelled into any angle before tightening secure, here it is being changed from a jug to an undercut.

the holds, gloves get in the way and are a positive disadvantage. A warm sweatshirt can be taken off when you climb, but it keeps you snug if you are waiting for your go on a climb. You are also likely to damage any rings or watches, since your hands and wrists get to ferociously grapple the rock. Long hair gets in the way looking down at footholds – use a hairband.

You could never design a give-it-a-go session for every indoor wall in the land, mainly because every climbing wall is different. Some are very high, some are overhanging, some do not have coloured plastic, bolt on-removable holds (so the routes cannot be made easy), and others resemble bat caves where you have to be an orangutang to even get off the ground. Therefore it is impossible to say what you are likely to find on your first session, but if we explain a typical day at a medium-sized climbing wall, it will give a good idea of what to expect, and what to look out for. The ideal walls for beginners, have areas with coloured plastic holds that are only just vertical. Because these type of walls are covered in a matrix of threaded holes, the chunkier plastic holds can be fixed intentionally to give enjoyable, beginners-standard climbing. The level of difficulty is determined by the person who attached the holds on the wall – called a route setter. It also depends on how 'mean and nasty' they were feeling on the day that they designed the route. One thing is for sure though, is that route setters are usually good climbers, and will know every type of move that a beginner is capable of, and are not planning to stitch you up. Note; some introduction walls do not have enough threaded holes for chunky plastic footholds, so you will benefit tremendously by using specialist rock shoes to grip the pebbly surface. Usually at

walls designed like this, they will have hire facilities for specialist rock shoes on your give-it-a-go session. More in section-1 indoor bouldering about shoes."

Most give-it-a-go sessions begin with a spell on a small wall at ground level, helping you can get used to the terminology of climbing and the types of hold that the coloured plastic offers. Many of the holds are cupped on one side, and then smooth on the other side. This enables a route setter to twist the hold into position that is most beneficial to the standard of the climb that they are aiming to set. The best type of hold that you are ever going to find is called a **'JUG,'** which is a lovely cupped shape that all your fingers nicely curl into. At once, you can find on the wall an assortment of jugs, and those that are definitely not jugs. In the climbing world, a 'jug' is a lovely cupped hold that you can hang off on one arm in a restful manner. I have to warn you even at this very early stage, that the term 'JUG' will haunt you for the rest of your climbing career. As you progress and get stronger, a slightly smaller version of this hold will become your new found jug. When you look at a very highly rated climb, and cannot see a single hold on it, just ask a top climber what the holds are like; you are likely to get the reply 'jugs all the way.' You will be no wiser since the term is completely relative.

With luck! the instructor will point you at a small wall covered in, lets just say BIG 'jugs,' so you can have a fun time beginning to climb. If you climb upwards, you soon climb high enough to hurt yourself. If you climb sideways, you can pick up a lot of the general climbing tips, and simply just step back onto the ground at any time. Climbing also is a bit like a game of snakes and ladders. Sure, going

An illustration of both hands coming to a match on a good jug, then leaving to another good jug.

up is easy if there happens to be a giant jug above your head. However, you can be assured that the mean and devious route setter will have a wicked sense of humour, and will not allow this to happen - all the time. This is good, since nearly all climbs, at any level - indoors or outdoors, on natural or artificial rock, will involve both climbing upwards and sideways. Climbing sideways is referred to as **'TRAVERSING,'** and in its simplest form looks like one of those fun aerobic exercises, that you get taught by an angelic flexible girl on breakfast TV. Reach out for a jug to one side and then move over – easy.

In climbing, when you bring both hands together on a hold, it is called a **'MATCH.'** Sometimes you may only get the fingertips of one hand on a hold, and consequently then have 'to match,' joining the ledge with the fingertips of the other hand. It is a term that is very useful to know when an instructor is explaining what you need to do on a wall – it's not an obvious term. When there are no obvious jugs, you have to improvise. This leads you to using jugs on their side. Any hold that we use in a side pulling fashion is not surprisingly called - **'SIDE-PULL.'** When a jug is mounted on a wall like this, you can see immediately see how climbing begins to work. You can use the same hold as the previous

jug, but instead of hanging vertically off it, you use your bicep and stomach to lock your arm. Your body will pivot on the foothold and the stiffness in your body will keep you in to the wall. In traversing, the use of sidepulls is essential, and makes the whole jaunt, so much easier.

The last basic type of hand hold is the **'UNDER-CUT.'** This is the upside down jug for want of a better description. It's the awkward one at waist level that you cannot see! It's a hold that is very dependent upon the positioning of the foot, because you can't hold an undercut without getting support

A lovely illustration of how to undercut, even in bendy trainers

A nice incut side-pull, great for beginning

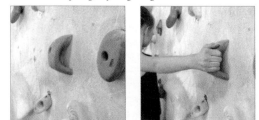

Padding with the feet   *A cute little move; the 'footswap,' conserving energy.*

from your feet. Find two good footholds a couple of feet apart, look for a good undercut at about waist level – for both hands if possible. Get onto the wall and hold the position to feel the dynamics of the undercut. Moving your feet in this position is very difficult indeed, since all the power is from the locking position of the body over the feet. In general, you keep your feet still when using an undercut, and only move one hand at a time – in and out of an undercut. Importantly though, it's a very useful move that can get you out of a lot of difficulty when the jugs seem to be elusive. It also uses different muscles-top biceps from jugs, so you may get a rest from aching and expiring forearms. For beginners though, strength conservation is of no importance. Go for it, grip like a bear and hug those holds. Staying on for as long as possible is a great challenge, and a lot of fun is to be had between the whole group of beginners. Start at one end of the wall, and just see how far along you can get. If you are on a really quick intro session - you might get onto a climb now, have a go and then go out to party. If you are enjoying the traversing, then stay with us a moment longer for some real climbing tips that will put you ahead of the class.

Climbing shoes are the business, but since they are not essential at this stage, we have illustrated our tips in training shoes. At this stage, it is the principle which is more important than the equipment. Your shoe has 4 different elements in climbing, and it is very important to understand the exact implica-

tions of each. The heel is obvious and very technical and for later on (p 119). The front half of the foot is split into 3 useable sectors. The toe, inside and outer edge. It is really important to understand that you do not use the other parts of the foot in general climbing, because it doesn't support your bodyweight. When you are resting on a wall you will be best supported by your inside edges. Using your outside edges gives huge support but requires good ankle flexibility and considerable hand strength. The toe at the front of the foot, is the only weak part of the foot and doesn't give you much structural support at all – so don't use it. The only time that beginners use the toe, is when there is a section without footholds. Here you rely on the friction created, between the sole of the front part of the foot and the wall; we call this **'PADDING.'** On a completely flat piece of board, the sticky rubber on a special climbing shoe will make friction, and as sticky as a racing car tyre. If you are traversing along and come to a section with only one foothold, using padding can be the way to crack the problem. You may pad your way across the wall to the foothold. Also if you have one foot on a hold and want to change it, place both hands on good jugs, pad the wall in front of you then place the opposite foot back on the hold. If the holds are not good enough for this, then you have to do another move called a **'FOOT SWAP.'** Here you very quickly take the weight off one foot with a skip like movement, flick one foot up and sneak the other into its place, on the hold. Definitely worth practising - low to the

INTRODUCTION

GIVE-IT-A-GO

IND/BOULDERING

OUT/BOULDERING

IMPROVEMENT

INDOOR SPORT

OUTDOOR SPORT

MULTI-PITCH

VIA FERRATA

WHERE TO GO

INDEX

The 'step through' is performed quite elegantly by tiny Rebecca

ground. When you get the knack it's easy, and is one of the best ways out of trouble in a traverse.

A better and smoother way of traversing, is to use the 'STEP THROUGH.' You will certainly need some good handholds to make this move initially, since it takes several years of climbing to develop very strong finger and hand muscles. The step through allows you to keep one foot on a hold (with the inside edge) whilst literally stepping through onto another hold with the outside edge of the other foot. Afterwards the trailing foot can simply swing around to either match the feet on the same hold, or go through to the next foothold. To finish, you end up with one foot of course the wrong way around on a hold, simply lift it up, and twist it around to regain a comfortable resting position. Finding the most comfortable configuration for the body to rest is essential whilst traversing; your forearms can use up all their muscle endurance in a very short time. To get good effeciency from your feet, you need good turn out, not as much as ballet requires, but an angle of 20° to the rock is about perfect. If your feet are perfectly level, you will get a lot of support from them. If you have a good jug for your hands, you can drop your ankles about 5° to the horizontal plane; this makes the body cantilever onto the foothold and therefore gain more friction and support.

Our little cartoon friend for this leaning series is called Dyno-mite. This little character is the very essence of enjoyable fun associated with indoor

climbing and bouldering, he bounces around and is full of energy, leaping for holds that are out of reach. The only rule for indoor traversing – is that there are no rules or boundaries, anything goes in an effort to go sideways without coming off. Eventually you get to a point where you can see the next hold, but it is just out of reach. Dyno-mite the cartoon character would always dynamically leap for this hold; we call this move, The 'DYNO.' There are 2 parts of obvious difficulty: 1 – to propel

Joanna here is demonstrating the double handed dyno; great fun and can go out of control completely - wild fun.

yourself in the correct general direction; and 2 - to actually hold onto the lump of plastic with your hand - when you have to catch it inbound at uncontrollable speed. Your body tends to carry on flying around at its own free will, and you can come off the wall very easily indeed. So try a dyno for a very short distance at the beginning, be near the ground, and have someone to catch you.

Using all these moves and techniques will enable you to get a lot more out of an hour on an indoor traversing wall. It's fun since you only ever need to be inches off the ground. When you can happily traverse across a jug infested traverse wall, see if you can start missing out a few of the jugs; or even keep your body twisted to one side the whole way – and use step throughs to complete the entire traverse.

INTRODUCTION

GIVE-IT-A-GO

IND/BOULDERING

OUT/BOULDERING

IMPROVEMENT

INDOOR SPORT

OUTDOOR SPORT

MULTI-PITCH

VIA FERRATA

WHERE TO GO

INDEX

A CLIMB, UP THE WALL

The second part of any give-it-a-go session, should be to make a complete climb of the indoor wall from bottom to top. You don't have to be a genius to look up at the wall, and realise that falling from the top to the bottom without a rope, could almost certainly kill you. You must be alert to strict supervision and care of from your instructor. Every indoor wall has its own regulations for instructors, because every wall is different from any other wall. Indoor walls are also completely different from general mountaineering or outdoors, and have different safety principles to adhere to. Any course run by a wall, should have quality assessed its own instructors, and should also have a procedure for vetting and authorising freelance instructors.

The whole idea of the give-it-a-go, is for you the fun loving bunny, not to have to worry about safety. The instructor will ask you to put on a climbing harness and check it over fully to see that it fits correctly and all the buckles are done up correctly. You often have the option of wearing a helmet if you

Special harnesses for small children are used on most walls

request, since some beginners feel a bit more confident with one. All beginners should start with the safety of a rope that comes from above. The instructor will make sure that you are attached to the rope completely securely. The rope will run up to the top of the wall and pass through a securely fixed point, and then down to the instructor. When you climb, the rope will be controlled by the instructor at all times, through a locking device called belaying. If you fall off, the instructor will simply lock-off the rope and you will be held where you are. The slightly un-nerving part is that all climbing ropes have some stretch in them, to absorb the shock of a sudden load in a fall. Even if the rope is fully tight when you come off, you will go down a couple of feet with rope stretch. This is completely intentional so do not worry (huh - you will). Usually before you start the climb the instructor will take up the rope tight so you can feel how the harness supports you, and see how comfortable it is.

When you've got the knack of tricks on the traversing wall, going up a beginners route should be a doddle. Climb up, remembering all the tips of matching, searching for sidepulls and undercuts etc. The major mistake beginners make, is to take giant steps up the wall. Generally you can climb most routes with small step ups. It is surprising how that a handhold just out of reach, can be grabbed by simply stepping up on another foothold. At about 3 times your height, most people start to get a bit scared. This is perfectly normal, in fact it is preferable, since you are appreciating that without a rope you would now be in a very serious position. All good climbers get scared, the real trick however is to control your fear. The more scared you are, the closer you will stand to the rock, and harder you will grasp onto the holds. Remember that you learnt to climb on the traverse wall, keeping your body away from the wall, and easily looking at what you were doing with your feet. You could see the whole climbing picture and were having fun. Now look at you, stuck right up flat to the wall and scrabbling about with your feet, too scared to look down for footholds. This is now crunch time, and there are nearly always two separate outcomes.

At Amersham Wall, the sections of wall can be mechanically tilted for an angle to suit beginners

INTRODUCTION

GIVE-IT-A-GO

IND/BOULDERING

OUT/BOULDERING

IMPROVEMENT

INDOOR SPORT

OUTDOOR SPORT

MULTI-PITCH

VIA FERRATA

WHERE TO GO

INDEX

Firstly you can continue scrabbling about the wall, shaking and getting some help from a good pull on the rope by the instructor, you get to the top and don't even know you are there. You are then lowered slowly down with shaking legs. When you get down, you say something completely ridiculous like – "Oh, I really enjoyed that!"

On the other hand, have belief that the rope attached to you will actually hold you in a fall. You are high up, but with the rope it makes no difference. It's a scary position, but importantly you need not have fear. You can think clearly, and start climbing the way you were on the traverse wall. You continue to climb and get to the top surprisingly easily, and feel a great sense of achievement. You still have one further test of nerves however. At the top, the instructor will ask you to tap the metal link, to show yourself that you got there. Then you have to sit back in the harness and let go! This is always unnerving, because you are relying on someone else directly for your safety, also at the highest and scariest point of the climb. Top tip, place a hand on the other rope that has passed through the top ring, and use your other hand flat against the wall to balance yourself (but not holding any holds). The instructor should check that you are comfortable in your harness; wriggle your hips to make sure you are in a nice comfortable sitting position. When you start to get lowered, do not tightly grip the other rope with your hand, just feel it move; this will help co-ordinate your brain, that the rope is moving and you will be going down slowly, and that everything is ticketyboo. Keep your feet apart, slightly bend the knees to stabilise your body. Make a backwards walking motion as you are lowered down. Get to the bottom and of course, thank the instructor for looking after you safely.

A nerve racking descent, holding onto the rope to calm the nerves.

You have now completed your first climb and will most probably have a very good idea if you like it or not. More importantly, you have given it a good go, and put in 100%. You can happily decide if you want to spend any more time or money on the silliest of pastimes. If you have caught the bug, I can recommend a full blown study of our second section – Bouldering indoors, it's essential climbing knowledge for just about any sort of climbing. After this, you will have learnt a huge amount about general climbing. Then you can enquire at the walls and climbing centres that run courses on bouldering, general climbing safety, advanced bouldering etc. Most centres that run these give-it-a-go sessions, will be able to advise on different courses and schemes to get you climbing.

INTRODUCTION

GIVE-IT-A-GO

IND/BOULDERING

OUT/BOULDERING

IMPROVEMENT

INDOOR SPORT

OUTDOOR SPORT

MULTI-PITCH

VIA FERRATA

WHERE TO GO

INDEX

Top: Vicky Hurley in mid-dyno, Boulder UK, Blackburn

Alice in Wonderland, dancing up Brunel Wall, Uxbridge.

Indoor Bouldering is all about body movement; it is like dancing on a vertical or even overhanging-surface. It's certainly a lot slower, but it still has the control and precision, freedom and expression, that good dancing has. When you step onto a good section of an indoor wall for bouldering, you could treat it like a small dance set from a Fred Astaire film. It's a stage covered in objects that you can stand on, pull on, and even make fun, twisting, movements across. It's your arena to invent, and make any movement that you want to. A beautiful wall, can also be used serenely, somewhere that you glide across effortlessly. Your skills will allow you to pull delicately on every hold, simply to stroke the footholds with your feet, and bodily flex your way through the physical problems. Some of the world's top climbers have done this on stage shows, a sort of vertical climbing ballet.

When you come across any type of hold in bouldering, it's your choice of how to use it, and where to go from it. At first you might be in extremis, just hoping to hang on for even a moment. But after a reasonable amount of time and practice, you do get the 'physical know how,' that will enable you to move comfortably and smoothly on a vertical wall. Outside bouldering is constrained by the fissures and ripples of the rock, which decides for you the movements that you must make. Inside it is different, there is usually an abundance of holds, edges and different forms to pull, push and twist your body around. Bouldering walls exist in vastly different shapes, angles and forms, and you have fantastic slabs, wave formations, caverns, and grotto's to be enticed into.

Indoor bouldering can also be about '**POWER**;' pulling on a handhold, and feeling every muscle and sinew that goes into the tension of going against gravity. There is a superb sensation when your fingers transform on a hold, from pure touch – then slowly creeping up to a full blown empowered grip. Then milli-seconds later, your shoulder and back cut in, and your whole upper torso can feel like an Apollo rocket launching off. This power surge sensation, is definitely one of the big attractions to indoor bouldering. Your feet cut loose on an overhang and will swing wildly out. With the huge crash mats at indoor walls, you can launch up pretty safely towards holds that are both out of reach, and almost impossible to grip when you get there. Falling is fun and looks ridiculous, which adds to the whole jovial nature of indoor bouldering.

You can use the indoor bouldering walls as a stepping stone to outdoor climbing. This use, will definitely improve your climbing awareness and balance, whilst building up your finger and arm strength quite quickly. It can offer huge benefits in learning to climb in control. There is also the competitive edge that can be found indoors, pitting yourself against other climbers on a specific set of holds leading up the wall; there are even world championships for indoor bouldering. If you climb with the world champion boulderers, you'll find that they consider indoor bouldering to be all about having fun, admittedly sometimes serious fun, but mostly just enjoying the movement. How seriously do you take your fun, well it doesn't matter a jot.

As a piano has 88 keys, and a tune is simply the combination of a select few notes used in a special order. A boulder 'PROBLEM,' is an individual way up or across a bouldering wall, and that uses a prescribed group of holds. The ultimate in bouldering, is usually a problem that consists of only a few holds, maybe only 5 or 6 - and is most probably only 4 metres in height. It is the complexity in the positional arrangement of the holds, which makes bouldering so special. It might be impossible to use any of the holds on their own, but together, they can be used in combination to climb up a wall. This is the magic of the purest form of bouldering, moving across five holds, locked in space.

INTRODUCTION | GIVE-IT-A-GO | IND/BOULDERING | OUT/BOULDERING | IMPROVEMENT | INDOOR SPORT | OUTDOOR SPORT | MULTI-PITCH | VIA FERRATA | WHERE TO GO | INDEX

SOUTHPORT WALL, a small wall that still feels big

There is a big difference between 'climbing walls' and 'bouldering walls.' They might look very similar to you, but they have different aims and objectives, and have many hidden qualities that you will find out about as you progress. Some walls are suitable for both climbing and bouldering, but most of the time, a wall is good for either one or the other. Big climbing centres, will have separate areas for roped climbing and bouldering; they can even have several different bouldering areas to offer assorted angles and surface textures. There are many reasons for this, which will become apparent throughout the book. Some walls have to make do with the space that they have, and are forced to combine climbing and bouldering in one area. This section hopes to explain and describe the different textures and surfaces of bouldering wall available. Here you can see what will be useful to you as a beginner, then as an intermediate, and eventually as an expert. If you turn up at a very demanding top bouldering wall, you will not even leave the ground – and then go home disheartened. You'll most probably give up. By knowing about the styles of walls, you will recognise a wall that is going to offer you fun at this stage, and know which types to keep an eye out for, as you improve. We have a section at the back of the book to show the major climbing walls that are in England and Wales, and give a red icon to show if they have dedicated bouldering areas. We also publish a Climber's Handbook, that gives specific technical details, information and photos for every wall in the country

KIDS PLYWOOD

The easiest way to make a fun climbing wall is to build a wooden frame, and then cover it on all sides with 22mm plywood. Then you can screw on blocks of wood, paint it and have a bright and funky little climbing wall. If you're only tiny, then the wall doesn't have to be very high at all. Any descent commercial wall for kids, should have very good crash padding at the base; and you really want a floor area that is completely padded out. At walls designed for more experienced climbers, you often find several crash pads that just butt up to each other, which are not suitable for bouldering novices! If an experienced boulderer falls, they will rotate their bodies during the fall, and look down at the same time. This way, they can plan their landing, to position their feet, either side of a crash pad joint. A beginner cannot cope with this, and may put a foot, straight down the joint; legs and ankles have been broken this way. A plywood fun area is great for kids and allows bouldering with simple training shoes, the holds should also be nice and large.

A bright and encouraging example of a kids wall at Bourne End, Bucks.

INTRODUCTION | GIVE-IT-A-GO | IND/BOULDERING | OUT/BOULDERING | IMPROVEMENT | INDOOR SPORT | OUT'DOOR SPORT | MULTI-PITCH | VIA FERRATA | WHERE TO GO | INDEX

INTRODUCTION | GIVE-IT-A-GO | IND/BOULDERING | OUT/BOULDERING | IMPROVEMENT | INDOOR SPORT | OUTDOOR SPORT | MULTI-PITCH | VIA FERRATA | WHERE TO GO | INDEX

A good example of high level flat panel bouldering with continuous crash matting. (Sunderland)

FLAT PANEL

This is the main type of cheap and flexible climbing wall construction that is used for both bouldering and sport climbing. Either single skin plywood is used in varying shaped forms to join together, or several layers of thinner ply, are bent over a frame to give a curved section. The real key to this type of wall is the way in which the holds are attached. This is achieved by using an ingenious spiked nut – called a T nut (see inset above). It rests in the hole with an internal thread, and as the bolt is screwed into it, the helix of the thread draws the spikes into the back of the ply sheet, to prevent it turning. T nuts are mass produced at low cost, and are used in enormous quantities for a big wall construction. Most climbing wall manufacturers will have a dense pattern of holes in a ply sheet, that all have T nuts attached behind. This way, a bolt on hold can be placed almost anywhere, and at any angle of rotation. They also remain behind the surface of the ply, and therefore do not affect areas with no holds on. With this type of construction, you are completely at the mercy of the person who bolts on the holds, and if they have been changed recently to give a particular style of bouldering. Some walls will cover an area with many holds, to accommodate a wide range of standards. For expert level however, too many holds in an area will often get in the way, so be cautious if there are not very many holds, on a flat panel bouldering wall. Another consideration for a flat panel wall is the surface texture. Many flat panel walls are painted to give a nice feel to the climbing area, but look closely at the finish of the paintwork. Many walls use a textured paint with grit, that gives a rough surface. In climbing, the technique of padding (p27), relies on friction between the flat sole of your shoe and the panel surface. So at an intermediate level, this rough surface is really beneficial and useful. At an expert level, you are expected to pad on completely smooth areas.

FREEFORM ROCK

This method of construction is to create a climbing wall that looks and feels like real rock. For the sake of artistic endeavour and climbing ingenuity, the shape and form will be of an imaginary piece of 'real rock.' Often, natural rock is often a lot flatter than you think, and of course, there just aren't any holds to grip onto. On the other hand, limestone caves in places like Thailand and Cuba, offer excellent climbing on bulging stalactites and flowstone forms. (**Flowstone** is where rock sediment in water solidifies, and forms pure solid rock again) These natural formations, give nice and chunky sized lumps that your hands can pinch around. When you get giant-smooth water worn holes, you can wedge your body into the rock and almost squirm up. To re-create these types of forms, the whole structure must be pre-planned. First, a strong steel skeleton in the broad shape of the final wall is built. Then a strong backing wall needs to be moulded, along with inset nuts, to accept additional bolt-on holds. The final surfacing part is the most critical and important,

and is when the wall is really created. When the final mixture of resin/sand/concrete etc, is still pliable, the wall builder can form pockets, edges, fingertip holds and gives the surface, a texture. Then it will set-cure "rock'ard," and you have your final wall. Additionally, the relative proportions of the mix, will naturally give a sandy concrete, or resinous feel. Pieces of natural stone can also be embedded into the surface, and can offer a completely different feel to a handhold.

Freeform is considered to be the true ultimate in bouldering wall design. It is the most expensive to build, and the most difficult to create. It can offer some of the best indoor and even outdoor bouldering on the planet. Its main disadvantage, is that it may not be suitable for all levels of climbing, and in particular - beginners. It also is a mixed blessing, since a badly constructed freeform wall, is not only a waste of money, but almost impossible to alter, once it is built. A freeform wall

A modern integrated freeform design; textured surface with features, plus bolt-ons; Castle climbing centre, London.

INTRODUCTION

GIVE-IT-A-GO

IND/BOULDERING

OUT/BOULDERING

IMPROVEMENT

INDOOR SPORT

OUTDOOR SPORT

MULTI-PITCH

VIA FERRATA

WHERE TO GO

INDEX

INTRODUCTION

GIVE-IT-A-GO

IND/BOULDERING

OUT/BOULDERING

IMPROVEMENT

INDOOR SPORT

OUTDOOR SPORT

MULTI-PITCH

VIA FERRATA

WHERE TO GO

INDEX

that is designed for beginners, with big hand and footholds, will be a complete waste of time for intermediates and above. Good freeform design, is invariably a compromise, and mostly ends up with hard problems on the freeform features, and easier problems on the large bolt-on's. Freeform does offer an attractive psychological boost to most climbers too. With a problem set in stone, the challenge is more permanent and therefore tangible, it's worth trying that extra bit harder, to get up it. When you do get up a problem – we call it a '**TICK.**' Climbers often like to return to a wall where they know, that they can easily tick a few known 'hard problems.' When you climb a problem over and over again, so that you look completely relaxed on it, we say you have it '**WIRED.**' You don't have this kudos with bolt-on's, because they get changed around so often. When you first go on a freeform wall, try to remember the holds that you use. You can then return in a few months after a lot of climbing, and be able to measure your improvement – or despair at perhaps your weight gain!

A very well crafted boulder section at Penrith Wall.

A superbly featured, giant pure freeform cave at Hull.

BRICK & INSERTS

Only very modern walls use freeform and flat panel, so it is highly likely that you might find another style of wall. These are the classic, old-style; brick walls, with inserts. There are literally hundreds of these walls around the country, and they still serve many useful purposes. At a very basic level, you have a vertical brick wall with a few odd bits sticking out, and these are really only suitable for a quick, give-it-a-go sessions (but hardly, inspiring!). Brick insert walls often come in a more advanced version, and are very good for intermediate bouldering – enough for the majority of climbers. They are often actually better for your climbing technique than most modern walls with bolt-on holds. This is because you have to make controlled climbing movements that are skilled and delicate. A lot of steep freeform bouldering, is just lunging from one brightly coloured hold to another, and is no more than chimpanzee frolics (but fun though). The only real disadvantage, is that all the holds are set in concrete and cannot move, so you get bored in the long term and end up knowing every hold on the wall intimately, I can promise. They are generally set out with quite a few easy problems, and the holds are quite chunky. The best sort of this design, are walls with concrete blocks that have inset pieces of natural stone in. You can create a lot

of problems with these if you are inventive. Before modern freeform walls, this was all there was, and climbing standards were superbly high. It is only your own lack of imagination that will limit your enjoyment on these walls. For a lot of climbers who are not over-strong gorilla's, they give a very delicate and testing bouldering session. You are less likely to ever suffer from finger and tendon injuries by climbing on vertical brick walls. A lot of these walls have been built on the outside of centres, which is non claustraphobic and preferable on a hot summers evening if you are stuck in the city. The main problem/attribute, that these walls suffer from, is 'POLISH.' Any natural piece of rock will polish up with use, and continued use by sweaty hands and boots, will create a mirror like, smooth surface. Climbing on highly polished rock is a very acquired taste, and is not to most people's preference. You do have to remember however, that popular climbs outside – can also polish up to a horrendous, slipperyness; so a bit of practise, does not go amiss.

The original limestone insert section, at Guildford Wall (you can also climb along this wall on the brick edges only!)

INTRODUCTION

GIVE-IT-A-GO

IND/BOULDERING

OUT/BOULDERING

IMPROVEMENT

INDOOR SPORT

OUTDOOR SPORT

MULTI-PITCH

VIA FERRATA

WHERE TO GO

INDEX

INTRODUCTION

GIVE-IT-A-GO

IND/BOULDERING

OUT/BOULDERING

IMPROVEMENT

INDOOR SPORT

OUTDOOR SPORT

MULTI-PITCH

VIA FERRATA

WHERE TO GO

INDEX

WOODIES

The easiest definition of a woodie, is a flat panel wall set at a ridiculously overhanging angle. This sums it up but not completely, because there is a lot of difference between a thoroughbred woodie, and a hybrid. The true thoroughbred only has smooth wooden holds, and is sought after by all the top boulderers. Bouldering in its entirety contains a huge dimension of physical exertion, using slabs to overhanging roofs. In a typical vertical plane, the feet and legs play a very important part to support the weight of the body. If you climb for a long time in this style, you're going to develop 'vertical' technique, which is superb fingertip strength, forearm stamina, and delicate tip toe precision. What you won't do, is to improve your real upper torso strength – because you never use it. The muscle groups that you use to climb an overhanging section are quite different, and come from the shoulders, back and stomach. This is why a climber who is superb on vertical rock, may be completely hopeless on overhanging walls – and vice versa of course. As a brick edge wall is perfect for training on vertical surfaces, the woodie is the answer to the baboon inclined climber. The requirements of a top class woodie are to supply the perfect ingredients for climbing steep angles, yet still to be of use to a wide variety of climbers whose strengths and arm-reach is hugely variable. Because of this, they are usually covered in a huge range of holds that are densely contained. The angle of a woodie is critical, and different angles give a completely different style of climbing. If the angle is 10-15º off vertical, you can still have small holds. At 20-30º you get a very powerful style of bouldering, but is still very reliant upon the use of feet. The critical angle is around 60º, which is when the feet almost become superfluous. They must have superb crash matting, since you are going to fall off them, every other second.

The woodie room at Broughton Wall in Manchester, a top venue for hard core bouldering.

INTRODUCTION

GIVE-IT-A-GO

IND/BOULDERING

OUT/BOULDERING

IMPROVEMENT

INDOOR SPORT

OUTDOOR SPORT

MULTI-PITCH

VIA FERRATA

WHERE TO GO

INDEX

Special competition cubes built by Entreprises, at an international competition in Birmingham arena

COMPETITION CUBES

Most areas of the UK have local climbing competitions that are run on a seasonal basis. They form the base of the pyramid to success in this style of bouldering. They are fun and a great opportunity for kids to see how good they are in relation to their pals from other nearby walls. The wall will simply mark up a set of holds in succession and call it a problem. You simply complete the problems in the least number of goes, and keep a tally of your own score. It is all pretty harmless and is done in good faith. Above the local level, you have regional area championships, which are done on a similar basis. Eventually you reach the dizzy heights of national and international bouldering competitions. These take place on specially constructed walls that are cubic in structure, and can be transported from one competition venue to another. They are designed to offer a superb array of possible bouldering problems in the overhanging style to say the least. They are built as flat panel design, with a complete choice of bolt-on placements, and usually have a very low friction surface. By making them a cube structure, each and opposite sides counteract and balance each other safely, allowing the cube to be com-

pletely freestanding. This also offers the spectators, an excellent all round view of several boulderers in action at the same time. The surfaces of the cubes will vary to give as many different types of overhangs and roofs as possible. An angle of 90° to the vertical is called a **'ROOF'** in climbing. A lot of the holds in competitions are usually quite large, which may look easy of course. But on the other hand, the angle is very, very steep; and the holds are a seriously long way apart. They are often, very rounded - which make them almost impossible to grip onto, especially if your body starts to swing. At this level there will be very good crash padding, and all climbers are very experienced in falling off! The problems will be set by other top climbers, who know exactly where to position the holds relative to each other, and create a good physical challenge. Some problems may be all about the gigantic distance between two holds, and involve a leap from one hold to another. Another type of move is where two holds can only be used together to reach another, making a problem that is all about body flexibility. To climb well at competitions, you need to be a good all round boulderer.

INTRODUCTION

GIVE-IT-A-GO

IND/BOULDERING

OUT/BOULDERING

IMPROVEMENT

INDOOR SPORT

OUTDOOR SPORT

MULTI-PITCH

VIA FERRATA

WHERE TO GO

INDEX

What to wear? One of the great things about bouldering, is that there is no silly uniform or particular games kit. Bouldering is a chilled out activity, and a lot of folk who do it go skateboarding, snowboarding and surfing; all those laid back and fun things to do. Some of the fashions of loose fitting and baggy trousers, have come into bouldering from boarding. When you learn to snowboard, you fall over a lot and get really hot; when your good on the other hand, you cruise effortlessly – so you have to wrap up well. Bouldering is the opposite. You are going to get cold as a beginner, since you are not strong enough to hold on for very long. You don't actually get that tired and therefore don't generate much body heat. When your fingers and forearms start to build up stamina, you get on the wall a lot more, and for longer periods of time, consequently staying warmer. Eventually, even in the coldest of bouldering walls, you are going to get pretty hot when you get '**CRANKING,**' (Climbing term for pulling hard on the arms only) and consequently, sweat like a demon!

By the time you have flicked through this book, you will have a good idea of the current fashions and designer wear for bouldering. When you travel to a wall, make sure you are warm because this keeps the muscles loose, relaxed, and ready to start working.

When you're starting out, take an extra sweat shirt along, and go for leggings or jeans, rather than shorts. If you keep your body warm and muscles warm, then you are less likely to strain anything. It certainly is a danger to be underclad and therefore get cold when you are a beginner. The temperature at different indoor walls will vary considerably. Your typical leisure centre is really warm, but a lot of dedicated bouldering venues are cold, and I mean COLD! It's a funny sort of national thing. In Spain for instance, everyone boulder's there in 35º, even at the very top level. In the UK, there seems something almost religious about 4º being the perfect temperature for top level bouldering; it's when you don't sweat, and your fingers 'only just,' don't turn to ice. Don't worry, most dedicated walls are generally in the 10-18º range, but the emphasis is to keep them cool. You need to wear loose fitting clothes since you will need good flexibility. You also need to see your feet well, so you can place them on footholds by sight. Big, floppy flares, either need to be rolled up or left at home. Sometimes you need to lunge or dyno for a hold, so you don't want to be restricted by anything tight. When you fall off, any metal tags could easily damage the surface of the crash pads, so consider that too. Keys in pockets, are another really painful thing to land on.

Experts at the Arethusa wall, in the latest designer wear - perhaps not! But having a lot of fun, a laugh, and some fiendish cranking.

So! What's with the white stuff, eh! Everybody calls it chalk, so it's known as chalk. It actually isn't chalk at all, but why let anything so mundane get in the way. It is indeed, "Light Magnesium Carbonate MgCO3," so you can appreciate why we just call it – CHALK. You do have to be careful though, since there is a similar looking substance, actually known as French chalk. This is a creamy-white powder (climbers chalk is brilliant white), which is as slippery as talcum powder, and horrendous for climbing with. Chalk is a drying agent and soaks up moisture in milliseconds. There are 101 uses for it in bouldering and general climbing; drying sweaty hands, moisture on the rock, marking a hold, drying shoes quickly, writing a message, etc. The only thing you don't really want to do, is to swallow it, because it's a laxative – the 102nd use.

Normal and Jumbo bags; A bag turned inside out, showing the fleece.

The most common and practical use for chalk in bouldering, is to soak up and dry out the sweat that oozes out of the pores of the skin on our fingers. It also seems to ooze out just when you don't want it to. You will be happily holding a good handhold, and it is guaranteed that your fingers will start to sweat, very quickly. This results in your fingers sliding, and if the hold is anything other than incut, you will quickly slide straight off. Hot climbing environments will increase your sweatability, and so will anxiety; so staying cool in the mind, is just as important as staying physically cool. It's practical to put some chalk in a small bag, tie it around your waist, and dip your fingers in it whenever they get a bit sweaty. Chalk bags come in all shapes and sizes, and a full array of colours. Apart from the cosmetic attraction, you need a bag that practically works. Loose chalk is put in a bag that has a fleece lining. The inner fleece traps the chalk, and you only have to dip your hand quickly to touch it, and your fingers are dry at an instant. You only need a small amount of chalk in the bag, otherwise you just pull out a load of chalk into the air, and upset any asthmatic in the close vicinity. Some good chalk bags have an instant 'clic' closing mechanism, so just before you jump off, you can close the bag and not let any chalk spill. If you can't be bothered with this, then go down the route of the muslin chalk ball. When using one, you need a slightly bigger chalk bag that is large enough for both your hand and the muslin ball. This has the disadvantage of being a lot slower to dispense the chalk. (Muslin balls are also naff for drying out wet holds, wet shoes etc.) When you are climbing dynamically, and land back on planet earth, you will create a cloud of white puff. Simply take your chalk bag off in this situation. JUMBO chalk bags are used by expert boulderers, and stay on the crash pad all the time. Chalk comes in different brands too, some manufacturers definitely make a lot more grippy chalk than others. At the beginning, you will find it almost impossible to differentiate the qualities, but eventually, you too may become a chalk aficionado – sad, isn't it. You can get it in powder form, or blocks that simply crumble into powder as you leave them in the bottom of your rucksack. Whatever form you buy it in, quickly transfer it into a good plastic container with a screw top, and one that isn't going to just pop open.

A chalk ball on the left - or loose chalk sold by the bag.

INTRODUCTION
GIVE-IT-A-GO
IND/BOULDERING
OUT/BOULDERING
IMPROVEMENT
INDOOR SPORT
OUTDOOR SPORT
MULTI-PITCH
VIA FERRATA
WHERE TO GO
INDEX

INTRODUCTION | GIVE-IT-A-GO | IND/BOULDERING | OUT/BOULDERING | IMPROVEMENT | INDOOR SPORT | OUTDOOR SPORT | MULTI-PITCH | VIA FERRATA | WHERE TO GO | INDEX

To any small kid who is just starting climbing, a pair of rock shoes are more likely to be a fashion accessory than a real aid to climbing. When you are very young and very light, you can easily support your body with your fingers and hands. It's when you grow to adult size that the alarm bells begin to ring, and you can't hang on any more. The heavier you get, the more reliant you are on your feet. In both climbing and bouldering, this also applies to your stamina and strength; the more tired you get, the more you rely on your feet. Climbing with your hands and arms like a baboon is fine for a while, but you limit yourself hugely. By supporting your body by your feet, you can get so much more out of your bouldering. You can climb harder, for longer, and are likely to remain more injury free, for far longer. The benefits of learning to use your feet in climbing are immense, it really is a part of climbing to take very seriously.

Buying a pair of rock shoes for a beginner is quite easy really. You have to like how they look, they must be a snug and comfortable fit, credit card to shop, and your done – simple. It's in about 6 months time when they may have worn out and you need to replace them, that chosing is more difficult. By then, you have learnt a huge amount about climbing, have seen all the different shoes on the market, and cannot decide on a shoe with 'this rubber,' or 'that heel shape,' or 'this lacing feature' etc. Enjoy your fun first spend, it's the last you are likely to get. Even if you get the wrong ones – you won't know it, so you won't despair. There are a few extra tips though for first time shoe buyers, that of course will be helpful. If you can first of all understand shoe dynamics, then you are halfway there.

This series of photographs illustrate why special climbing shoes are far more effective when using the smaller holds on climbing walls.
Top: Trying to stand on a small hold in everyday training shoes is almost comical. The foot-toe inside the shoe will slip back, and as there is no stiffness inside the sole, the boot simply curls up under pressure.
Centre: The bare foot is a lot more efficient at gripping the small hold. The toes can feel the shape of the hold, and then claw in the best way to support the foot. The problem is however, that in this case, all the weight will be taken on the single joint of the big toe - which is never going to be very strong.
Bottom: Here the foot is trapped tightly inside a rock shoe. The edge of the shoe is made to 90° so that it will fit precisely onto small square shaped edges. There is also stiffening in the shoe which supports it from side to side, but allows it to bend from front to back. In this instance the foot will superbly support the whole body weight.

SHOE DYNAMICS

There are two main types of foothold in climbing, the edge - and a smear. (There are also several weird ones, called hooks, locks and jams!) The 'EDGE,' is the main foothold that you use 90% of the time. It can vary in size, but you realistically need to stand in comfort on an edge, that is about 2cm

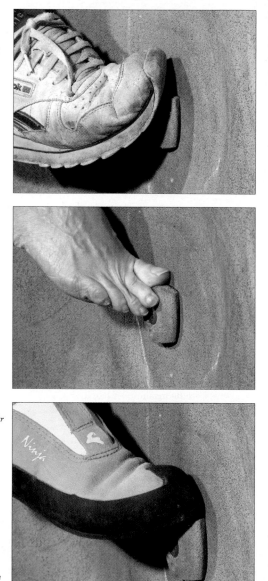

wide in comfort. In normal shoes or trainers, this is completely impossible. What happens is that your foot simply rolls off the edge. The photos illustrate the difference between a foot in trainers, and a foot in a close fitting rock shoe. By getting your foot as close to the rock as possible, and completely containing it in a shoe that is shaped to fit into a natural rock edge, you get massive support. Rock shoes can continue to give fantastic support on tiny edges that are only a few millimetres in size. You will be completely amazed by their performance. They don't perform however, if the foot is allowed to move around, inside the shoe. The second main foothold is the '**SMEAR**.' This is when you have a slab, and you put the sole of your shoe, flat onto the rock (A slab 'technically' is - angled rock less than vertical). With this sort of foot placement, there the edge does not grip at all. The rubber on the sole of the shoe comes into contact with the rock surface to create friction. If there is enough friction, then the shoe will not move. The physics are simple; the more rubber in contact with the rock, the more friction is generated. A completely flat piece of rubber on a completely flat piece of rock, will generate maximum friction.

ANKLE DYNAMICS

This is the most important part of footwork in any sort of climbing. It is perhaps easiest to understand with the smear. By placing your foot, flat on a slab and generate friction – you stick. As you move your foot, the sole will lift, and the friction goes, swisshhh – you fall. Somehow, you need to move your body up, yet keep the sole of the shoe, perfectly still in the maximum friction position all the time. The answer is so simple, you bend your ankle continuously as you move, so that the sole of your foot stays perfectly locked and still. The ankle is such an amazing joint, because not only can you bend it back and forth, you can also roll it from side to side. Whenever you place your foot on a hold, the part beneath the ankle will remain perfectly still – it has to, to work. It is the rest of the body above the ankle that moves. If you keep your feet still, when you move your body, you have just improved your climbing by about 100%.

For indoor bouldering, white circles allow easy identification of holds.

SHOE FITTING

Fitting a pair of climbing shoes to see if they are right for you, is completely different to fitting a normal pair of everyday shoes since they have a completely different purpose. An everyday shoe is mostly a fashion accessory. It should perhaps protect your feet from puddles, and not give you a blister if you walk half a mile. Climbing shoes would fail spectacularly on both of these tests. You need to find a shop with a good selection of shoes to choose from, and get the attention of a shop assistant who has a good personal knowledge about climbing, and who can assist you in making a good choice. It will also take more than a few minutes, so set a reasonable amount of time aside, maybe half or even a whole hour. Should you be influenced, by how they look? Climbing is a hugely psychological activity and you must feel comfortable in how you look and feel. I would advise to steer clear of shoes you just hate the sight of, but if it is down

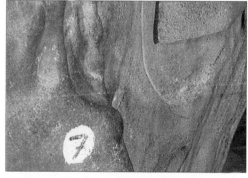

You often come across downward sloping foot holds that don't allow you to easily stand on them. By flexing the front part of the sole, and using ankle flexion, they can be used very efficiently and securely.

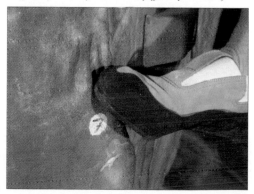

INTRODUCTION

GIVE-IT-A-GO

IND/BOULDERING

OUT/BOULDERING

IMPROVEMENT

INDOOR SPORT

OUTDOOR SPORT

MULTI-PITCH

VIA FERRATA

WHERE TO GO

INDEX

to a choice in the end that is marginal, be a bit brave and go for the one that is the better fit. A climbing shoe should fit skin tight, ideally so you can feel it on every part of your foot. On the basis that every person's foot on this planet is different, the climbing shoe manufacturers have an uphill struggle. There is hope however since none of the shoemakers use a standard shaped foot. Each company will have different pattern shapes for different models etc; and because a lot of shoes are separately hand finished, two - identical size 42's for example, can end up having different internal shapes anyway. There are most probably around 20 different internal shapes of shoe on the market, and each year there are changes to these designs too. Your objective, is finding a shoe out there in the shops that fits your foot exactly. Climbing shoes sizes have been historically bizarre and the shop assistant will know that and assist you. Every shoe manufacturer claims to have the stickiest rubber in the world, but then you'd expect that anyway, and at this stage, it's the fit that is by far the most important factor. Your feet expand half a UK size when you stand up, so unless you want to be crippled, try them on standing up. You may not be able to find the perfect shoe, and therefore have to make the decision to go to another shop, it' is difficult. If there is any area of compromise, then it is the heel, I find it doesn't have to be an incredible fit; but the front half of the foot, that's critical. Get shoes that are perfectly snug, and comfortable to walk about 10 paces in. We all know that shoes stretch and there is nothing more comfortable than an old pair of shoes Modern rock shoes do not stretch very much, so getting a really tight pair might not be wise. A final consideration is your

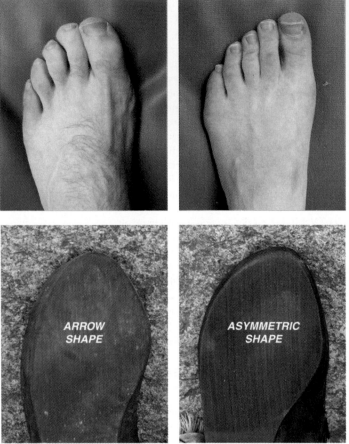

Here are two examples of different shaped feet and how they are suited to completely different shaped shoes. Top-left; there is a foot of a very experienced climber, whose feet seem to have been curved into the shape that fits an arrow shaped shoe - over many, many years. The ideal shoe for this foot, is one where the point of the shoe is just right from the centre line. On the other foot, the prominent big toe is completely over to the right side, with the emphasis being over to the instep. Here the person will look for a shoe that is termed as having an asymmetric shape, where the point of the shoe is nearer to the inside than the centre. The difference in the final shoe will look slight but critical. It the left foot wore an asymmetric shape, there would be an air gap to the right of the toe; the other way round would cramp and hurt the big toe.

achilles tendon. There are some shoes on the market with a severe heel cup that grips the heel of the foot strongly. This is to grip the heel of your foot in extreme circumstances. If the power of this is too strong, it could damage your achilles tendon which certainly is not an injury you want. Be very wary of any shoe that grips aggressively in the heel area, again – it may not be a good design for your foot.

SLIPPERS

The cheapest form of climbing shoe, is a non lace-up style. Most manufacturers make these and there are many different models. In a basic form, they have a simple elastic section to keep the foot in the shoe. When you try one on, you must get your toes completely touching the far inside end of the shoe, otherwise you will find it desperate to get on. They perform superbly, and are highly precise shoes. Some have velcro straps which are handy, because you can easily reduce the tension across the foot when you are not actually climbing. Their disadvantage, is that they do not grip the heel very well, and can easily come off when you do a 'HEEL HOOK,' a clawing action with the heel. On the plus side, because they are cheaper; a lot of shops stock them in most sizes, right down to tiny kids sizes.

COMFORT SHOES

This category has no particular boundaries, except that it contains a huge variety of shoes that are not classified as high performance shoes. Even though expert climbers can climb just about anything in these, their design is more for comfort and longevity, than pure performance. They will have a good 5mm of rubber on the sole which should take quite a bit of wearing away. The tongue of the shoe will be nice and padded to give extra comfort, and their may well be a lining inside to aid extra comfort. A reccomended choice for a 1st time shoe.

The Sapphire shoe, is one of those designs that is certainly well known to fit womens feet well - a popular and comfortable shoe.

You can get slippers usually either in an elastic or velcro version, both seem to work well and it is more down to foot shape in the end. When new any shoe will have a very sharp edge that will soon round off on its own to work on these smooth, dish shaped smears.

Above: Some shoes have a moulded one piece sole. These have massively improved in recent years, allowing comfort shoes with very good performance and heel hooking features. Below: A good padded tongue is a comfortable asset in any shoe.

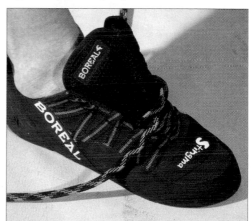

INTRODUCTION
GIVE-IT-A-GO
IND/BOULDERING
OUT/BOULDERING
IMPROVEMENT
INDOOR SPORT
OUTDOOR SPORT
MULTI-PITCH
VIA FERRATA
WHERE TO GO
INDEX

INTRODUCTION | GIVE-IT-A-GO | IND/BOULDERING | OUT/BOULDERING | IMPROVEMENT | INDOOR SPORT | OUTDOOR SPORT | MULTI-PITCH | VIA FERRATA | WHERE TO GO | INDEX

PERFORMANCE SHOES

These are the cutting edge of shoe technology and employ the latest ideas. The rubber on the sole will be a lot thinner than other shoes, so you can feel every pebble of the rock. Each model will have a characteristic sole that is either soft, medium or hard: Soft - so that it can mould over a particular rock surface like gritstone; or medium dish shaped, to maximise on sandstone scoops. They will have complicated lacing patterns, to give tension control right down to the toes.

An example of a modern high performance shoe. The upper will be soft and able to wrap around the climbers foot, and deform in the toe section for claw shaped toes. It must have a good lacing system to get tension in the right places. The sole will have been curved and shaped to support the foot in an ideal climbing position. It will be made of very sticky rubber and may have its own style of ridging or varying compound. There can also be a stiffener incorporated in the sole to keep some areas rigid, and other parts flexible. A hugely complicated construction and difficult to perfect. Below: a concave sole.

HYBRID SHOES

These are a relatively new development, where the front half of the shoe is a comfort shoe, and the back half is more like a training shoe. They are not intended for doing much walking, but more of an outdoor bouldering shoe, where you require extra protection to the heels when you fall off. For pure bouldering, they do not offer the ideal heel for some techniques, you just have to consider what is more important to you.

A very good example of a Hybrid shoe, and in the convenient version of a velcro slipper too.

MODERN SOLES

There are many different soles coming onto the market, so much that it will certainly confuse any beginner. If the rockshoe fits well, go with it. Some newer soles '**CONCAVES**,' have a concave centre in the centre of the front part of the sole. This is so that when you put pressure on a flat surface, it deforms under your weight and keeps the whole sole still in contact with the rock. keeping the friction high. Classic-style slightly curved soles, generally curve up on the sides and loose friction in this particular instance. However, on a slightly dish shaped slab, the concaves will not deform enough, and you are then at a positive disadvantage. Some manufacturers use only a 10mm wide, front edge, so you can hook this over the rock, to get extra support. In conclusion, all soles have their plus and minus points, and it's generally, more a case of how well you can use your feet, than as to the performance of the shoe.

Spider

IRS 2002

IRS (Integral Rand System): The biggest revolution since sticky rubber

< - Sole, rand and heel in one piece!! >
< - Natural and anatomical fit of the heel, arch and forefoot >
< - Different thicknesses and shapes across the toe, rand and heel >
< - Anatomical hole in the front part of the IRS sole >
< - Revolutionary heel for extreme climbs >
< - Different thincknesses depending on the size >
< - No deformable y de gran durabilidad >
< - Eliminates the sole delamination and deformation >
< - Increase the durability of the sole >

Boreal UK
Phone: 0114 209 6220
borealuksouth@hotmail.com
borealmiduk@hotmail.com

BOREAL
www.e-boreal.com/spider.htm

INTRODUCTION

GIVE-IT-A-GO

IND/BOULDERING

OUT/BOULDERING

IMPROVEMENT

INDOOR SPORT

OUTDOOR SPORT

MULTI-PITCH

VIA FERRATA

WHERE TO GO

INDEX

Plastic is the popular name for the brightly coloured holds used in climbing walls, and in photo's they often look very much like plastic. The process to make a hold is relatively simple. First you design a mould to be the shape of your final hold, either in 2 parts so that you can get the final hold out; or of a stiff rubber that will peel off the final set hold. The shape of the hold depends on the actual crafting of the mould, and is dependent on the strength of the resin mix. Resins are very advanced and can be designed to stick to almost anything, and cure in almost any required time scale. Their disadvantage, is that they have no frictional quality, and are expensive. In making a climbing hold, the main ingredient used is sand which comes in a huge variety of granular sizes. A hold manufacturer will decide which sands they want to use, which grain sizes to pick, how to blend them. Then with testing, decide which mixture is most appropriate for particular holds. Dyes can be added to make different coloured holds, and all sorts of wonderful patterns can be created. (Formulas secret to each manufacturer). If you look closely, you will see the supple variations of texture from one hold to another. For general recreational climbing it doesn't matter very much, but if your skin is looking pretty rough after an hours bouldering, try to climb on a few problems that have plastics with a low abrasive texture.

A lovely theme style hold to add a bit of fun to a wall. You can get lots of different shapes and styles of holds, from letters of the alphabet - to animals and even giant toilet seats!

This hold broke when being attached to the wall. Breakage could be a fault in the resin mix, bumps on the wall forcing the hold to bend, or caused by a countersunk bolt - splitting the hold.

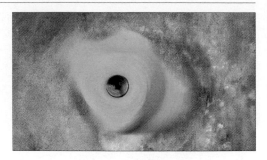

SPINNERS, SNAPPERS & CRACKERS

Pulling on a plastic hold is hardly rocket science, but there are a few things to watch out for that can leave you flat on your back – or worse. The main contender is a spinner. All plastic holds are attached to the wall by a central M10 bolt with a 6 or 8mm allen key head. Many climbing holds are fixed to a wooden plywood panel that contains moisture, and will both expand and contract. As wood heats up, it dries out and contracts, effectively leaving a space between the hold and the panel, and the hold becomes loose. If you grab a loose hold and pull on, it spins and you instantly fall off. It is not something that the wall management can do anything about, it is all in the fun of bouldering. On an older wall, most of the wood will have stabilised and you don't get so many spinners. On new walls, watch out. Your other nasty waiting, is a hold that simply breaks in half, or the bit you are holding snaps off. This is not likely to happen on a small bouldering nipple, but if you are under a roof, or in a grotto, most of the jugs will have a good incut to them. The mix of sand and resin, although strong, simply cannot withstand year after year of cranking, and will eventually break. With a crash pad below you hopefully will be saved. This is

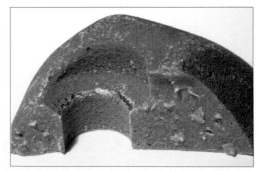

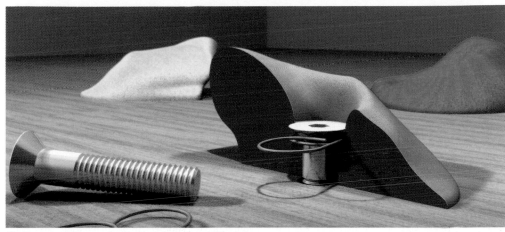

The Entreprises EPS system, of a wire loop inside a plastic hold

more of a concern to sport climbing indoors, since if you are high up, you might well drop the piece that broke off and it could hit someone below. The most dangerous hold of all is a cracker. This is when a hold develops a crack through the centre hole. It can be due to overtightening, not being on a flat surface, or just that the crystals of sand have set in a straight line -which makes the hold unpredictably weak. Then what happens, is that the hold breaks and you end up with one half in your hand, and the other half falling back to earth. With a large hold on a high overhang, it can present a dangerous proposition. Also when you are pulling hard on a hold and it breaks, for some strange reason, it seems to come back and thump you on the nose – and it's a nasty ouch! The climbing hold manufacturer Entreprises, has already started to put wire inside their holds, so as to keep them attached to the bolt, should they crack in half.

UPS AND DOWNS OF PLASTIC

There are plenty of good points about plastic. They generally come in bright colours, so you can spot them a mile away, and they're big, comfortable and designed to actually to hold onto. What more could you want for? They're rounded, which makes them far less injury provoking, and they don't often trap your fingers inside. They can be changed from week to week around the wall, and give never ending different problems. They can be used in coloured problems. ex. reds only to give a certain problem,

blue for extra footholds to make it easier – nice and simple. They have excellent friction, so your feet don't ever slip off them, and your hands stick like glue. I can promise, that if you are a beginner, they're perfect. There is a downside of course, they're not enough like real rock, and don't prepare you so well for going bouldering and climbing outside. Don't let it worry you for a while, get on and enjoy your bouldering on plastic.

Plastic holds that get well used, become clogged up with chalk in their granular surface, and then get slippery. They also get darker with shoe rubber deposits, eventually making it hard to spot the different colours. Most commercial walls therefore, wash their holds at regular intervals.

INTRODUCTION
GIVE-IT-A-GO
IND/BOULDERING
OUT/BOULDERING
IMPROVEMENT
INDOOR SPORT
OUTDOOR SPORT
MULTI-PITCH
VIA FERRATA
WHERE TO GO
INDEX

INDOOR ROCK - HAND HOLDS

Bouldering indoors on a well designed wall can
be as good as climbing outside on real rock. If
you travel far and wide, you may find some bolt-
on holds from natural rock, but for most of the
time, you get specifically selected, natural pieces of
stone, set in a freeform wall. Immediately the wall
becomes more dangerous! You have sharp edges
that naturally occur, ready and waiting to cut your
fingertips. You also wonder why the person building
the wall, left only that tiny little bit, protruding.
"You expect me, to pull on that!" I'm afraid so.
When you leave the bouldering world of plastic,
and head onto natural rock, you certainly go up
in the world of climbing difficulty. At this stage
in your bouldering there are 3 grades; easy, hard,
and desperate or perhaps impossible. Even the
easiest problems on natural rock holds, will seem
invariably desperate.

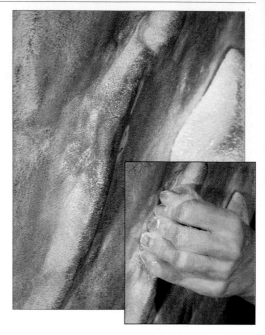

You need to learn how to use an indoor rock edge.
You cannot just flop your hand onto it and hope for
it to grip; that doesn't work. You need to gently feel
the edge or feel the rounded nature of the hold all
over. You do this by gently placing your hand on the
hold, and then very slightly gripping it in different
ways. You don't need to put your full strength on
at this point. When you are sure that you know
how you are going to hold the edge, think and
ask yourself 'has my hand sweated up, and is the
hold dry enough.' When you commit yourself to
the hold, it may then be too late to take a hand off
and chalk up. Good preplanning will mean you
probably chalk up first, and then carefully place
your fingers on the hold. You then transfer your
weight onto the handhold in a gradual, but quick
manner. Just like the principle with the foot and the
ankle; the hand combined with the wrist, works in
a similar way. If you tense all your fingers with the
palm and hand, it becomes locked, firm and strong.
If the rock edge you are using is polished and shiny
and your fingers are dry, with your hand locked
- you will hold the edge. If you can't hold it, don't
worry, you're just not strong enough yet. Try on a
few bigger holds instead.

*When using a long sidepull like this, your body and eyes are never
in a good position to see behind the edge. Be sure to feel for the best
part of it. This edge is made from the actual wall texture and is
therefore rounded, a very comfortable hold to use.*

*Rough aggregate has been used in a concrete mix for the wall surface.
Sometimes it takes a lot of feeling around to get the best pattern of tiny
grains to make into a good-ish hold! Painful, and can cut the skin.*

INTRODUCTION | GIVE-IT-A-GO | IND/BOULDERING | OUT/BOULDERING | IMPROVEMENT | INDOOR SPORT | OUTDOOR SPORT | MULTI-PITCH | VIA FERRATA | WHERE TO GO | INDEX

INDOOR ROCK – FOOT HOLDS

This is when it really starts to get hard, and it's baptism by fire I'm afraid. Indoor rock footholds are always polished, and your feet will skid off them sooner than you can even think. I recommend that you continue to use a lot of plastic footholds, even when you are using rock handholds. Sooner or later though, you will have to take the plunge, because you have to learn how to properly use natural footholds for any substantial progression in bouldering. You might have to invest in a pair of glasses, since looking for footholds is essential, and then placing your foot exactly on the hold is the key. Any tiny edge of rock bigger than 1mm counts as a foothold in bouldering, so you always need to look carefully.

When you place your foot on a natural foothold, it is almost the last part of the operation. You spend time looking at the edge, ripple, indent, pocket – whatever it may be. You have to imagine how the foot is going to work on the hold, before you actually put your foot on it. Why? It's obvious, because when your foot is on it, you can't see it anymore and don't know if it is the best way you are using the hold. It is the classic mistake for a

beginner, to just casually cover up the foothold with a casual misplacing of a foot, somewhere in the vicinity of the hold. A climber learning, might not have the leg control and agility to place their foot, exactly in the right place first time, and might need to adjust it slightly – that's allowable. But you must always look very carefully before you use any foothold. When you gain experience, you can just look at a foothold, know how it will support you, and judge very accurately where you will be able to reach, once you are standing up on it; that's the beauty of practise, leading to experience.

The nasty side to footholds on an indoor wall - also on an outdoor cliff, when the footholds get polished by lots of people using them over the years. Even carefull placement of the shoe, will not always prevent it slipping. If there is any dust on the hold, it will prevent the rubber from creating friction. All the tiny pieces of grit, will then act like little ball bearings, and the foot will quite simply roll off the hold. You can usually feel this happening, and in bouldering you just clean the hold and the sole of your shoe. In the case of smooth polish, a point will come where there is not enough weight on the rubber to create friction, and the contact will be instantly lost. This results in the shoe, literally shooting off the rock. If you are directly above the hold, and your waist is turned into the rock over your foot; your knee usually comes down and crunches on the hold. After some experience, you can see this sort of thing coming, and work out the best way to avoid these painful knee crunching moves.

INTRODUCTION
GIVE-IT-A-GO
IND/BOULDERING
OUT/BOULDERING
IMPROVEMENT
INDOOR SPORT
OUTDOOR SPORT
MULTI-PITCH
VIA FERRATA
WHERE TO GO
INDEX

INTRODUCTION

GIVE-IT-A-GO

IND/BOULDERING

OUT/BOULDERING

IMPROVEMENT

INDOOR SPORT

OUTDOOR SPORT

MULTI-PITCH

VIA FERRATA

WHERE TO GO

INDEX

You most probably won't find that many wooden holds on your beginners wall, since they're not the easiest of holds to grip, and rarely do they come in big sizes. Wood will also polish up with traffic, so you are not really likely to find them on popular indoor sport routes. So why use them? Wood, simply is the most favoured surface for training on by the majority of top level climbers. This is because of its low frictional properties. Put enough French polish on wood and it turns to glass, but in its natural smooth state, it offers ideal friction – not too little, not too much. What really makes it superb, is that the smoothness of the surface is just right, and doesn't tear your skin very easily. Eventually, when your hands become tired, your grip starts to fail. But it doesn't just instantly fail, the hand slowly starts to open (almost in slow motion), and your fingers start to creep over the hold. The coarse, granular surface of plastic holds, start cutting up the top layer of skin, and very effectively, remove it. Do this enough times, and you will start getting through your layers of skin – and eventually, with gnarly results! However, when you slip on a wooden hold, then you rarely loose any skin at all. Climbers wanting to improve greatly, really push themselves. Consequently, their hands will take a lot of punishment, and will slip on the holds a lot. By climbing on wood, a top climber can have a good 4 hour training session, and not have big worries about skin abrasion. OK – they might wreck their tendons, muscles, ligaments etc, but at least they still have skin left. There are two other very good assets to wood. The way it can be shaped and made into climbing holds, gives another large variety of shapes to test your skill upon. And secondly, because the surface is smooth, gripping onto it when your body is moving becomes an skill-art. It's not easy, and requires very strong stomach muscles with co-ordination. Climbing on wood is pretty advanced, but at least you know what the folk on the woodies are up to.

A full-on angled ply panel. To make pockets on this wall, big blocks of wood have been attached to the back of the ply, then holes and be drilled out and carved to make realistic pockets. By coating them with lime and resin mix, the finish can be made identical to limestone, to minimise skin wear. Naming the holds is popular, to identify different problems.

A fully bespoke and tooled wooden bolt-on hold. This is about as mean as they get, with only some of the pockets being much good, but having nice curves to slide out of easily. Rotation of the hold gives endless possibilities.

59

INTRODUCTION

GIVE-IT-A-GO

IND/BOULDERING

OUT/BOULDERING

IMPROVEMENT

INDOOR SPORT

OUTDOOR SPORT

MULTI-PITCH

VIA FERRATA

WHERE TO GO

INDEX

Asking climbers to warm up first, is like getting a kid to read through a 60 page user manual when the new playstation has just arrived – no hope. Also to be quite frank, when you're a beginner, you are very unlikely to have enough muscle power to do damage anyway. The people who do need to warm up, are those in the one arm pull up, or a two finger '**LOCK OFF**' club. (Lock off, is the term used when you just hang motionless from a hand hold and generally with no footholds.) Any top climber will take a good hour to warm up, phew! Most people can't even climb for an hour, they're exhausted. It's a lovely phrase, 'that you have to get fit enough – to warm up.' And it's true. Most climbers of course, only discover about warming up, after they have pulled their first tendon – eeeek! There isn't any magic about warming up, stretching etc. It is, what it says it is, and there isn't, a fast track way around it. A watch is certainly the best gauge to help you, just a nice cheap plastic one that can get trashed on the wall. As we said earlier, arriving at the bouldering spot in a warm and relaxed state is the most essential part. If you're not, go for a jog around the block, maybe a couple of press ups, sit ups, squat thrusts. Just get warm. Don't ever stretch cold muscles either, it does them damage, only try stretching them after you have been climbing a while.

Your best way to warm up your climbing muscles, is just to get onto the wall and climb. Stick to all the big holds, and stay on for only around 1 min. Don't let your arms get tired before you step off the wall when you are warming up. It's a good time to chat with friends, getting on and off the wall, having a few jokes and a laugh. After about 15 minutes, set yourself another spell of 15 mins using the smaller holds of the wall. When you're mate lurches up a desperate problem, don't try the same, you'll regret it if you pull something. Spend the 30-45 mins warm up, repeating some problems you have done before, not the hard ones. Target the problems that need control, and maybe do them 2 or 3 times to feel strong on them. The last part of the 45-60 min period, should be used to start warming up your flexibility. Start to leap for a few holds, but don't concentrate on trying to hold them, just get the body moving and loose. Now is the time to perhaps sit down, stretch the back of the legs and try the splits, hamstring stretches, etc. Any good fitness video will have the lot of these exercises in, and with a very attractive model no doubt. After an hour, you are ready to get stuck into some good, hard, boulder problems –oohps, time to go!

What is of serious importance though, is the need to warm down whilst your muscles are still warm, this prevents you becoming muscle bound and inflexible. It only takes a few minutes and can easily be done whilst chatting at the end of a good session. When you boulder hard, you work your muscles and then they contract, and should be stretched.

For most of the body it is not that important, but you must attend to: Forearms, Biceps, and Pectorals. These will definitely contract unless you look after them properly. We have shown in photos how to generally stretch each one in a common practical way. If you are interested on this subject, or are perhaps even concerned, visit a physiotherapist who should be able to advise you personally, on exercises that will be useful to your particular body.

World Ace-boulderer - Jerry Moffatt, happily stretching in a relaxed manner.

Amira, demonstrating a good warming down exercise for the biceps-upper arm, and the pectoral-front of the shoulder muscles. You simply place your flat hand on a wall around shoulder height, then slowly twist your body away from the wall and feel the muscles jently stretch.

Gary, litterally taking his performing thank you bow. Linking the hands together behind his back, and then lifting them back as far as possible to get a good all round shoulder stretch.

Garrett, giving a very good strech to the inside forearm muscles, and also importantly, the inner hand muscles. Very flexible people will be able to bend the fingers quite a way back, muscle bound climbers often can only just straighten their hands!

INTRODUCTION

GIVE-IT-A-GO

IND/BOULDERING

OUT/BOULDERING

IMPROVEMENT

INDOOR SPORT

OUTDOOR SPORT

MULTI-PITCH

VIA FERATA

WHERE TO GO

INDEX

There are a lot of different types of climbing that you can do, back and forth along a traverse wall, or up and down the naturally easy ways of the bouldering wall. Eventually you will be drawn into the real nugget of bouldering, what it is all about – 'THE PROBLEM.' There will be no shortage of enthusiastic boulderers at a wall to show you an endless number of problems, and particularly objectionable boulderers can be a problem themselves! So what is a problem, and what makes it either good or bad. Firstly, trying to move from one hold on a wall to another, is called a 'MOVE.' This describes the combined body movement, rather than any individual limb, hand or foot. A boulder problem consists of 2 or more moves in succession. Each move should be around the same level of difficulty, if not, then you only practically have one move anyway, since the other is so easy in relation.

So what then makes bouldering so attractive and addictive? A very simple answer – 'NO HOLD IS JUST A HOLD.' This is what makes bouldering fantastic. Let me explain. We consider a plastic hold bolted onto the wall as our hold. The rules are very simple, you can use any part of that hold in any way that you like, and with any part of your body. The magic is that everybody will use a different part of that hold, and most probably in a different way. You the boulderer have all the freedom in the world to utilise the hold, however you want to. At this stage, you will most probably not realise how influential this is. We all not only grip holds differently, but are allowed to use holds in completely different ways. If a hold has a good small side edge, you may prefer to use that, rather than a poorer but bigger – top edge. You decide for yourself, how to use the hold.

On a problem, all the holds will be marked so that you know which holds are in the problem, and if there are any in the surrounding area that are not allowed to be used. A typical problem may have 10-15 holds on a wall, going up, across, or even in an S shape over the wall. The holds are 'the problem,' and it is for you the boulderer to decide, which ones you want to use and how you want to use them. A lovely way of describing a boulder problem, is to call it, 'Three dimensional, physical chess.' You have to think a lot, since a big kudos of bouldering, is to do the problem on the first go, and if not – at least in the least number of attempts.

There is no real definition of what a good boulderer is. I suppose it is someone who really enjoys their bouldering, and generally gets up a lot of problems that they try, in very quick time. There are a few slang words to describe certain types of problem seekers! ANIMAL, is someone treating bouldering as a purely physical activity, trying a problem endlessly until they build up enough strength to get up it with minimal technique. ONSIGHTER, is by choosing a reasonable problem which you don't

Here we have Chris Cubit, one of the very best climbers in the world, kindly demonstrating a very simple problem that would suit a beginner. A lot of problems actually start with you sitting on the ground, called a sitting start (SS). Since a bouldering wall will only be 4-5 metres high, you want to pack in as much climbing as possible. In this instance, the problem uses a set of green holds which go up the wall.

INTRODUCTION
GIVE-IT-A-GO
IND/BOULDERING
OUT/BOULDERING
IMPROVEMENT
IND/OR SPORT
OUTDOOR SPORT
MULTI-PITCH
VIA FERRATA
WHERE TO GO
INDEX

INTRODUCTION

GIVE-IT-A-GO

IND/BOULDERING

OUT/BOULDERING

IMPROVEMENT

INDOOR SPORT

OUTDOOR SPORT

MULTI-PITCH

VIA FERRATA

WHERE TO GO

INDEX

Just because you reach a hold with one hand, doesn't restrict you then using the hold. Chris matches his hands and then shuffles them around to prepare for the next move. The less you shuffle, the less energy you waste, but the style of grip that you need for the next move is the most important factor.

Chris will know from experience, exactly where to place his feet, in order to get the most height with ease. Generally a problem on a wall will involve coloured handholds, but allow feet to be used anywhere.

know. This gives a mental challenge, because they are meant to get up it first go. PAIN IN THE ARSE, suggests someone who watches everyone struggle on a hard problem, then afterwards, shows them their way, which is far easier. CELLAR DWELLER, a boulderer who works out on a woodie all year long, and then does a single problem that is perhaps the hardest in the world. To be a good boulderer, you therefore have to know all the moves that you are going to need on your bouldering problems. We hope to cover, most of the unique ones for you.

This next move may look very simple, but is far from it. The hold Chris is reaching up for is an undercut, and is completely useless to him from his lower position. By really pulling on his right hand, and stepping up on the left outside foot edge, he can stand up independently; the left hand is only used for balance. As he gets higher though, the lower hold becomes useless, but by this time, the high undercut is now working as a hold and he can completely stand up. You can often get a move, where exactly in the middle, you can't hold on with either the top or the bottom hold - just like jumping a gap. In this problem, a beginner might only just hold in the middle of the move.

As the next hold is a long way up and Chris has a good left hand undercut, he can step up onto the right handhold. This move requires good flexibility and technique to keep your body close to the wall.

He has now very skilfully dropped his right knee across his body and down to the left. This makes his whole body work in the very powerful closed position, and although it is slightly overhanging, he can easily reach up to the next right hand hold. In this case, the right hand hold is sloping so he couldn't lunge for it either, finding a good position in balance was essential.

Here Chris has to quickly reach out and grab a good jug to the left before his feet swing off.

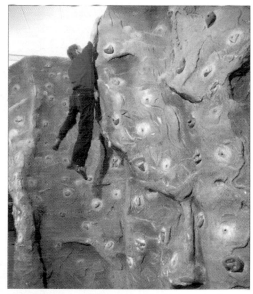

To make the last move really hard, he had decided not to use the green undercut hold, and make a dynamic leap for the top; a fun problem.

INTRODUCTION

GIVE-IT-A-GO

IND/BOULDERING

OUT/BOULDERING

IMPROVEMENT

INDOOR SPORT

OUTDOOR SPORT

MULTI-PITCH

VIA FERRATA

WHERE TO GO

INDEX

INTRODUCTION

GIVE-IT-A-GO

IND/BOULDERING

OUT/BOULDERING

IMPROVEMENT

INDOOR SPORT

OUTDOOR SPORT

MULTI-PITCH

VIA FERRATA

WHERE TO GO

INDEX

If you are actually able to hold onto the first hold of a problem, then the first difficulty you are likely to encounter, is reaching the second hold on the problem. If you can't reach it – welcome to the fun of bouldering. An instant way to overcome this difficulty is to leap, but we shall leave that for the next section because it is a bit unsubtle, and uses a huge amount of energy up in one go. Why leap when you don't have to. If you are trying to do a problem on the first go, then you could easily blow it with a leap that goes wrong. The intelligent approach is to maximise your possible reach, in the easiest possible manner. When you reach up with your hand in either bouldering or sport climbing, you can be said to be reaching up in the open or closed position. The 'OPEN POSITION' is like the 'stick your hands up' pose. Your hands can be in any position, but your body is flat onto the wall. It is an ideal position to hold when there are handholds at shoulder height, and especially in front of your face. It's very much the natural way you are going to hold on, and generally – it's how you move around the wall. When you reach up in the 'CLOSED POSITION,' you turn your body sideways onto the wall, so that your arm goes across your body. Although you can hold onto the wall with a jug in the closed position, you will naturally always hold onto a sidepull or an undercut hold. You also change your foot position to use the outside edge of the shoe on the hold for the highest foot. Your weight goes onto this foot, and although the lower foot can be rested on, it is usually just used as a counterbalance, and is said to be flagging (p 214).

The two positions could be mistaken as the same, but they are very different and have hugely different pros and cons. It's not vitally important that you know everything about them, but a basic understanding will really help you to solve many of the simpler boulder problems

Here Jessica illustrates a simple problem of going from one handhold to the high pink one. In the open position, the move gets progressively harder if you use a higher foothold. In the closed position, you need a relaitvely high foothold, but it is easier and usually gets you reaching further.

OPEN POSITION

CLOSED POSITION

when you are learning. The open position will always get you the furthest reach, especially if you start to dynamically leap, but the closed position is a much stronger and securer technique. Often, you will see a strong climber do a move in an open position. You try, but simply cannot hold on. Apply the technique of the closed position. Use the handhold in a sidepull manner, use the outside edge of the foot, turn your body around, so that you are pulling across your torso in a closed position. You will find it far easier this way, and may well be able

to do the problem. Often, the foothold and sidepull may be small and terrible, but because the position is such a strong technique, you don't have to pull so hard, and consequently it works. I can't guarantee that this will work every time, but it's a very good general rule of thumb. You will learn a lot now from watching other better climbers, just look how often they turn their bodies into the closed position.

INTRODUCTION

GIVE-IT-A-GO

IND/BOULDERING

OUT/BOULDERING

IMPROVEMENT

INDOOR SPORT

OUTDOOR SPORT

MULTI-PITCH

VIA FERRATA

WHERE TO GO

INDEX

INTRODUCTION

GIVE-IT-A-GO

IND/BOULDERING

OUT/BOULDERING

IMPROVEMENT

INDOOR SPORT

OUTDOOR SPORT

MULTI-PITCH

VIA FERRATA

WHERE TO GO

INDEX

There comes a time when no matter how high that you try to reach, you simply cannot get to the next handhold on the problem. Apart from jumping – see the next section, there is one last avenue that you should explore. This is know as the 'HIGH STEP UP,' or sometimes the 'ROCKOVER.' There has to be a foothold in the area between the waist and the shoulder that is allowed. Try it on a low foothold to start with (like above), so that you can get the action worked out, before trying the impossible with a foothold around your ear hole! First of all, simply match your hands on the good handhold and throw your foot onto the foothold. The next part is a double action, first pulling down until enough weight is over the foot, so then you can then push down on the hands to straighten the arms. So long as you use a low-ish foothold, you will do this OK. The higher the foothold you use, the more flexible you have to become.

The really technical way to climb a high step up, is to use your hand on the hold as well. Now you have to work on your flexibility to do this, but there are a few tricks that will help. Often, the easiest way to get your foot up, is to lean back and sort of throw your foot out sideways, high onto the hold. The only problem here, is that you might not be flexible enough to reach in and grab the hold! The alternative version is to grab the hold first, then try to lift your foot high enough to go onto the hold (photo). If you are inflexible, you will struggle mercilessly. However, if you can nearly do it but not quite, then try swinging your foot a little, getting it higher by a good couple of inches with momentum, then sneak it onto the top of the hold. In this position the leg is not in its strongest range of movement, and you risk pulling a hamstring if you are not warmed up! By pulling on both hands at the same time, you give a huge amount of extra help to the leg which is trying its hardest to work in a weak position. This really does make a difference and you will soon be pulling upwards, then you can easily let go with the lower hand. It is one of the most beautiful movements in climbing to do. Not only is it elegant, but it also leaves you in perfect control to reach for the next hold.

A classic problem at Brunel Wall, where the handhold really can be used to hold the body close to the rock, whilst the foot is brought up onto the hold. Rocking up onto the foothold is still initiated by pulling on both hands before letting go with the left hand, thanks to flexible Jon Partridge.

INTRODUCTION

GIVE-IT-A-GO

IND/BOULDERING

OUT/BOULDERING

IMPROVEMENT

INDOOR SPORT

OUTDOOR SPORT

MULTI-PITCH

VIA FERRATA

WHERE TO GO

INDEX

INTRODUCTION

GIVE-IT-A-GO

IND/BOULDERING

OUT/BOULDERING

IMPROVEMENT

INDOOR SPORT

OUTDOOR SPORT

MULTI-PITCH

VIA FERRATA

WHERE TO GO

INDEX

Neil Gresham, a specialist climbing coach and Masterclass teacher, demonstrates a perfectly controlled lunge on a steep section of an indoor overhang. (Westway)

There are three stages of mid-air movement in climbing; Lunge – Jump – Leap; and they're all called '**DYNOS.**' (See section 2-3 for jumps & leaps). It's what makes bouldering fun, hence our little cartoon character Dyno-mite, who loves to make fluid movement wherever he goes. You'll have great fun throughout your bouldering life with all sorts of jumps and leaps. If you were to make a dyno that is effectively 'a movement past the point of no return,' high up on a mountain cliff, it would be suicidally dangerous. Fortunately, we are in the world of bouldering, where if you don't quite make it, you simply fall back onto the soft crashmat. In bouldering, the dyno is cute way to solving many problems, instead of resorting to 'bulldozing by strength into submission.' A good comparison can be seen in gymnastics. The men with humungous muscle power on the rings, power their way around. However, the girls with minimal strength on the asymmetric bars, flow dynamically from one bar to another, and seemingly effortless with agility and fluidity. You often see the same in bouldering.

Where a problem can simply be solved with movement, you don't need to build up the muscle bulk of an Olympic male gymnast.

If you make a dyno to any handhold within practical reach, it's called a lunge. There isn't a totally strict definition, but you generally keep your feet on the same footholds. A lunge is also a movement where you almost feel that if you were a bit stronger, you could grip the lower hold better to reach the upper one in complete control. A lunge is also a movement that with practise, is made fluid and exact, but retractable – i.e. You can still keep hold of the lower hold during the movement, so if you don't make it, you are still able to hold onto the wall. This certainly takes a lot of practice, but is something that all top boulderers excel at. On the first attempt to a problem, you are allowed to keep lunging, so long as you don't come off - one of the nice quirky rules in bouldering.

A lunge requires three separate skills, dynamic planning, co-ordinated gripping, and final body flow. Every movement in climbing is different, so it is completely impossible to say this or that, but there are a few principles which will help you lunge with a certain amount of success. '**DYNAMIC PLANNING**,' is the foundation, you have to look up at the next hold and work out how you are going to use to grip it. From below this is not always easy. (Think crash pad, landing – it may be a spinner, or outdoors it may even be a loose block.) If you are in doubt, it is best to take the cautious approach, and not go for the onsight. A lot of experienced boulderers will do a pre-dyno, where they lunge up for a hold, but instead of trying to hold it, they tap it in mid air (whilst passing), to hear if it is hollow and may be dangerous. They also know that they are coming down, and will have planned where to land, and how their feet will be placed. This method also gives you a bit of confidence and practise, to fall in reasonably controlled manner. To make the dyno and reach the hold, you often have to put your foot on an intermediate hold around knee or waist level. Exactly where to put your foot may depend on wherever there is a foothold, but after a while, you will get to know how your body works, and get your foot in the right place, every time.

Although Neil looks moderately strong, he uses very little strength at all during this move. By pulling up in a co-ordinated fashion on both hands at the same time, his right hand can simply flick up to the somewhat 'diabolical' hold.

Very few climbers will be strong enough to reach out from under a roof or a cave, and get the hold on the lip in a static manner. Here a small lunge is really handy and a good way to get used to using and holding the move. Nice too, since you are near the crash pad and can get a lot of practice. Do remember to take off your chalk bag whenever you are practising lunges or dynos.

INTRODUCTION
GIVE-IT-A-GO
IND/BOULDERING
OUT/BOULDERING
IMPROVEMENT
INDOOR SPORT
OUTDOOR SPORT
MULTI-PITCH
VIA FERRATA
WHERE TO GO
INDEX

CO-ORDINATED GRIPPING, is the art of arriving at a handhold on the move and gripping it – now, does that sound easy! It would be if you were arriving at it; but you're not, you're simply just passing through, and on the way back down. When your body is stationary at a hold, the force on your hand is your bodyweight. If you are a millisecond late and are on the way back down, the force of gravity multiplies your weight, and the force you have to hold becomes far greater than just your weight. Usually, your hand is only strong enough to hold your weight, so it is critical to grip at the exact point of equilibrium. Of course, the slower you arrive at a hold, the easier it is to take a grip of it, - how so many boulderers forget this! If you plan to lunge a couple of inches past the hold, it will give you a few more milliseconds to get a grip of the hold – on the way in! Not everyone has immaculate co-ordination, so think about yourself and plan

Here Chris demonstrates the key basics to perfect dyno technique;
1) You must select the perfect foothold to use. It may not always be obvious or big, it is all about position.
2) Getting the correct momentum by pulling on both hands together equally, but also whilst keeping your body close to the wall.
3) You mustn't over cook it; you need to arrive at the top hold, almost in perfect balance.
Done like this, the dyno uses far less energy than any other method of climbing, and feels great.

accordingly. A lot goes on when you arrive at a handhold during a dyno. Your fingers will touch the edge, and you need to develop cat like reactions. How good is it? How comfortable is it? Is it chalked up or moist? Am I on my way up so I have a good chance of holding it? Am I on the way down and have no chance of holding it? What happens next, is that you put all of you're body weight on the hand. If you have got it wrong, it can be excruciatingly painful – your hand simply rips over the hold,

Handhold preparation

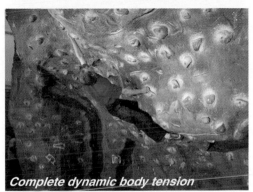

Complete dynamic body tension

Powerful and accurate holding

and down you come. It is better not to grip, than to try gripping when you don't stand a chance of holding the hold. A lot of beginners can get nastily cut up if they are too ambitious with their lunging, I recommend that you start to lunge early on in your bouldering life, and slowly work up to bigger lunge's and then onto holds that are not so kind.

FINAL BODY FLOW, is why a lot of beginners cannot hold a dyno-lunge. Unless you've made a dyno where the hold is at the absolute peak of your flow, then grabbing the top hold is only one part of the move. A lot of the time you are arriving at a hold from an angle, and it is when you have to quickly pull the dancing feet out of the bag. The most popular method to stop your momentum, is to throw a leg behind in a flagging movement. The other popular technique, is to match your hand on the hold you are arriving at. It is often comical to see a climber make a dyno and presume they can grip the final hold with one hand. At the last minute, the other hand quickly makes a match to keep them there, it looks juddery like the old silent movies – but it counts, because they're still on and that's all that matters.

Key elements for good dyno technique on a very hard and continuous dyno problem.

Fast reactions and continued movement

INTRODUCTION

GIVE-IT-A-GO

IND/BOULDERING

OUT/BOULDERING

IMPROVEMENT

INDOOR SPORT

OUTDOOR SPORT

MULTI-PITCH

VIA FERRATA

WHERE TO GO

INDEX

You can get nice layaways and difficult layaways - yet we seem to have found a particularly nasty finger layaway, to illustrate how you use one! The word layaway is used to describe a hold that is vertical in nature, and one that you have to push against. Sometimes the term 'TO LAY OFF' is used, to indicate that you push off a hold, rather than grab it in the palm of your hand. For the beginner, layaways are difficult to master because they are usually small, and require some awkward body movement techniques. It is far more natural to pull on a big jug, than to push away on a small edge. They require two elements, 'FINGER STRENGTH' and 'BALANCE.' You need good strong fingers, to pull the body onto the rock in a reverse action. This really works the triceps muscle on the outside of your arm, and the lower back muscles – be sure to warm down after a good session of layaways. You also need good balance, since a lot of your weight is over your leg, and the foothold you have may not be all that positive. Problem setters just love to combine a layaway with a high step up, a great but desperate combination. Outside, you can look at a piece of natural rock that seems flat and with no incuts at all. Peeping a bit closer, you can see that there are layaways on it so it can actually be climbed. This is the magic hold of climbing, it makes the unclimbable, climbable.

A useless hold for anything except a layaway

A fiendish layaway hold, but fortunately situated in a perfect position for a layaway, above - but only just to one side of a good foothold. When layaway is more out to the side, you need more tricep and back power.

INTRODUCTION

GIVE-IT-A-GO

IND/BOULDERING

OUT/BOULDERING

IMPROVEMENT

INDOOR SPORT

OUTDOOR SPORT

MULTI-PITCH

VIA FERRATA

WHERE TO GO

INDEX

INTRODUCTION

GIVE-IT-A-GO

IND/BOULDERING

OUT/BOULDERING

IMPROVEMENT

INDOOR SPORT

OUTDOOR SPORT

MULTI-PITCH

VIA FERRATA

WHERE TO GO

INDEX

There are many more techniques to learn for indoor bouldering, but what we have shown you in this section will be plenty enough for you to get stuck into a good season's fun and exploration. By mixing with a lot of people at your local wall, you will start to pick up tips and tricks, all over the place. The last topic for us to deal with before propelling you into an indoor fun competition, is to check out the different ways to come down off a climbing wall. Learning to climb downwards is not that easy, but certainly comes with practise. In our next chapter when we go to outdoor bouldering, where there isn't going to be a big bouncy crash pad, so you will need to start making preparations to sort out your down climbing skills, and your jumping technique onto a portable crash pad.

A good idea is to incorporate down climbing into your warm up routine. Try going up to a nice high point that you are comfortable with, and then climbing directly downwards. It's certainly a lovely privilege to do this at an indoor wall above a mat. This is a very bad time for spinners. If you are pulling up to a spinner, it will often spin as you touch it, but you still have most of your weight on the lower hold. Often when you are climbing down, you automatically put your weight onto the hold that you're dropping your body onto. If the hold spins, you are off in an instant, and are generally uncontrollable in heading to the deck – head and shoulder first. The best way around this, is to always use the same holds for hands and feet. When you put your weight on holds with your feet, they can spin or break, and you have the luxury of still holding onto good handholds. Then when you come to use them for hands, you are at least fairly confident of their performance.

There is an art to 'JUMPING OFF' from a great height. Pick a height that you want to practise jumping off from, which may be as low as 2 metres, but it is important to be comfortable with what you are attempting. Try a simple jump. Now get back onto a slightly overhanging section and drop off. The best technique, is to let go of both hands

A typical problem that finishes a bit higher off the ground than you want. Always down climb to a place where you are happy to jump down from, Steve taking a good look at the landing area, then perfectly landing with feet apart, bending the knees, and steadying himself with the palms of his hands.

and one foot, whilst just keeping the other foot on a hold for a millisecond as your body starts to fall. This also has the effect of stabilising you, and almost feels like stepping down. In some instances, you can even push on the foothold to take a slight step, and therefore direct your landing into the exact area you want to. If you are going to land and roll, make sure it is sideways. If you roll forward, you thump your head on the mud outside, or into the rock in front of you. If you fall backward, you get a lovely roll – until you head thwacks the ground. This has the added stupidity, that by then you will have just rolled off your portable crash pad and be hitting the ground. If you roll sideways, you can absorb a lot of the shock in some horizontal movement. Needless to say, please roll sideways – downhill. If you land with your feet together, you

generally fall over like a tree being felled, and your hips take a massive crunching, followed by your shoulders. The finest falling technique, is to seemingly glance the ground, whilst rolling sideways into a ball, and do a complete 360º roll with your head tucked in, and then spring back onto your feet. It looks fun, and works well - so long as there isn't a tree in the way. It works amazingly well on a slope. Some boulderers fall up to 7 metres, and roll in this way. Beware, some boulderers like visiting hospitals too and don't mind legs full of pins. Certainly the most critical part to falling in bouldering, is the angle of the ground that you fall onto. If it is level, then you don't have to fall from very high to be in big trouble. If the ground slopes away, you are in a far luckier position – so long as you can use the slope to your benefit. Don't wait until you get outdoors to try out your rolling technique, utilise the Indoor mats.

Below - Hayley's foot being used to direct her landing away from the wall; casual but critical.

INTRODUCTION

GIVE-IT-A-GO

IND/BOULDERING

OUT/BOULDERING

IMPROVEMENT

INDOOR SPORT

OUTDOOR SPORT

MULTI-PITCH

VIA FERRATA

WHERE TO GO

INDEX

You may find this hard to believe, but if you've studied up to here carefully, and enjoyed about 10 really intensive bouldering sessions, then you could now be ready for your first competition. You're highly unlikely to win it, but then again, the whole idea of competitions for 99% of climbers, is to have a great day out and enjoy some new boulder problems set by professional route setters. You can get it wrong at a competition and have a horrible time, but these few pages should put you in the picture and enable you to know just what goes on and how to go about it. With this information, there isn't any reason why the first comp you enter, shouldn't be anything other than fun.

First ask at your local wall about competitions and when they occur. If they have the words 'World championship' or 'International' in the title, then you leave your rock shoes at home and go as a spectator! These events are for super bionic boulderers who are stronger than you can believe. You most probably wouldn't even be able to leave the ground on their problems. If there is 'local or Southern etc.' in the title, then this is the one for you. Today there are competitions like this all around the UK, and they have a nice mixture of categories for kids, adults and veterans. The comps

T shirts on sale and registration time, early and bleary eyed often.

are relaxed and have an easy-going atmosphere to them. You may get a couple of whizz kids, but they usually just get hot under the collar with each other anyway. Comps are usually held at the larger walls because of their popularity, and you may expect up to 100 entrants. You get all sorts of people turning up; lots of kids, plenty of juniors, adults, veterans and the golden oldies.

Most comps are about a 4 hour event, which can get extended for various reasons. Most local comps don't require you to register before the event, but popularity could change this in the future, hopefully not. There's usually a registration period in the early morning when you turn up, pay your entry fee and get a competition card that you carry around the comp with you. Make sure you let the organisers know if you are a newcomer to competitions, they will most probably suggest the easiest of the categories for you – regardless of age, sex etc. This way, you will get up a lot of problems and enjoy it. If you end up in a high category, you will get despondent because you simply can't do any problems. They often sell T shirts for the comp, and might have a sponsor's stand with the latest bits of equipment to have a look at. It looks chaotic with 100 boulderers warming up, but you get a good chance to say hello to friends, and get moving on the rock.

All the problems will be set in the bouldering area, and the idea is not to do any of them before a set time – usually around 10-11am. All the problems will be marked up with a system particular to the

No age limits. (Michaela & Hannah getting ready to crank)

comp. This is often done by putting a circle in chalk around the holds or putting masking tape around the holds. There will be quite a few abbreviations that you have to get familiar with. Importantly, if it's your first comp, it doesn't matter at all if you get anything wrong, you're not going to carry away first prize so don't feel under any pressure. A lot of the easier problems will be marked up as MH-any footholds. This is simply hands only on the Marked Holds, and you can use any footholds on the wall. FO, means Features Only, this is any part of the wall that is not a bolt on, or screw on hold. MF-MH, means Marked Footholds and Marked Handholds only. SS, means start with both hands on this (or a single S on two separate holds). FF, means finishing hold. When you get to the finishing hold, you must grab it with two full hands if it has two F's, and actually hold onto it. Outside of this, there isn't a lot more.

Competitions can be organised in different ways. Sometimes you have to do your own scoring, but at bigger events, there is usually a good gathering of judges. Around the start time there will be the general announcements of any particular rules for the competition, and you will hear how many problems there are, and how long the comp will run for. You are likely to have between 15 and 25 different problems, and around 4 hours to complete them all in. A common system for many competitions is to have a judge on each problem,

Main briefing at the Southern Indoor league comp - The Castle Wall.

Judges getting a very thorough briefing of the problem from a route setter, normally a world class boulderer who will know how to create difficult, but not impossible problems.

usually a parent, friend, or a keen climber with an injury. Here you simply give your scorecard to the judge, attempt the problem and they mark your card. They can also keep cards in order to help queuing on busy problems.

The basic comp rules. You are allowed to watch other climbers do a problem, or fall off it of course. You are not allowed to touch any of the holds on a problem – prior to your actual go on the problem. Each go starts, as soon as your feet leave the floor, A restart means 2nd go etc. If you are moving along the problem and your foot touches the floor, you are considered to have fallen off. You are allowed three attempts to do each problem without falling off. You can climb forwards and backwards along the problem, so long as you only use the designated holds. No help or outside physical support is allowed of course. It's very simple, and after each go you can mark your score card accordingly.

The basic scoring rules: Points systems can vary from comp to comp, but as an indicator you may get 10 points if you do the problem first go, 7 for a second attempt, and then 3 for a third. There may also be a bonus point system operating, where if you do a problem with or without a certain hold, you get an additional point.

INTRODUCTION

GIVE-IT-A-GO

IND/BOULDERING

OUT/BOULDERING

IMPROVEMENT

INDOOR SPORT

OUTDOOR SPORT

MULTI-PITCH

VIA FERRATA

WHERE TO GO

INDEX

The junior girls category, being keenly being judged by a parent.

A well laid out competition, with clearly marked holds and numbers.

You can do the problems in any order, to avoid queuing and congestion. The keen climbers will walk around in the warm up and look first at every problem. Because they are experienced, they can often see exactly how to do a problem without even touching the holds. They will be planning how to approach the event, do some easy ones first, then mentally prepare for the harder ones. If you're a beginner, I recommend you to find any problem without a que, and just get on it and have fun. Think about it, somebody else has spent considerable time setting 25 new problems, just

for you to have a go at and enjoy. They are likely to be very well set and will have a great range of techniques – simply paradise. Certainly take a bit of time to watch the strong boulderers in action, see how they grip holds, how they can change hands and dyno for holds. You will often be surprised by the strong looking guys doing well, but then being superbly outclimbed by someone who looks completely weak. There is nothing so bewildering as to how well some casual laid back people, can climb.

There will be a set finish time in the afternoon, and all the cards are handed in to the computer number cruncher. Hey presto, out comes a score sheet with everyone in order of points. There is often a mini competition held after this for the very top boulderers who come in the top 3 or 5. This is fun to watch, and the climber who does best – wins of course. A comp is often sponsored by companies who then gives prizes for various categories. For most people, comps are about having a nice day out, catching up with friends, and picking up tips from watching other better climbers. It's fun to have a learning day which is very much 'hands on.'

INTRODUCTION

GIVE-IT-A-GO

IND/BOULDERING

OUT/BOULDERING

IMPROVEMENT

INDOOR SPORT

OUTDOOR SPORT

MULTI-PITCH

VIA FERRATA

WHERE TO GO

INDEX

As usual, the top mens category is uncomfortably difficult in many places, with slopers and awkward dyno's.

It's not a actually necessary for anybody who takes up indoor bouldering, to then go outside and make the transition into outdoor bouldering. They are separate activities which of course are linked, but they are very different indeed. To go outside can be considerably more dangerous, and we rate outdoor bouldering at an insanity level of 4, compared to a measly 2 for indoor bouldering. You may simply adore your indoor wall bouldering just around the corner from your home, convenient and a handy work out for times when life's stress just gets to you. So why change it? Do you really want the hassle of travelling hundreds of miles to a bouldering location, only for it to rain all week? Now that's never happened at your lovely centrally heated wall, or has it?

The move into the outdoor world of bouldering, is the beginning of a real life adventure. It's not about waving goodbye to the inner city rock grotto where you've almost become an insitu stalactite, or the abandoning of friends who you've bouldered with and learnt so much from. It's simply taking everything that you have learnt so far, and putting it to the test in the big wide world. Then you can enjoy the elation from returning home, with wonderful stories of this boulder from heaven, that overhang from hell, and the slab that was flatter that you could ever, ever imagine!!

If you've been used to an indoor freeform rock environment, you will be a tiny bit conditioned to the bizarre nature of rocky shapes and weirdy holds. But nothing will really prepare you for the wonderful complexity in rock that our mother earth can produce. When you arrive at your first proper boulder, place your flat hand on it. You can enjoy the rock as a true friend, it doesn't bite you, it doesn't tax you, and it doesn't fire bullets at you either. But on the other hand, it can cut your fingers and hurt you, give you the most physically and mentally taxing problems around, and indeed kill you if you don't respect the heights and dangers on offer. A boulder is everything imaginable, it's up to you how to interpret it and get out of it what is enjoyable for you.

You can learn how to boulder on indoor walls in about 6 months, it may take a few more years to become an expert. When you start to boulder outside, you have just begun a lifetime's apprenticeship. There is an incredible amount to learn, and even the old masters are still learning in their retirement years. The basic techniques still apply outdoors and will serve you well, but there are now two more additional aspects you have to get to grips with, those of TEXTURE and FORM.

On an indoor wall of plastic's, you can develop a limited range of strengths to work on certain shaped holds. You can even improve on freeform, but nothing will prepare you for the variation of rock texture that you get with outdoor hold shapes. You will be confronted with everything from the tiniest flake edge, to the smoothest, giant frictionless slopers. The boulders themselves hold the majestic presence of form; shapes that are beautiful, awesome, ridiculous, deceiving, enigmatic, serene, etc... You can go on forever. Every face of every boulder, gives a new problem that requires its own technique, All the famous rocks of Granite, Sandstone, Gritstone, Limestone and Gneiss, offer different styles of problems. Every type of rock comes in a million different shapes, textures and sizes. The geological and geographical enormity of bouldering is immense. It's not something you can capture or complete, you can only sample a bit here and there. You can't take it home with you, but the memories – yes, they last forever.

Outdoor bouldering, it certainly beats sitting behind a desk.

Top: Pedra do Urso, Portugal. Covilha 6a; Jerry Moffatt
Bottom : Rocher aux Sabots, Fontainebleau, France. Morceau de Choix 5a; Tyler Landman

INTRODUCTION

GIVE-IT-A-GO

IND/BOULDERING

OUT/BOULDERING

IMPROVEMENT

INDOOR SPORT

OUTDOOR SPORT

MULTI-PITCH

VIA FERRATA

WHERE TO GO

INDEX

INTRODUCTION | GIVE-IT-A-GO | IND/BOULDERING | OUT/BOULDERING | IMPROVEMENT | INDOOR SPORT | OUTDOOR SPORT | MULTI-PITCH | VIA FERRATA | WHERE TO GO | INDEX

At your local wall there will be good standard problems that everyone knows, and often there is a book which will list a whole set of problems using this and that hold. A popular way of marking holds is to paint a white dot where it can be seen but not rubbed off, then write a number or letter on it for reference. Even with a simple sharp edge on a freeform wall, you can place a dot just beneath it for identification. Simply by following the numbers, you have a set problem.

You then arrive at one of fun parts of bouldering, 'GIVING A PROBLEM, A BOULDERING GRADE.' Well, you can't beat the simple system of 3 grades; easy, hard and desperate. So why make grading any more complex? Well, standing at the bottom of a desperate boulder problem, can be the equivalent of waiting at the receiving end of a West Indian, fast test bowler - a perfect example of pointlessness, intimidation and danger. Yet standing beneath a problem where you are most likely to get up it with a struggle, is both fun and something you're going to want to do – again and again. Just like most sports, you can get a tremendous amount if you operate around your comfortable, yet testing level. The spectrum of climbing ability is far greater than 3 broad categories without doubt. The physical measurements of our world, like the kilogram and centigrade, are directly derived from the weight and boiling point of water. For the indexation of bouldering, we take a mystical trip to France.

If there is a yellow brick road in bouldering, then it certainly leads straight to Fontainebleau, just south of Paris. Simply get on your magic carpet and zoom off there. It's where both bouldering and grading began, which makes it perhaps easiest to explain. Measuring difficulty of a problem is always going to be subjective. It can easily be influenced by your reach, bendy flexibility, and if you are particularly strong on a certain type of move. At Fontainebleau, bouldering started with a broad spectrum of climbers; whole families bouldering together, tiny tots, strong adults. They needed a grading scale for everyone. They took all the problems that there were, and placed them in an order of difficulty, starting at 1, and went up to 5. To separate the grades, each number was subdivided into a plus and minus, e.g. giving you 4-, 4 and 4+. This gave 15 grades to

separate out the different problems - which worked very well for very many years. In the 1940's, standards went up so much that a 6th grade was invented, but rather than use a plus or minus, 6a, 6b, 6c was used. With the addition of a plus grade to each, this made 6 new grades. Eventually came even harder climbs, and the 7th grade was opened in 1960. By the 1980's, the 8th grade became the cutting edge level and today there may be a 9th grade. It's all quite academic, since only a handful of climbers in the world ever hope to reach this level.

Good things always take a while to catch on here in the UK, and Fontainebleau grades are still having to compete with around 6 other grading systems here. Certainly around Europe, Font grades are popular because most climbers can go to there, understand the grading, and then make good relative comparisons for their home patch. You will find them in Portugal, Spain, Italy and Germany; and they are very likely to be of an identical standard.

In the UK things used to be nice, fun and quirky, with funny grading systems everywhere. Now we are a bit of a chaotic state, with the popularization of the American bouldering scale that simply goes from V1 to V15, (and which doesn't help to dispel the myth that UK boulderers can only count in a straight line from 1-15). It also a scale which doesn't pretend to be any other than elitist. It starts at V1, the equivalent of Font 5a and English technical 5b; which is certainly beyond the ability of a lot of climbers to onsight. It also doesn't even categorise problems for kids, families, and anyone with disabilities of course. So in the UK, we have to combine UK technical grades for general problems.

V grades originate from Hueco in America, where 99% of any European boulderers haven't been to. This consequently means that any climber in Europe grading a problem. has no real bench mark and therefore you will get wild variances from area to area! It will not take you too long to discover that most bouldering areas are very well graduated from easiest to hardest, regardless of any numbering system anyway. However, unless a problem gets a Font grades, it is unlikely to be actually 'GRADED.'

The first thing you need to do, it to find your boulders. When you are a highly experienced boulderer and know all there is to know, a computer search engine on your mobile phone-gps, would be the business. But if you want the privilege of having life easy, and having someone do all the work in finding you the best problems in an area, then a guidebook is without doubt the cheapest way to do it. Because bouldering is slightly more esoteric than Football, you won't get a bouldering specialist guidebook in your local newsagents, or even bookshop. The best place to go is to a specialist climbing shop that stocks climbing books. (All listed in our up to date Climber's Handbook).

There are a great many different types of climbing guidebooks, and like any typical sales pitch, they are all the best and what you need most. Most styles of climbing will have their very own guidebooks, so you get some for ice climbing, others for alpine, etc. At other times you get a guidebook to a whole area, which covers all the styles of climbing in that region. These are not so common, because few climbers other than instructors, will have need for the full scope of local climbing information. Also publishing trends continue to change, and now sport climbing and bouldering seem to be more commonly found together in the same books. There are of course, many guidebooks dedicated solely to bouldering problems, and even some which only cover certain difficulties of problems (usually friggin 'ard).

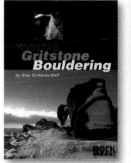

Alan Cameron-Duff, superb Yorkshire boulder guide

Bi-lingual - dedicated love of bouldering in North Wales

Cosiroc -The Bible, every problem in an area at Fontainebleau.

Portugal - combined sport and bouldering guidebook

Sometimes, guidebooks can be very low on content! But then again, they can usually stand on their own artistic merit as a lovely book. Some are purely functional; others are purely dysfunctional unfortunately. Perseverance is not only a asset that you need to develop into a good boulderer, it is often a major quality in keeping hold of a guidebook, instead of chucking it over the nearest hedge in frustration. You normally get a map of the bouldering area, with every boulder drawn in outline. Then there are little arrows to indicate where problems are. Most are given a name, grade, and have some fun little icons to show what sort of problem it is. Some areas may offer 100 problems not worth doing, others may have 3 that are worth travelling hundreds of miles to. Only you can decide what you are looking for. Guidebooks for the most part, are meticulous to detail, and offer a fantastic wealth of climbing information. The value for money that you get, is usually immense.

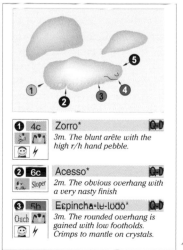

1 4c **Zorro***
3m. The blunt arête with the high r/h hand pebble.

2 6c **Acesso***
Sloper *2m. The obvious overhang with a very nasty finish*

3 5h **Espincha-le-todo***
Ouch *3m. The rounded overhang is gained with low footholds. Crimps to mantle on crystals.*

A JW-bouldering guidebook layout, with problem icons, and quick drying indicators.

When you climb on an indoor wall, it is important to get good friction from the soles of your climbing shoes, but rarely is it critical, since the plastic holds are so grippy anyway. When you start climbing outdoors, your feet are suddenly in a grimey and mucky environment – yuk! When you place a climbing shoe on a foothold, via a cowpat, not only does it stink, but it shoots off, like '....' off a shovel. For the first time you will realise, how useless a climbing shoe is when it's wet. There are two big enemies to outdoor performance, one is damp, and the other is sand. Both are equally as disastrous and will limit your ability hugely. So many beginners fail to see this and have a frustrating time, floundering about the bottom of the boulder. If you watch any good boulderer, they will make sure that their feet are immaculately clean. A few may try to fool you so beware, their feet may look dirty and covered in sand, but just before they climb, they will skim the edges of their shoe, squeaky clean. They afterwards proclaim that the problem was easy with dirty shoes. But you will have noticed that they only used their pristine dry edges.

You certainly don't clean your shoes by rubbing them on the ground, or even worse - the rock, because it causes unneccessary erosion. It is simple, you sit down and place your ankle across your knee, then you rub all the dust and sand off with an old beer towel. Make sure your sole and the strip 'RAND,' around the side is dry. This works for most abrasive rock and will be grippy enough. You can however gain a significant amount of extra friction, by rubbing the sole of the shoe with the palm of the hand. You only need to do this once, and you can see the rubber change colour, to a far more blacker and deeper colour. If you do it more times, you just wear away the boot, and end up with very black hands. Now when you step onto the rock, they will stick like glue. It is really useful to have a small piece of carpet to stand on, so you can go straight from cleaning onto a magic carpet. There are not excuses left if you fail now!

At Fontainebleau where there is no shortage of sand, you soon become accustomed to cleaning. On the lower photo you can see just the top part has been taken down to the very dark black rubber.

One of the essential pieces of kit for outdoor bouldering, is a crash pad. It is used, to 'IMPROVE,' the softness of the landing area, but does not come anywhere near the safety of your big indoor crash pads. It also plays a hugely significant part in preventing ground erosion, especially when you repeatedly fall off. Many climbers who are not planning to fall off, simply use a piece of carpet or a small doormat to stand on. In a lot of cases, there are other nasty shaped pieces of rock sticking up. Fortunately,

boulderers usually respect Mother Nature, and are prepared to enjoy a slice of chaos. Thank goodness that boulderers are prepared to climb around such dangers, or accept them for what they are, instead of bulldozing them down at every opportunity. The crash pad is used both as a cushioned landing platform, but sometimes as a glancing surface. They

come is 3 forms, all which have pros and cons. The complete flat pad is the best, and good for both falling and glancing. It is a complete pain to carry around, and you have to fight with it to roll it up, and it doesn't go on a bicycle! Two section pads are practical. If you fall onto the joint that is over a branch, you could become a cropper. Some have an angled joint, but for most of the time it is not an issue, and there are far more immediate concerns. Three section pads with 2 joints? You have to be that more careful where you place them, but they still work superbly. They have the advantage of being easy to carry, and even fit in the boot of a some Ferrari's.

Crash pads come in all different colours and different surface textures. They are very robust and have to take a real hammering.

INTRODUCTION

GIVE-IT-A-GO

IND/BOULDERING

OUT/BOULDERING

IMPROVEMENT

INDOOR SPORT

OUTDOOR SPORT

MULTI-PITCH

VIA FERRATA

WHERE TO GO

INDEX

Transporting a crash pad to a location in the forest is easy, they are very light, and most come with rucksack straps for ease of carrying. You can keep a piece of carpet, your shoes, chalkbag, and pof in the middle. A lot of climbers also have a small shoulder bag that can loop over the top of the pad. It has to be said though, that when you are bouldering, the job of carting a giant postage stamp between the boulders is a complete pain! I've fallen off enough, with and without. A pain they may be, but they do save your body, big time.

A secondary advantage, is that they give you an expansive dry area to step off onto. We live in a real world where it rains from time to time, doesn't it? Rock only takes a few hours to dry at the most, ground takes at least a day. On the sand of Fontainebleau, the surface maybe dry but you sink in slightly, beneath it is all wet and can stay that way for a couple of days. With a nice large crash pad, you can walk around the bottom of a problem on the mat, check out the moves, try it this way and that way, and keep your feet clean and dry.

If you're short, then a simple folding mat is good, you simply fold it over when you can't reach the start, and then your mate flops it back when you are off it. Multiple crash pads are another phenomenon that you often see. If you're on the short side and can't reach the starting holds that everyone else is using, build up a stack of pads until you can step off onto the top of the boulder! I jest, but it is useful. If you want to do a long traverse, then 2 or 3 mats are very handy. Work out which areas you are likely to fall, and place the mats at the critical points.

At a quick glance, the piece of ground on the left looks quite harmless and appears to be a good landing. Experience pays here, by looking closely and in a differnt light, there is a horrible tree root just above the surface. If you land on this with your heel, it can do you tremendous damage. Without a pad, you can fall onto these with the instep of the foot, and it is very painful.

By using 3 pads here, the gap is well covered, but you still want to be in control if you fall.   *6c+, Capuchos, Portugal; André Neres*

INTRODUCTION

GIVE-IT-A-GO

IND/BOULDERING

OUT/BOULDERING

IMPROVEMENT

INDOOR SPORT

OUTDOOR SPORT

MULTI-PITCH

VIA FERRATA

WHERE TO GO

INDEX

This outside malakey is starting to sound a bit grim; cow pats, rain, spikes to spear yourself on. Now I'm going to tell you that the rock isn't even clean either. Fortunately if you're a beginner, then just about everything that you go on will be popular and zizzingly clean. If you want to enjoy climbing on some boulders away from the madding crowds, then you might well have to clean the holds prior to launching up onto the problem. Deep in the forest, you often get pine needles covering the rock and mosses growing. Even on mountain tops, black cornflakes seem to grow on granite in there thousands. Cleaning is a delicate subject because it is so very easy to clean the rock, but also destroy the surface that you are then needing to use. It is a serious problem for a lot of un-educated beginners, and stupid others, who simply don't think of their 'BARBARIC' actions.

Good cleaning still allows all the mosses to grow under the trees. Only the hand and footholds are cleaned, keeping the texture of the beautiful forest. (Sintra, Portugal)

Full on pumped up action, for hard mountain Gtanite. Even the wire brushed only last a few daus!

There are two ways of cleaning, a heavy way for compacted rock, and a gentle light way for encrusted rock. Compact rock is strong and granular throughout, e.g. Granite and Limestone. To some extent, you can go at this hammer and tongs, at least if you do chip a bit off, then the granular structure remains as hard. Also bear in mind, that the incredibly hard quartz in granite, is still only held together by relatively weak mica and feldspar. The biggest erosion problem, are encrusted rocks like sandstone and gritstone. Here the inner rock is very soft, and it is only the outer skin that has become hardened by weathering. Should the outer skin be broken, it's like a hole in the road, and you end up with a pothole in a week. If you need to clean any encrusted rock, you must only ever use the lightest of pressure. At the very most, you would use a light nylon toothbrush for one or two light strokes. Look closely for yourself, if you see a grain of sand or grit come away, then you have VANDALISED the rock. All boulderers know, that the rock and problems they are enjoying, has always been left for them by other – responsible boulderers.

Some of the small handholds at Fontainebleau will get greasy even after one pull on them. As the friciton is critical, chalk can be lightly sprinkled on the holds to dry the moisture, then gently brushed off with a soft tooth-brush. Sometimes the toothbrush is simply dipped in the chalkbag prior to rubbing, since this keeps the area cleaner. Extensions are often required.

INTRODUCTION

GIVE-IT-A-GO

IND/BOULDERING

OUT/BOULDERING

IMPROVEMENT

INDOOR SPORT

OUTDOOR SPORT

MULTI-PITCH

VIA FERRATA

WHERE TO GO

INDEX

Standing on your crash pad and ready for launch off, almost. Go to the haven ground of Font, and you will see climbers thwack the rock with a pof. No, it's not April fools day, it's true. If you distil the leaves of Pine trees, it's amazing what you come up with. From this you get rosin, but with solvent extraction from the tree stumps, you get a thick and sticky wood rosin, which is known as Colophony – and in the climbing world, we call resin. It's something that climbers for years have sprinkled on their fingers, which makes them sticky. Wow! Drive home after a day's bouldering, and your hands stick to the steering wheel, it's fun. It's a natural substance that has been used at Font, well before chalk was invented. It comes in a block from the chemist, but then turns into powder easily. It has the benefit of not colouring the rock, and certainly decomposes in sunlight. It dries your skin slightly, but it's not really a drying agent like chalk, whatever anyone tries to tell you.

Even though resin was discovered and has been used for ages now, some interesting observations have been made. Nearly all of the old problems that have been climbed for years, are showing very little wear. However, all the newer problems climbed only with chalk, are all wearing away very rapidly. Certainly, the technical explanation seems quite sound. If you examine the surface of sandstone under a microscope, there are small undulations, and grains of sand sticking up. There are usually, free floating grains of sand, on the surface too. When you stand on the surface, your foot moves the free floating grains, and they abrade the surface. If you wipe the surface first, you reduce abrasive action; however, your weight can still break free the grains embedded in the surface. If you 'pof' the surface with the pof, then resin dust spills into the space between the grains. Your shoes and hands compresses this, and with some water-dampness solubility, there is a build up layer of resin on the rock. OK - so eventually the surface will become smooth. Half of the area, will be the resin that locks in the remaining grains on the surface. Now what you have, is quite a slippery hold, but still with around 50% of the sandstone showing. Although this is nothing like as frictional as a pure sandstone surface, it will be locked in place, and incredibly

Accurate mid air poffing, needs a lot of practise to get a hit every time.

hard wearing for a few weeks. The same resin is from the family as shellac – used for a gloss finish on pianos! Leave antique furniture outside in the sun and rain for a few days and you can certainly see how instantly biodegradeable the resin is.

When you come across a polished hold in bouldering, it can be a bit ghastly, but you do have to make decisions about erosion, sooner or later. It certainly shows at Fontainebleau, that resin does help to protect sandy textured rock. Anybody who climbs on sandstone should have to answer a very strong case as to why they don't want to use resin to protect the holds from erosion. Our Gritstone in England is now in a terrible state, complete hand and footholds have worn away – that's undisputed. I just ask everyone who learns to climb, always think if there is a way that you can prevent your actions

from eroding the rock. If you cannot, then should you really be climbing on it? Using resin is very simple, you make a pof as illustrated, and then tap it on the relevant hand and footholds of a boulder problem. The rag end of the pof can be used to swish away, excess resin dust. Tapping the ball of the pof on the fingers, adds resin to your fingers, which helps them grip too. It also has a lovely woody smell to it. Note: If you are at all concerned with using chalk, resin or any substance on your hands, check with your doctor who can advise you medically on an individual basis.

First take the solid lumps of Colophony, and put them in a thick plastic bag. Then with a rock, shatter the resin into small crystals. Pour this onto a large 1msq. of cotton, in the centre. Then scoop up the mass to make a ball (tennis size), and secure with an elastic band. The crystals will slowly shatter in time, and allow the dust to pregnate slowly through the cotton. Keep an eye on the ball for splits in the cotton, and move the wearing area around.

The inside of a pof.

INTRODUCTION

GIVE-IT-A-GO

IND/BOULDERING

OUT/BOULDERING

IMPROVEMENT

INDOOR SPORT

OUTDOOR SPORT

MULTI-PITCH

VIA FERRATA

WHERE TO GO

INDEX

Every time that you stand at the bottom of an outdoor problem, you should survey the landing area. If you fall off, where will you fall? If things go wrong, where are you most likely to end up? After many years of falling, you get to know the pitfalls quite well. A friendly tree only 2 metres away, can turn very nasty. If you fall and bounce off a 45° slab, you will charge into this column at incredible speed, wiping out any piece of anatomy that crunches into the immovable trunk. At times like this, you need catching. If in doubt, hail a spotter!

The job of spotting is hardly rocket science, but you see terrible examples everywhere. There are two essential parts to the job of spotting. The first is staying alert and concentrating. When someone is pulling over the top, they haven't finished the problem; they are in the most dangerous position imaginable. The second demand is always to catch someone's waist, 'BEFORE' they touch the ground. If you approach with this attitude, you have every chance of being successful in your task.

A perfect spotting example; Cul de Chien, Fontainebleau.
(Kareen Bouvrais spotting Audrey Leveque)

The whole point of spotting with a crash pad, is not to catch someone, but to make sure that they land on their feet and make the pad do the work. Tips: When they fall, shout so they know you are going to catch them. Your principal aim is to get your hands either side of their torso, just above the waist. You need to grab them when your arms are fully outstretched. As they fall, your arms will then bend, and with pressure you can direct where they fall to. (Not by much, but it's often the difference between - on or off the crash pad). If you are on the pad, then you simply guide them comfortably into you. It is no use at all being off the pad; invariably you won't be able to reach them. Often with quick reactions, you can really help to slow down somebody's fall. Keep your head a bit back, so you don't clash skulls of course. If a climber comes spinning off and waving their arms, do your best!

Macau perfectly poised to guide André onto the crash pad

Superb co-ordination between boulderer and spotter. The climber (Ben Moon), on a 7b that demands a really awkward heel hook, that puts him in a really dangerous position. In falling, Ben manages to twist his body, and 'critically' unhook his heel. Ths spotter (Jerry Moffatt), brilliantly guides Ben's waist, and tips him into a perfect upright falling position. If Ben kept his heel hooked, he would pivot on the lip. Jerry would have no option, but to fully catch Ben's upper body. You really need a spotter that you can rely on in a situation like this.

INTRODUCTION

GIVE-IT-A-GO

IND/BOULDERING

OUT/BOULDERING

IMPROVEMENT

INDOOR SPORT

OUTDOOR SPORT

MULTI-PITCH

VIA FERRATA

WHERE TO GO

INDEX

INTRODUCTION

GIVE-IT-A-GO

IND/BOULDERING

OUT/BOULDERING

IMPROVEMENT

INDOOR SPORT

OUTDOOR SPORT

MULTI-PITCH

VIA FERRATA

WHERE TO GO

INDEX

The first technique that you need to learn in outdoor bouldering, is a way to get finish the climb and get standing on top. If you make a mistake here the consequences are the worst, so you want to practise on small boulders with a good spotter. It is a move, that can go terribly wrong when you are a beginner, and you will most probably go completely out of control. I cannot stress enough how

important it is that you be very careful. Eventually when you have perfected your technique, you can happily go bouldering on your own.

At the top of the boulder there may be a big jug, you simply pull on it to get standing up. A lot of the time it is completely flat, just like the edge of a swimming pool. If you can't get out of a pool

*Our thanks to the wonderful Nicole Flint in demonstrating the **Grovel or Beached Whale Mantel**; tummy, knees, anything goes with this one.*

without the steps, hike off to your local pool and get practising. Indoor, heated pools, are a great place to learn the easier mantelshelf techniques, and you get plenty of splashing around when it goes wrong. The basic method is called the 'STRAIGHT ARM MANTEL.' You begin with flat hands over the edge, then pull your body up and turn your arms into a press up movement until they are straight. In this position, all your weight goes down your arm effortlessly so you can rest. From here you either put your knee on the edge, or better still the sole of your foot. Then you can transfer your weight onto your foot and stand up quite easily. The buoyant water in the pool will make getting up into the arm locked position quite easy, especially if you sink down a bit first. Really work hard on getting your foot straight onto the edge, you only get even wetter if you get it wrong at this stage, and every boulderer does it this way. So long as you lean forward at the end, you won't fall back.

*Tyler Landman making the **straight arm mantel** look so easy.*

*Here, Jingo demonstrates a **Heel Rockover Mantel**. The hands are first positioned to one side on the best holds available. You then keep your lower foot, flat on the wall and throw your heel up onto the ledge. Then in a quick rocking over motion, you pull your weight over your foot and attain perfect balance. In this case the other edge can be used to help you pull over into balance.*

The big problem comes when you go outside, and there isn't any buoyant water to give you that initial lift. It's a real test of how overweight you are; featherweight children simply put us all to shame. If you start pulling on your arms quite quickly, you can get momentum going so that you zoom up to lock your arms. If you're not that strong and only get 95% of the way up, you won't make it. It's in the the very last part where your arms are in the weakest position that you will fail. The fortunate part however, is that ledge you are using is usually quite good, and your arms are in a technically stronger position lower down. This enables you to cushion your descent, and try, try, try again. The easy mantelshelf is a nice move, reversible and effortless, but there are some nasties out there too! There are perhaps more variations of the mantelshelf than any other climbing move! It can be the most elegant move, or the gruntiest and grovelleyest of moves. It can be made to look so simple – be warned. To list a few: Grovel mantel, straight arm mantel, heel mantel, lip

mantel, sloping mantel, double inverted mantel. When you get to the top of a boulder, you have to choose between any of these. Certainly the grovel is the safest, followed by the straight. The heel version is elegant, but needs practise. A lip mantel takes an acquired skill to prevent it from becoming a grovel. A sloping mantel is for those who can keep their nerve. A double inverted is for those with ridiculously supple bodies. Get trying and puffing.

*Carla Duarte demonstrates the **Overhanging Rockover Mantel**. This is made difficult, because the wall beneath the ledge is overhanging. It's very easy to hang below the lip and flick a heel over. You can even hang off one hand quite easily. Pulling up on both hands for a while seems quite easy. At the top you can get your arms straight, but because your leg is pushing under the overhang, your body has not passed through the vertical position, and you will start to fall back. The only way to prevent this, is to place the palm of your hand, close and in front of you, and to push down. When you start pushing, you will feel the pressure go off your toe, which is touching the rock under the overhang.*

INTRO
GIVE-IT-A-GO
IND/BOULDERING
OUT/BOULDERING
IMPROVEMENT
INDOOR SPORT
OUTDOOR SPORT
MULTI-PITCH
VIA FERRATA
WHERE TO GO
INDEX

GIVE-IT-A-GO | IND/BOULDERING | OUT/BOULDERING | IMPROVEMENT | INDOOR SPORT | OUTDOOR SPORT | MULTI-PITCH | VIA FERRATA | WHERE TO GO | INDEX

A mantel that you do need to perfect is the **Undercut, Shelf Mantel.** *Perfectly performed and executed by Mark Edwards at Sennen Cove, Cornwall. You start with your body hanging from the lip to get the hang of it. Throw your leg over which ever side is lower - the left in this case. You can actually get quite a good rest on your calf with straight arms. Because the shelf is so undercut, you don't get any assistance from your right leg at all. Pulling on your left heel, you twist your left arm around and place the palm on the edge of the lip. You only have to get your body a small way over your left hand, and then the right hand can join and push you straight over. A lot of weight goes onto your knee and toe combined. When you have this wired, it goes really easily.*

If you want a ridiculous mantel, then this is the one for you; the **Double Handed, Inverted Mantel**. Perfectly performed and executed by Caedmon Mullin at Hound of the Baskervilles Tor on Dartmoor! Pulling on the rounded granite hold to even leave the ground, will floor most. Then, being able to backwardly invert your arms is an asset. A complete freehanging pressup is then required, followed up by superb flexibility in hopping your foot onto the ledge by your hands. An excellent party trick.

ERR' TRICKEY

INTRODUCTION

GIVE-IT-A-GO

IND/BOULDERING

OUT/BOULDERING

IMPROVEMENT

INDOOR SPORT

OUTDOOR SPORT

MULTI-PITCH

VIA FERRATA

WHERE TO GO

INDEX

INTRODUCTION

GIVE-IT-A-GO

IND/BOULDERING

OUT/BOULDERING

IMPROVEMENT

INDOOR SPORT

OUTDOOR SPORT

MULTI-PITCH

VIA FERRATA

WHERE TO GO

INDEX

If you can stand on any two footholds when you climb and take your hands off completely, then you are said to be bridging. Your legs can form a natural arch; either a narrow bridge, medium bridge and wide 'eek' bridge. If you can take your hands off, then it's effectively a rest of course. When you're sport climbing and your forearms are throbbing with exhaustion, start looking for footholds in positions that can allow you to bridge across them. After a while, you get very good at spotting them, especially if you are unfit or enjoy life too much to be a lightweight. Bridging in bouldering, is a technique used to climb up a groove.

You're more likely to learn how to bridge, by down climbing, rather than actually climbing up. Most of the problems on boulders are up the faces, but to get down, you scramble off the back or side where often there is another boulder. The boulders together form a narrow corridor so you can put a hand either side of the gully, then lower your body down and search for footholds, one on either wall. Often, there are horizontal bedding planes in the rock which give lovely natural footholds. First your hands bridge the gap, and then your feet. You can push on either side of the corridor to wedge your body, and allow movement of the feet. By pushing out sideways – as if you're trying to push the boulders apart, you effectively lock your body in position. As you can easily do this, you generally feel confident. Also, because your feet are bridged, your arms are resting and you can stay there for hours, not like your forearms ticking clock, tiring on an overhang.

When you get a narrow corridor in between two boulders, we call it a '**CHIMNEY.**' In bouldering areas, they tend to be damp and cold, and they're often covered in gunge too. If you can find a clean chimney, take the opportunity to try and climb up it. Beware, if they flare out at the bottom, getting off the ground can be either desperate or even impossible. With the experience of down climbing,

Sandy Ogilvie enjoying the superb chimney section of the yellow circuit (grade 3), at Cuvier Rempart, Fontainebleau

you should have the basic bridging idea. You put a foot on one side, then try to wedge your upper body on the other side. This is an effective bridge in itself. Then you can lift up the other foot up to find a foothold. (Top tip: nylon jackets don't grip the rock since they just slither all over it, and worse still, they grip to the rock and you then slither out of them, wear soft cotton clothing - it sticks well.) By wedging a combination of body, knees, hands and head, you can squirm up the chimney. A good chimney climber will notice all the little footholds on either wall, then almost tip toe up, keeping a foot on either wall and pressing flat with their hands on either side. When you get the knack of it, it's very easy indeed.

The principles of bridging are funda-
mental to a lot of climbing. It's where
you let your feet do all the work, and
give your hands a nice rest. When
you bridge, you can either balance
your feet on two holds, or push in an
outward direction. In the same way
that you can climb a wall with no
'holds,' by using layaways; you can

*A superb problem on the yellow circuit (Grade
3), at Franchard-Hautes-Plaines (Fontainebleau). There aren't any holds in this scoop, but
you can climb it by bridging the whole way,
using alternative palm and footholds.*

INTRODUCTION

GIVE-IT-A-GO

IND/BOULDERING

OUT/BOULDERING

IMPROVEMENT

INDOOR SPORT

OUTDOOR SPORT

MULTI-PITCH

VIA FERRATA

WHERE TO GO

INDEX

A fine example of bridging a groove. Here, Jingo's weight is spread between the left foot, and the palm of the right hand. The left hand is simply resting on the wall to form a stable tripod position. The right foot can then be easily moved up to another small footledge. It is far easier to take lots of small steps and movements in a situation like this. Moving the foot next to the right hand could overbalance the climber, and force tipping back.

also climb a groove-scoop, without any incut holds for the feet. You simply use your feet to bridge across the gap in the groove. Foot control is the key. You need to be very well in control of your feet, and know how to flex the ankles. If the sole of the shoe is not at the perfect angle to maximise friction, then your foot won't stick. If you get it right, you simply tip toe up the groove. If there is a foothold to use, then you can also use the depression for the palm of your hand. This way you can form a bridge between a leg and an arm, which will allow you to move your other non-weighted foot. You have to have quite strong leg muscles and flexibility to bring your foot up to your palm, but with practise, it soon becomes quite easy. Good balance for climbing holdless grooves is a real asset. It is something that improves with a lot of practise.

You rarely get boulder problems with bridging moves, simply because the shape of most boulders is cubish and without substantial grooves. When you do get one, you usually get a goodie so watch out for them. Chimneys are pretty uncommon too, since they are usually quite easy ways up and down, and would quickly fill and entire guidebook on their own. The great benefit of an area like Fontainebleau, is that the whole forest is full of non listed problems, chimney's etc, for you to play on. It's knowing where to start and what are the best problems to pick out, which is the difficult part.

Visiting Fontainebleau for the first time is quite an experience. The forests are a mixture of pine, oak and silver birch trees. The whole area around the town of Fontainebleau was once a royal hunting forest, but is still full of long avenues and bridal tracks - but no royals. These avenues all look the same! When you go there, you need a map, compass, guidebook, and preferably – someone who knows the place. In the hundreds of square kilometres which is forest, there is only climbing in about 1% of the area. So if you just turn up, it's like finding a needle in a haystack. That 1%, does admittedly contain around 100,000 boulders!

The local hot shots are called 'Bleausards,' and have explored the secrets of the forest and found it's wonderful possibilities. The most impressive asset you get, is the formation of climbing circuits. The Bleausards look at a whole area, and work out around 50 very good problems of a roughly equal standard to form a circuit. They give the circuit a colour which represents an overall middle grade. An orange circuit would generally have problems from 3a-4a. You might even have one of 4c to really test you out, but the point of the circuit is to enjoy a large amount of climbing, with a terrific variety of styles and techniques.

Each problem is simply indicated on the rock with a tiny coloured number. At the top of the problem, you often find a tiny arrow to where the next problem is. This is where the circuits grow and grow. On the way to the next problems, you will be given lots of little arrows on the rock which lead you up and down chimneys, traversing around blocks, all over the place with lots of other easier,

The numbers are painted on the rock, but slowly peel off over the years. Only at the start is the number of the circuit. They are also very small, so you really have to look closely for each problem. Circuits range in difficulty from 1a-7a

but good problems. By the time you've reached number 5, you've done around 15 problems and you're exhausted. The beauty is, that there are lots of grooves and fun problems at Font, which are easily accessible for everyone. There are even blocks right next to circuits without marked problems on. You just have to go there and explore.

INTRODUCTION
GIVE-IT-A-GO
IND/BOULDERING
OUT/BOULDERING
IMPROVEMENT
INDOOR SPORT
OUTDOOR SPORT
MULTI-PITCH
VIA FERRATA
WHERE TO GO
INDEX

INTRODUCTION

GIVE-IT-A-GO

IND/BOULDERING

OUT/BOULDERING

IMPROVEMENT

INDOOR SPORT

OUTDOOR SPORT

MULTI-PITCH

VIA FERRATA

WHERE TO GO

INDEX

Separating the words edge & crimp is going to be slightly confusing to the beginner, because it describes both small holds, and the way that you grip them. Additionally, not all small holds are edges & crimps, hence the word crimp is often used to describe a way of holding another type of handhold – all will be clear, I promise. When you look closely at a flatish piece or rock (Slate excepted), there will be little ripples and rugosities all over it, we call these edges. The wonderful understatement of the English language, still allows you to describe a ledge as a big edge. In difficult bouldering, when someone suggests that you use an edge, start by getting out your magnifying glass. It is a very relative term: A beginner's edge is around 1cm wide, then ask an 8a boulderer to show you an edge, you are talking about 2mm - max. You can also use an edge for either your feet, or your hands.

When you stand at the bottom of a nice flat slab, you can take your time to spot all the little edges there are. You have the opportunity to picture in your mind how you are going to use them to unlock the problem of say, climbing directly up the centre. The easiest way to do this is when the sun is perfectly in line with the slab. The sun's rays won't light up the slab, but they do pick out any tiny little edges, because they stick out and also leave tiny shadows. On a grim day or in the shade, you just have to look closely and have a very keen eye. Now, because climbing on small holds is very tiring and most slabs are too flat to bridge on, you have to move quite quickly and confidently with your moves. You start up, and almost immediately are stuck because you can't find the little edges for your feet that you had spotted before. Jump off, you've blown the onsight. There is a real trick to this, you

need to mark the fine edges with chalk. You need just enough chalk to see the edge, and no more. Your thumb is handy, dip it in your chalk bag, and either run it along the top of the edge to highlight it, or gently press it just beneath the edge to make a small white dot. The white dot method is good since it doesn't put any loose chalk on the tiny edge which would compromise your friction, and if you decide to use a different foot edge, you can very easily wipe the little dot off.

When you are climbing a wall or a slab on small edges, the sequence of moves starts to get critical. Most of the time there are too many edges to use, but it is the ones in the right places that are vitally important. You have to work out for yourself, which edges work best, and that allow you to climb a problem in the easiest way for your shape and flexibility.

On a large slab like this, you will have to mark the footholds as you climb, Sennen Cove, Cornwall; Mark Edwards

A font 7b traverse at Sennen Cove, Cornwall; Mark Edwards

INTRODUCTION

GIVE-IT-A-GO

IND/BOULDERING

OUT/BOULDERING

IMPROVEMENT

INDOOR SPORT

OUTDOOR SPORT

MULTI-PITCH

VIA FERRATA

WHERE TO GO

INDEX

One of the best ways to hold an edge with your hand, is to crimp it. Our photograph shows this best - where you bend the fingers and squeeze your thumb onto the tip of the forefinger. This configuration of the hand, works on the same principle of the sea anchor. At the second joint in your fingers, you effectively have the pivot where your weight hangs from, and the front two pieces (metacarpals), are literally angled and driven into the back of the edge. The thumb stops the hand from opening up and works like a brace. When you take and edge like this, you are said to be crimping it.

The crimp also has another great asset, which is flexible wrist movement. When you take an edge with a crimp, your hand is locked in position over the hold. As you move your body, you can also move your wrist. The shape of your fingers will change for sure, and the thumb used in bracing will move. But the strength from the linking mechanism will always be there. This makes the crimp, the common useful way to grip a small hold. When your whole body is below the hold, take a crimp that you can pull up on, then as your body moves up the rock, you can still keep your hand on the crimp – turning the pull into a push. This is a move you will use all the time in climbing slabs.

When you start crimping, don't expect to be very good at it – you won't be. It's not magic either, it's a skill, but is also muscle related. The more you do within your sensible comfort range, the stronger your fingers will become. At this stage, doing finger damage is always possible, but less likely since you won't have enough strength to grip onto

much anyway. It's as you grow stronger with your climbing, that then you start having to consider not pulling hard to prevent self-inflicted finger injury.

Crimping is also an art, and one that will confound you too. It can be painful, but should never be too painful. Some climbers have been forced to give up climbing from the damage incurred to their fingers under self inflicted crimping – so be careful. Small sharp edges and big bodyweights don't go together, you cannot expect to crimp up a wall that only a very lightweight climber can do. The real art of crimping, is in being very light on the crimps. This requires you to use your feet in the most effective way, and apply superb body supplety for your weight to be taken mostly by your feet. It is very easy for your fingers to uncurl and slip, with the skin then tearing on your tips; go very carefully and inspect your fingertips after every crimp. You most probably will learn the hard way by getting the odd cut to your fingertips, but you don't benefit at all from split fingertips. I've bouldered with the best climbers in the world on the roughest of granite crimps, then after a day of crimping hard 7c boulder problems, their skin is always immaculate. If you are ripping your skin, you're trying too hard, try something easier – you will get better in time.

When you get on a 7a crimp route at Fontainebleau, you certainly need to have good eyesight! Jus d'orange 7a, Roche aux Sabots; Sylvain Dion

INTRODUCTION | GIVE-IT-A-GO | IND/BOULDERING | OUT/BOULDERING | IMPROVEMENT | INDOOR SPORT | OUTDOOR SPORT | MULTI-PITCH | VIA FERRATA | WHERE TO GO | INDEX

Eventually you reach a point in all parts of climbing when there just aren't any footholds at all! Huh, so you have to invent some eh. Fortunately, you don't have to resort to sculpture, you just have to interpret the rock in a different way. If you examine the surface, you can see where the rock goes in and out, and here you get scoops and dimples. Not all rocks are as generous with their scoops - slippery granite offering the least amount of dimples. However, with hard sandstone and limestone, you nearly always get a superb choice. Having found your dimple/scoop, you can now use it as a foothold.

The lower half of a dimple will always dish outwards, and it is this part that you put your foot into. In bouldering terminology, we call a smear because it resembles a small blemish. You certainly don't however smear your shoe onto it, as you would smear your finger to get a mark on a window. Just like using any other foothold, you make sure that your shoe is pristinely clean, and then place it exactly on the right spot to give you maximum friction. Because the smear takes the shape of a curved scoop, a new climbing shoe with a 90° edge will only have about 2mm of rubber contact. If the toes of your shoes are curved, then you will get a good 6mm of rubber on the smear. It's not a lot,

Any of the dimples in the rock on the left could act as a smear. The cleaned up, is tiny and awful. However, to make the dyno for the top, you must have something to push off with your right foot. Without using this, the problem is impossible. (Balancier dyno 6b, Franchard Isatis; Jeff Landman)

but it's 3 times the amount of a new shoe. So an old pair of worn shoes are worth keeping, just for a problem that involves using a critical smear.

The most important part to smears though, is their location – think, location, location, location. So often in bouldering, you get a good foothold that just 'isn't,' in the right place. By utilising a smear that is in a great place for your body dynamics, you can do can actually do the problem. When you become an experienced climber, you will realise that body position and movement, is far more important than where all the obvious holds are located.

If you take a nice angled slab, it may be covered in cracks and little edges. You can climb this in your familiar way, crimping and layawaying as you go. Sometimes however, there isn't anything except little scoops and sloping holds. You can tip toe up the slab on the tiny little smears that are available. It's often fun climbing and teaches you an enormous amount about the friction that you can get from your feet.

Steep angled rock, simply doesn't support your weight on a smear. If you take a good handhold and place your feet on smears, you instantly see that it doesn't help a huge amount. It does however help a lot more that just padding a flat wall with the soles of your feet. If you pad a wall with your feet and pull up, you get to the point when your arms are level and stop. Because there is no upward force at all from your feet, you will find it almost impossible to launch your body in an upwards direction. If you put your foot on a smear, however bad, the angle will be helping you. This will act superbly when you pull on your arms, and so long as your stomach muscles are strong, you will be able to reach up. A very good tell tale sign is that all smears will be blackened by the rubber from other climbers shoes. If you are on a well known problem, look closely, it makes life a lot more simple when you are learning. The smear may look like a small foothold and seem insignificant, but in the end, it makes all the difference.

A no-hands-allowed-problem, smears only , with a very tricky crux involving a foot crossover - great fun; RAC Boulders, Snowdonia; Jingo

INTRODUCTION

GIVE-IT-A-GO

IND/BOULDERING

OUT/BOULDERING

IMPROVEMENT

INDOOR SPORT

OUTDOOR SPORT

MULTI-PITCH

VIA FERRATA

WHERE TO GO

INDEX

There are cracks on boulders everywhere, but are completely avoided by most sensible boulderers. The plus side for those climbers, is a pain free life and no real great loss to be honest. If you aspire to go on and become successful at sport climbing, then I'm afraid that jamming is a technique, which you are best off learning sooner rather than later. If you can be bothered to learn the technique of jamming your hands and fingers into cracks successfully, it actually will help your bouldering fun of course. There

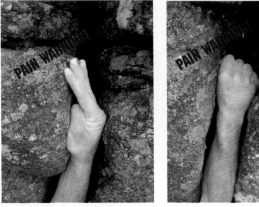

Left: A wide hand jam, that uses the thumb under the palm to make up space, so the wrist, knuckle and fingers can splay out to create a good jam.
Right: A perfect narrowing for a fist jam.(Cad's fist)

are a lot of problems that start under overhangs which are far easier to start with a good jam. You'll find it a lot less frustrating if you get this sorted. Sometimes you may also be on a high boulder problem and things start to go a bit wrong! You want to be good at every sort of climbing technique in this position, I promise.

I think that it is fairly obvious to say that when you place any part of your body in a crack, you may well experience a reasonable level of pain! On the other hand, if you can find a nice smooth crack, get your technique polished up, then you'll find that '**JAMMING**,' can be completely 'pain free!' It's the practical simplicity of getting the right size of crack, for the exact piece of your body. I tend to avoid jamming unless my hand fits perfectly and the sides are comfortably smooth. If you put a hand in a crack with your thumb up, it is called a JAM. This is because to make it grip, you have to push with

A very good example of a finger lock, the fingers would have been placed in the crack, when the elbow was out to the left, as the arm is now below, they are locked in place. (Luc Percival)

your fingertips and palm against one side, and the back of your hand-knuckles against the other side. It's the squeezing of the muscles in the hand which jams you in place. Keep your hand still always, and just pivot on your wrist. If you find a crack which is the exact size, you don't have to do much pressing, and if it has a bend to help you, even better. A 'LOCK' is when you place your hand in the crack the other way up. By twisting your elbow and hand together, the hand twists in the crack and locks with the top edge of the hand on one side, and the bottom thumb knuckle on the other. The lock relies on a twisting of the arm action, so it hardly uses any strength, a great way to rest on a sport route. The jam uses hand muscles which is more tiring. For jamming the fingers, you just poke-em-in. If they grip, you're fine.

A classic problem on the Blue circuit at Cul de Chien, Fontainebleau. Even though the crack starts early, it is far easier to climb it by laying off to the left. The fingers are in a jam here, but nearly all of the weight is taken as a layoff. Higher up, the crack flares out and becomes a perfect size for a hand jam. By moulding the right hand on the curve of the crack, the back of the hand is getting a lot of comfortable friction which makes the jam easy and comfortable.

INTRODUCTION
GIVE-IT-A-GO
IND/BOULDERING
OUT/BOULDERING
IMPROVEMENT
INDOOR SPORT
OUTDOOR SPORT
MULTI-PITCH
VIA FERRATA
WHERE TO GO
INDEX

INTRODUCTION · GIVE-IT-A-GO · IND/BOULDERING · OUT/BOULDERING · IMPROVEMENT · INDOOR SPORT · OUTDOOR SPORT · MULTI-PITCH · VIA FERRATA · WHERE TO GO · INDEX

There are parts of the climbing world such as the Yosemite Valley in the USA, where you get granite cracks that go on for hundreds of feet. The cracks come in so many different sizes and shapes that you could almost write a book on technique for 'The Valley' alone. For bouldering and sport climbing, there is really only one technique that you need to know, and that is the horizontal foot lock. It is a very simple procedure and can be done with either the toes facing in, or the foot on its side with the heel going in first. Both achieve the same effect of twisting the foot in a horizontal crack. Put a good twist on the foot and it will not come out. The huge danger with this in bouldering, is that if your hands come off whilst your foot is inserted, you are in big trouble. Your body is likely to be then falling horizontally – if not head first, and your foot might get stuck in the crack. This is likely to break your ankle, before smashing your head onto the blocks below! Of course it's a risky move, and unless you are of a superb standard, don't try it without a big team of catchers.

A very good example of a foot lock in action on a spectacularly hard boulder problem, and one that is a bit too high
and dangerous for the majority of boulderers. Climbed by
Dave Henderson, who just happens to be one of the best
boulderers in Britian. The lower wall is taken quite easily
to reach the horizontal break beneath the roof. From here
the move out to get the hold on the lip is a very tenuous
one, relying on the palm of the hand to keep hold of a very
flat and flared break. If the climber were to then reach
out with the second hand to the lip, the feet would most
probably swing off. As the hold on the lip is curved, the
climber would easily hold it to start, then have difficulty
as their body swung underneath. The disaster would be at
the end of the outswing, when there is nothing to grip with
the hands, and the momentum of the body would pluck
the poor climber off into space. By placing a foot in the
horizontal break and twisting, the climber can then move
all their weight under the hand on the lip. The climber can
also move both hands onto the lip. In this case the climber
can even reach the next break up, even with the foot locked
into the crack. Now with two hands on different holds
that are both good, and the climbers bodyweigh hanging
vertically down, the foot can be released without any fear of
swinging. A simple toe step up, and our magician finishes
this attractive little problem.

INTRODUCTION
GIVE-IT-A-GO
IND/BOULDERING
OUT/BOULDERING
IMPROVEMENT
INDOOR SPORT
OUTDOOR SPORT
MULTI-PITCH
VIA FERRATA
WHERE TO GO
INDEX

INTRODUCTION | GIVE-IT-A-GO | IND/BOULDERING | OUT/BOULDERING | IMPROVEMENT | INDOOR SPORT | OUTDOOR SPORT | MULTI-PITCH | VIA FERRATA | WHERE TO GO | INDEX

A technique that you don't often get a chance to learn on indoor walls, is the '**HEEL HOOK**.' It's a skill that anybody who isn't strong, or carries a bit of weight, is going to love. Most boulderers can hang off two good handholds, and dangle in space. But to actually move from this position, you either have to find some good footholds, or do a pull up. Even when you do a pull-up, you then have to lock one arm completely, whilst you move other hand off to get another hold. This is incredibly difficult, and for most of the time is unnecessary. If you have both hands on the lip of an overhang, just simply swing one leg up, and place the heel on the lip to one side. By dangling your body like this, you can take one hand off, moderately easy. The power in this move, comes directly from your steel-like stomach muscles. The slight disadvantage with most climbing moves, is that if you can do them too easily at first, you never get enough practise to build up the necessary muscle strength. If you're a kid, do a lot of heel hooks; then when you become a proportionally heavier adult, you'll have nice and strong stomach muscles.

In sport climbing, the heel hook is an essential part of technique. On a long sport climb, you can imagine the strain in hanging off a lip of an overhang, then the relief that you feel by throwing a heel over it to take some weight off your arms. In bouldering, you tend not to need rests, but often find that a heel hook can give you that quick breathing space, before you have to tackle a fiendish, finishing mantelshelf. Flexibility counts for a huge amount if your heel hooking is really going to work in your favour. Also, accuracy with heel placement is important. To lift your whole leg up and place the heel in the perfect spot first time, will save a huge amount of energy. Although you'll often find that a lot of problems can be done without heel hooking, the grade will be given for the easiest way, which may well involve a secret heel hook. On many of the problems in the higher grades 7a (V7) upwards, you are forced to heel hook on the most miserly smears, and again - it's just enough to let you move the hands.

A nice example here of Ben Moon showing the full use of the Heel Hook on a 7b problem at Pedra do Urso, Portugal. By using a heelhook early on, he can save a lot of strength. This eventually gives him a long reach to the right, using the left hand and foot, working together. (Eventually, the left foot gets even closer and you stand up - the holds in the groove being dreadfully poor.)

INTRODUCTION | GIVE-IT-A-GO | IND/BOULDERING | OUT/BOULDERING | IMPROVEMENT | INDOOR SPORT | OUTDOOR SPORT | MULTI-PITCH | VIA FERRATA | WHERE TO GO | INDEX

INTRODUCTION

GIVE-IT-A-GO

IND/BOULDERING

OUT/BOULDERING

IMPROVEMENT

INDOOR SPORT

OUTDOOR SPORT

MULTI-PITCH

VIA FERRATA

WHERE TO GO

INDEX

Jude Sprachen, perfectly heel hooking, Cromlech boulders, Wales

INTRODUCTION

GIVE-IT-A-GO

IND/BOULDERING

OUT/BOULDERING

IMPROVEMENT

INDOOR SPORT

OUTDOOR SPORT

MULTI-PITCH

VIA FERRATA

WHERE TO GO

INDEX

The heel hook does come into play big time, when you are climbing a problem traverse. It can reduce the grade so much, that sometimes two separate grades are given, 'with' and 'without' heel hooking. Needless to say, some traverses – even with heel hooking are completely desperate. A tricky, but often advantageous move with traverse heel hooking, is to place your heel between your hands. This will enable you to cross over your hands and make a lot more distance in one go with your move. You should consider also, that it's a very dangerous movement, since you can actually kick yourself off the rock if you catch the lip with your foot. Falling off in this position with your back and head so vulnerable, doesn't bear thinking about. Call up the team of spotters for 'learning' this one.

Jingo climbing a classic Font roof (4c) at Jean des Vignes. A lovely problem in 3 parts; first to reach the lip involoves a long reach onto a sloping hold. To grip this without coming off is possible by jamming both feet stacked together in the back of the roof. Then finally a heel hook is used to start the mantelshelf which will finish the problem. Very concentrated and technical.

INTRODUCTION | GIVE-IT-A-GO | IND/BOULDERING | OUT/BOULDERING | IMPROVEMENT | INDOOR SPORT | OUTDOOR SPORT | MULTI-PITCH | VIA FERRATA | WHERE TO GO | INDEX

There is one hold in bouldering which is multi-use, and that is the pocket. You rarely get them on indoor bolt on walls, but you will find them on the better quality freeform walls. Another good name for a pocket is the 360° hold. This is because it has a use in every direction. When you first feel a pocket, you slot your fingers in and naturally pull up, then look for another different hold. So often, you just don't have to. This is because either the top or the side is incut, and it then turns into a sidepull, and finally an undercut. For a while, you'll kick yourself everytime you forget this – eventually it sinks in. Pockets come in all shapes and sizes;

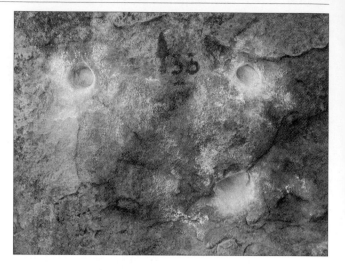

from giant buckets that you can put your hands and feet into, down to single finger pockets called 'MONOS.' A good incut pocket the size of a tennis ball will have a 1 metre zone of climbability around it. At this size, you can dyno up into it, and then use it as an undercut to reach a long way up. It is a tremendously versatile hold.

If the edge of a pocket is sharp, you must to be very careful and aware your finger joints. Even the sharpest of jugs and incuts will only have a 60° edge. The lip of a pocket can form an unusually sharp angle of around 30°. Most pockets will have their razor sharp edges removed by the odd passing stone – fortunately! This still leaves a 2mm radius edge (like a plate edge) which isn't going to cut your skin, but will pulverise and even cut your tendons and ligaments. A simple pull up on this sort of hold can do you damage. Genuine weakness in your arms and fingers will most probably protect you from self inflictment at this early stage. However, it is not pull-ups that are the largest worry. Most normal climbers can only do relatively slow pull-ups, so they will feel any damage being done to their fingers very quickly. The biggest danger for this type of hold, is when you use it as an undercut. Here you can grip with a very strong fingers curled underneath, and pull on a straight arm. This is a very strong position when you push up with the

thigh muscles. You can start generating forces easily in excess of twice your body weight this way, and do immense damage to your finger joints.

The muscles that support your fingers are relatively weak and you need to get them strengthened up, so try to start using finger pockets early on in your bouldering life. A very good precaution to consider for the first 6-12 months as your tendons get stronger, is always to make sure that when a problem uses pockets, that it also has good footholds. A single finger is very prone to injury if you use it on it's own, be careful. When you use a medium pocket, use your 2nd and 3rd fingers together, they make a very strong unit. Generally speaking, your forefinger and 2nd finger, is not as strong. You will find out quickly enough, but your 1st and 2nd together up to the 1st joint, is the most effective way of gripping a small pocket. Even wrap the thumb around the top of the 1st finger. You also want to consider the consequences of falling off with your fingers in a pocket! Only use half of your fingers in the pocket if you think you are going to have trouble getting them out in a fall.

Tyler Landman getting to grips with La théorème de Pascal 6a, Fontainebleau. This is a classic problem on the red circuit at La Roche aux Sabots, an area that is world famous for its pockets and powerful moves. Starting top right, a multi-crashpad lift off is needed for young climbers like Tyler. Immediately he uses the pockets in their best configuration for his small fingers as a pull up. Then he gets his feet high onto smears, and then locks off the left arm - using the pocket as a side pull, and to reach up for another pocket. Because there is nothing over the top, the problem has to go left, and you are forced to use the pockets as undercuts as you move left. Eventually you can reach up to the finishing holds

INTRODUCTION

GIVE-IT-A-GO

IND/BOULDERING

OUT/BOULDERING

IMPROVEMENT

INDOOR SPORT

OUTDOOR SPORT

MULTI-PITCH

VIA FERRATA

WHERE TO GO

INDEX

INTRODUCTION

GIVE-IT-A-GO

IND/BOULDERING

OUT/BOULDERING

IMPROVEMENT

INDOOR SPORT

OUTDOOR SPORT

MULTI-PITCH

VIA FERRATA

WHERE TO GO

INDEX

A classic fontainebleau sloper. There is a ripple here to almost crimp on, but the climber in this case feels a lot more of a grip by placing flat fingers on the area and holding it as a sloper. You can see also how the sweat/moisture from the hand immediately soaks into the rock, and this was on a perfect morning of around 5 degrees. In hot weather, this hold would be impossible to use. (The hand of 'Loïc Fossard')

These are the nastiest type of holds to get to grips with, you put your fingers on them, and slowly you slither off. The harder you begin to climb, the more often you come across them. When you first started to boulder, all the holds were bright plastic and obvious, now the game has changed upside down, and you're struggling in trying to use imaginary holds. A sloper is generally a flat area of rock, where you are best off putting your fingers, completely flat on the hold. Whilst it relies on a lot of friction, the main locked component of holding a sloper, is the shape of the fingers and wrist. The power on the other hand, must come completely, from the locked tension of forearm-bicep and inner shoulder (Pectoral).

Because you are using the flats of the fingertips on a smooth hold, you are incredibly likely to slip. The only way to stay gripping to such a hold, is to force downward pressure onto the hold. It's a straight equation; more pressure equals more friction, and hence greater sticking power. So the more sloping the hold, the more downward pressure you need to exert. As a beginner, you just won't have the power in your forearms to really power down on a sloper and hold onto it. This is an acquired strength; one that you gain over many years in using lots of different slopers. Eventually, most climbers love slopers because they really test your skill in a very subtle way.

Here at Kings Tor on Dartmoor, Steve is on one of those classic skin scraping traverses, on slopers! The skill here is obviously to have good sloper muscle strength, but to also feel for all the slight dimples in the granite, and utilize the weaknesses that the rock has to offer. By using a series of heel hooks, you can also save a considerable amount of strength. Be very careful though to twist your body and wrists as you heel hook, and keep you hands perfectly still - well, if you want to keep your skin!

A real classic example of, (F6a-V4) 'horrible slopers,' or 'superb slopers,' depending upon your viewpoint. Smallacombe Rocks, Dartmoor; Ian Hill

INTRODUCTION

GIVE-IT-A-GO

IND/BOULDERING

OUT/BOULDERING

IMPROVEMENT

INDOOR SPORT

OUTDOOR SPORT

MULTI-PITCH

VIA FERRATA

WHERE TO GO

INDEX

1.

2.

3.

4.

This V2 (t-5c) problem at Porth Ysgo in Wales is a very good example of using slopers and how you have to think ahead. The temptation is to try and get your foot up onto the big ledge early! Because you are using slopers, and you need to be below your hands, keep your feet low as much as possible. The key technique of using slopers is to keep your elbows low. 1) Starting with a dead hang this is easy, especially here where there is good friction and a few tiny foot edges. 2) When you first reach up, keep your body as low as possible and artificially keep your elbow (left here), very close to the rock. 3) When you have a good grip of both slopers, then move your body to help your hands, here by moving to the right. Here if you lifted your left foot onto the ledge, you would find standing up with the right hand desperate, because it is a sloper. Instead, you slap up right again and then move your left hand up onto the good sloper. 4) Now you can dead hang quite easily and are in a very good position to put your foot up and rock over to finish. A good rule of thumb with slopers, is to get your hands of top of a problem, before thinking of trying to rock over.

MASSA EXPANSIVA, Font 7b, Peninha, Portugal; Ben Moon. A full on dyno with atrocious footholds, leads up to a sloper from hell for most climbers - except Ben of course, who at least manages a puff on this occasion.

Slopers are as kind as they are nasty. Most of the time they are very friendly to your muscles, with perhaps exception to the stomach. After a really hard day on slopers, you will really feel it on the stomach muscles. However, it's on the skin that you get the real grief. Just the slightest bit of moisture on the hold, and you're going to start sliding around on those fingertips. If you slip once or twice on smooth sandstone, you don't really feel it and can happily come back for more punishment. Do the same on grainy sharp granite, and you will be lucky not to draw blood. The crystals of quartz in granite, have a hardness level of 7/10, in relation to about 1 of your skin – no competition. They are generally big enough to really bite into your skin and cut it up badly. On the other hand, go out with some of the top climbers in the world for a day on granite, and they come home with perfect skin, no cuts or abrasions at all! The key to longevity in climbing with slopers, is to push yourself hard, but not right to your limit when you are in danger of slipping and damaging your skin.

INTRODUCTION

GIVE-IT-A-GO

IND/BOULDERING

OUT/BOULDERING

IMPROVEMENT

INDOOR SPORT

OUTDOOR SPORT

MULTI-PITCH

VIA FERRATA

WHERE TO GO

INDEX

You have to be selective about using slopers. Climbers refer to the ambient weather as 'GOOD or BAD – CONDITIONS.' If it's hot and sunny weather (bad-C), stick to problems with good incuts and holds that you can easily chalk up on. When it's very still, you can often feel the humidity in the air (bad-C), and after rain it's the same too (very bad-C). This moisture is the enemy to holding a sloper and it is quite silly to try and use slopers at this time. The time to go out and climb on slopers is when you have good conditions. This is usually, when a good strong drying wind is in the air and temperatures of around 5-15 degrees. At this time, the rock maybe cold and not so pleasant,

but the friction you get will be superb. A lot of the harder problems in bouldering can only be done in these perfect conditions. A nice hot summer's day in a forest without wind, can give you some of the worst conditions imaginable – the rock simply sweats and you grease off everything. Some of the best conditions are surprisingly before a storm. Here you are often at the end of a dry spell and the rock, ground and trees are tinder dry, then a wind blows away any moisture from the air. In about 3 hours everything is swimming of course, but always remember to take advantage of these times, it's maybe worth a soaking, getting back to the car late - for those extra perfect minutes of bouldering.

Conditions! Technique! Foresight! Sometimes, you simply need pure upper body power. Ian Hill at Willy's Farm boulders, Snowdonia. V5.

For this climber, the day on Dartmoor granite has left a few scars and flappers, don't let it get this bad.

This is a very tricky subject. A potion that may be good for some people's skin could be terrible for someone else's, so we are not going to recommend any particular products. Anything that you put on your skin to improve it, make it grow stronger or quicker, is up to you. There are a few basic points that are worth mentioning and should help everyone. Your skin in bouldering will take a real bashing, especially on slopers, as you can imagine. The first level of pain that you'll get, will be bruising to the fingertips and insides of the hands. Be sensible about this and don't try to be too superhuman. If your climbing is beginning to hurt, stop and go for a cup of tea. The pain is there to protect you – so listen to it.

Dry skin will stick to the rock a lot better than wet skin, so make sure your hands are always dry before you try a problem. Use chalk sensibly to always dry out your skin before a move. After a go on a problem, look at your skin to inspect it for abrasive damage. The first signs of tearing you will see, are tiny little 1mm nicks that pull up from the skin. If you see one of these, stop and think. By doing the problem again and again, and using the same holds in the same manner, it's definitely going to get worse. Either try another problem, or use the handhold in a different manner. Any of these little nicks sticking up from the surface of your skin are a complete waste of time, and do not help friction at all. They're also attached to the rest of the skin on your finger, and if pulled, will start to rip away at the skin leaving a flapper. Most boulderers carry a mini sanding block for this reason, to simply sand away these bits of skin, when they occur.

If you need to put protective tape on your fingers – see our section in sport climbing outdoors for the best methods of finger taping (p259). At the end of the bouldering day, wash your hands thoroughly as soon as possible. You therefore clean the skin and the pores quickly and efficiently, so it can grow and replenish itself. Only after washing, do you apply any hand cream that revitalises the skin and you are happy with. You should also plan your bouldering days on alternative rocks if the weather allows it. Nobody's skin can last for 7 days in a row on hard, mountain granite.

INTRODUCTION

GIVE-IT-A-GO

IND/BOULDERING

OUT/BOULDERING

IMPROVEMENT

INDOOR SPORT

OUTDOOR SPORT

MULTI-PITCH

VIA FERRATA

WHERE TO GO

INDEX

INTRODUCTION

GIVE-IT-A-GO

IND/BOULDERING

OUT/BOULDERING

IMPROVEMENT

INDOOR SPORT

OUTDOOR SPORT

MULTI-PITCH

VIA FERRATA

WHERE TO GO

INDEX

An arête is simply the edge of a boulder, where
two faces of rock meet at an angle. You can have a
sharp arête or a blunt arête, and the word itself is
French. In climbing terms, they are considered the
ultimate shapes to climb, because they are striking
in shape, and the climbing line is obvious – straight
up. They also make for stunning photographs,
where a climber in silhouette can seem to barely
be hanging on except with their fingernails. They
demand specific techniques that are a combination
of all other bouldering moves. You will often find
that to get up an arête, you need all of the climbing
moves; crimping, sidepulls, undercuts, slopers, and
even heel hooks.

*A lovely quiet arête in the forest of Fontainebleau, not even a marked
problem. Jingo in the top photo, gets quite easily established on the
arête by the low foothold and palming with the hands. Then comes
the classic move where you have to pad the face of the bloc, and just
lay-off your hands. At his point you are very likely to barn door. The
situation is kept under control, by keeping all your weight to the right,
and twisting the ankle out to the left. Then by heel hooking with
the left foot, it is relatively easy to move the hands around. This will
be essential for the final reach to the top. If the hands were kept in
the original position, then reaching up simply wouldn't work. When
you have a foot flat on the rock and are palming with the hand, you
cannot reach very far - your foot always slips off. You are always better
off moving the whole position up, so you don't have to over-reach.*

INTRODUCTION

GIVE-IT-A-GO

IND/BOULDERING

OUT/BOULDERING

IMPROVEMENT

INDOOR SPORT

OUTDOOR SPORT

MULTI-PITCH

VIA FERRATA

WHERE TO GO

INDEX

INTRODUCTION

GIVE-IT-A-GO

IND/BOULDERING

OUT/BOULDERING

IMPROVEMENT

INDOOR SPORT

OUTDOOR SPORT

MULTI-PITCH

VIA FERRATA

WHERE TO GO

INDEX

They also have a habit of being on the large side, and you definitely have to consider the consequences of falling off a big one. Arête's also have the habit, of needing very delicate moves that can go wrong, and consequently make this larger problem – somewhat of a considerable mental, and physical challenge/disaster. Sometimes they are very straightforward and only a couple of moves. At other times they can be frustratingly difficult; do you climb it with your body on the left, or the right? They can also be often climbed in different ways, and most bouldering guidebooks will have grades for climbing up one side or the other. Some have tiny little incuts, and are dispensed – simply as a vertical wall that ends up in an arête. Alternatively, you can use the edges for your feet, and use the edge of the arête as a layaway. Sometimes you may have an overhanging arête, and if it is made from limestone there might be jugs all the way up it. This you climb as a normal overhang. The only difference is that it just looks very spectacular.

This arête is a classic 6b example of climbing 'a cheval,' like riding a horse with your legs gripping both sides. Pulling on the left hand low down is a very difficult crimp, but to actually grip with the left foot, you need to squeeze with the right foot on the arête too. Only then can you let go and move you hands up, one at a time. A pinch on with the right, then a sloper with the left, then a pocket to finish - just about every hold on this route. Ooohps, yes a mantelshelf to finish.

The comic failure with an attempt on an arête, is the '**BARN DOOR.**' We use this term in climbing when you have clasped one hand around the arête, and then your body starts to swing out from the wall and you pivot on your wrist. If there is no hold on the wall in front of you to grab, your body just swings under its own momentum like a barn door. The difference is that your hand, although pivoting, is not a hinge. As you swing around, the layaway becomes useless and you fall off. You will go through many stages of – I think I'm gonna barn door, phew, just managed to stay on. There is a big disadvantage to taking a barn door high up, you tend to come off the arête in rotation and cannot control your fall. This is immensely dangerous. If you feel that you are about to barn door, take the sensible action to simply jump off. Out of control barn dooring, is something you only want to do at an indoor wall.

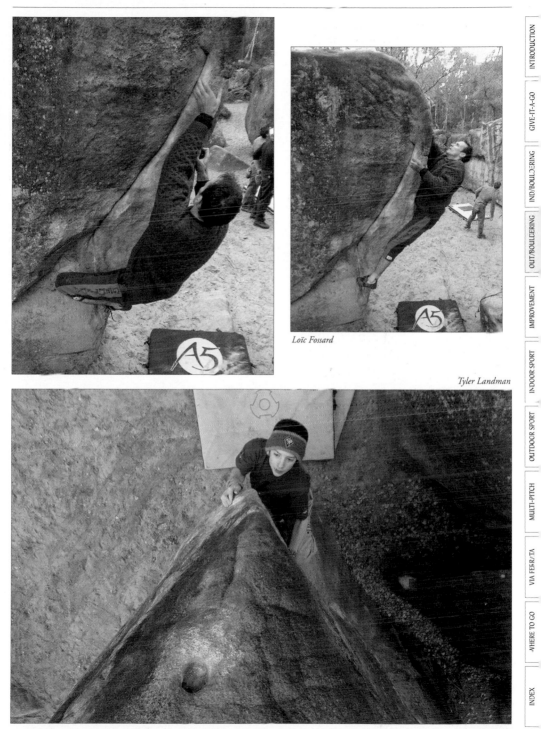

Loïc Fossard

Tyler Landman

INTRODUCTION

GIVE-IT-A-GO

IND/BOULDERING

OUT/BOULDERING

IMPROVEMENT

IN-DOOR SPORT

OUTDOOR SPORT

MULTI-PITCH

VIA FERR/TA

WHERE TO GO

INDEX

INTRODUCTION

GIVE-IT-A-GO

IND/BOULDERING

OUT/BOULDERING

IMPROVEMENT

INDOOR SPORT

OUTDOOR SPORT

MULTI-PITCH

VIA FERRATA

WHERE TO GO

INDEX

Mark Edwards on this lovely arête, situated on a low sea platform at Sennen Cove, Cornwall. A touch on the highball side for most climbers.

133

INTRODUCTION | GIVE-IT-A-GO | IND/BOULDERING | OUT/BOULDERING | IMPROVEMENT | INDOOR SPORT | OUTDOOR SPORT | MULTI-PITCH | VIA FERRATA | WHERE TO GO | INDEX

ABILITY TO PULL UP - *Q-Fix: Try 10 pull ups a day on a doorway lintel.*
Improvement: Full sessions of pullups, hands close together and long way apart; pull entire length of arm movement, pull on a machine bar and continue by pushing it down to straighten the arms.

FINGERTIP STRENGTH - *Q-Fix: Get a little finger exerciser, use it watching telly.*
Imp: Buy or make a specific finger pull up board, comfortable with a smooth wood texture. Pull up on different sized small edges, use both a crimp grip and an open extended grip with the thumb low down.

SLOPER STRENGTH - *Q-Fix: Just rest your fingertips on the edge of a desk, push down and hold.*
Imp: Do pullups with open hands, but then hang halfway down, and lift the legs nice and high.

DYNO CO-ORDINATION - *Q-Fix: Do 10 dynos every bouldering session.*
Imp: Use a rope ladder footless, quickly grab the rungs going up and down, improve quick grip strength.

ANKLE FLEXIBILITY - *Q-Fix: Gently twist your ankle around, helping with your hands.*
Imp: Traverse on a wall only using an outside edge for one foot, get the edge working for you.

3 DIMENSIONAL AWARENESS - *Q-Fix: Watch good climbers work out problems.*
Imp: Work out a problem visually from the finish-backwards, work out the holds, and the reaches involved. Try to climb the whole problem visually before you even touch the rock.

MANTELSHELF SKILLS - *Q-Fix: Go swimming and have fun getting out.*
Imp: Go out with a friend to spot and really try those awkward problems, repeat them a lot too.

FOOTHOLD AWARENESS - *Q-Fix: Ask a friend to shout out when you miss a foothold.*
Imp: Always examine a problem for pockets, and check where bulges make footholds invisible.

BODY FLEXIBILITY - *Q-Fix: Yoga lessons with the opposite sex.*
Imp: Get a general fitness book or video. 6 months of dedicated stretching will get you sorted.

INGENUITY - *Q-Fix: Play a few lateral thinking games at the pub.*
Imp: Climb with a good group of top level climbers, who will show you all the sneaky tricks in the book.

ROCK VARIATIONS - *Q-Fix: Go to different climbing walls, especially ones with good freeform.*
Imp: Climb on many different rock types, even the ones you don't like - at first.

SOUND MENTAL HEAD PSYCHE - *Q-Fix: Stay up longer on high walls, and look down a lot.*
Imp: High level traversing above mats is good since you get used to more exposure. Do easy highballs.

FOCUSING CONCENTRATION - *Q-Fix: Countdown from three before a hard move.*
Imp: Work on 3 levels of concentration; diverse-1st go, well committed-2nd go, and then full on psyche.

WEIGHT LOSS - *Q-Fix: Cut down on beer and cookies and stop watching telly all the time.*
Imp: Keep an eye on your diet, and take exercise 5 days a week. Resist those 10 cream buns!

SHOE PERFORMANCE - *Q-Fix: Buy a better pair and tighter pair of shoes*

CHALK PERFORMANCE - *Q-Fix: Get nice and gritty, dry chalk.*

Now, we can presume that you have fully mastered 'all' the techniques so far! Maybe not, but at least you know the basics and can reference this book. In bouldering, there is a huge difference between using a technique poorly, and really having it at your disposal in any situation. Some people are quite happy to learn a couple of mantelshelf techniques, and only ever use those ones. Other climbers want to extend their repertoire, so they can develop into full, all round boulderers. This section is intended to help you continue in your learning phase, and to improve your wide range of skills.

A lot of eager kids and even adults, quickly get to grips with bouldering and become very good at one or two techniques. Then what happens! Is that they fail miserably on something a bit easy that isn't their style, and pass it off as an embarrassment. The last thing they want their mates to see, is them still having a hard time on the silly little problem – a whole week later. Unfortunately, this is exactly what they must suffer if they want to improve. Walking away from a problem that you could do, but can't do, is definitely NOT the way to improve. The great Jerry Moffatt, one of the world's greatest boulderers, gave me a lovely quote, "Climbing strength is always about how hard you work on your weaknesses." All great boulderers work on their weaker points, and keep training at all their techniques until they are perfect.

Knowing the movements is important, how to place your hands correctly, when to twist your body etc. But just going to the gym, wall or any bouldering area without focus, is 'not' going to improve you very quickly. To improve, you must have concentrated focus. Alternatively, always going to the wall and being totally focused on improvement, is going to make you into a dedicated bore! Climbing is all about a different combination of sessions; relaxed fun and joking with mates, bouldering on your own for some peace and quiet, but also focused 'sessions,' on improving a technique, mad dynos etc.

On the left is a chart that Dyno-mite uses. These are the well known weak points of climbing, and ones that you can work on. We give ideas for improvement in the short and long term. The rest of this section should help you become aware of some more advanced techniques, and ideas on improvement.

THE BOWDERSTONE, Borrowdale, Lake District. One of the famous and historic improvement spots for English bouldering. (Caleb Reid)

INTRODUCTION · GIVE-IT-A-GO · IND/BOULDERING · OUT/BOULDERING · IMPROVEMENT · INDOOR SPORT · OUTDOOR SPORT · MULTI-PITCH · VIA FERRATA · WHERE TO GO · INDEX

INTRODUCTION | GIVE-IT-A-GO | IND/BOULDERING | OUT/BOULDERING | IMPROVEMENT | INDOOR SPORT | OUTDOOR SPORT | MULTI-PITCH | VIA FERRATA | WHERE TO GO | INDEX

RAC boulders classic traverse, Snowdonia. Here you can find a superb pump with at least 10 different types of hand hold; Ian Hill

A lot of sport and traditional climbers go traversing, they use it as a means to get the forearms pumped and improve their levels of arm stamina. It's also a convenient way to work at improvement for these types of climbing without a partner. For bouldering, you have to be a lot more discerning since stamina is not going to get you up a hard problem. You can use the traverse to far better effect, when you devise a super techno traverse. You can do this indoors, inner-city, or if you're lucky, on a remote quiet boulder set in a beautiful location. You need to devise a traverse that involves lots of different moves, and which requires precise movement of both hands and feet. Dispense with any big footholds completely; use smaller ripples next to them, this way you get used to placing your feet exactly where they have to go. The wall may be covered in one type of hold, look for various different holds – search out a pinch, a sloper, a jam, and even a guppy (see photo). By incorporating all of these into the

traverse, you can come up with a problem which is both tiring and most of all – interesting. You'll be amazed how hard the problem is the first time you invent and try it. Then after a while it becomes easier and easier. You can start eliminating footholds to make it harder, and for the final pump challenge – do it from both ends. Always work on technicality and different holds, it pays off in the end.

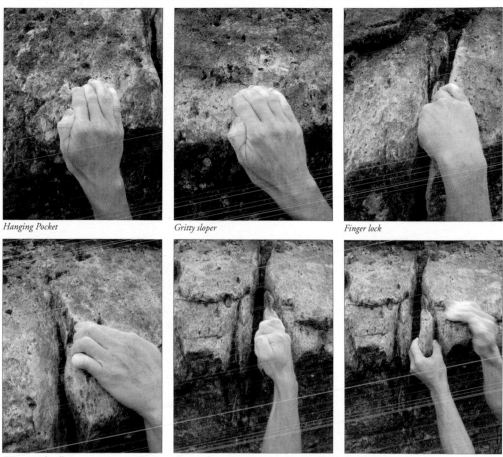

Hanging Pocket

Gritty sloper

Finger lock

Fingertip sidepull

Guppy, where you cup your hand over a spike

Pinch - forearm strength

Good slot for a rest and to match on.

The traverse goes around the corner with even more desperate moves. It is also simple to change the way you use each hold on each traverse, to technically develop your skills.

INTRODUCTION

GIVE-IT-A-GO

IND/BOULDERING

OUT/BOULDERING

IMPROVEMENT

INDOOR SPORT

OUTDOOR SPORT

MULTI-PITCH

VIA FERRATA

WHERE TO GO

INDEX

INTRODUCTION · GIVE-IT-A-GO · IND/BOULDERING · OUT/BOULDERING · IMPROVEMENT · INDOOR SPORT · OUTDOOR SPORT · MULTI-PITCH · VIA FERRATA · WHERE TO GO · INDEX

A lot of boulderers miss out on good rounded technique, especially when they go to an outside bouldering venue. They get carried away and hone in on a desperate problem, slapping for this and grabbing that, often with their feet trailing everywhere. Sure, it's good to have a problem that you can't do, and work away at it, you build strength in the muscles every time that you try it. But the disadvantage is that you only build up muscle strength, and are you're wasting a golden opportunity to improve on technique. You have the indoor gym and wall to train on and have 6 months of winter for this. Your time on the rock is always precious and you have to use it wisely; work on 3 dimensional awareness, ingenuity, head psyche and rock texture.

All problems from the blue circuit (3b-5b) at Roche aux Sabots, Les Trois Pignons, Fontainebleau. This is one of the most diverse circuits demanding all round technique and skills. (Nat Kelner)

Going on a trip to Fontainebleau is perfect for this. The guidebook will give you a wide variety of problems to choose from, and grade them from easy to desperate. The most unique part of Font, is the creation of coloured circuits.. They are designed to cover a wide variety of grades, but also have a complete variation of technical moves. The visionary climber who wants to improve, doesn't go off to do hard problems; they simply pick a circuit and try to do 'every single problem' on it. Even on the easiest of yellow circuits, there can be problems of grade 3 whcih can easily catch you out. The circuits are designed to encourage all round technique. They also give you a wonderful lift, because you end up climbing a lot of problems, which is always mentally satisfying.

This problem - Quartier libre 4c, demanding ingenuity of crack climbing and heel-toe hooking on the arête, a real testpiece for the grade.

Pense bête 5a, the roof demands is a desperate dyno to even reach the lip, then you get the mantel from hell. (Jeff Landman)

Tout en grattons 3c - All the tiny holds, an excellent combination of balance and fingertip strength. (Rowan Kelner)

INTRODUCTION

GIVE-IT-A-GO

IND/BOULDERING

OUT/BOULDERING

IMPROVEMENT

INDOOR SPORT

OUTDOOR SPORT

MULTI-PITCH

VIA FERRATA

WHERE TO GO

INDEX

climbing without failure. You might not get it first time, but you should get up it within half an hour. For want of another name, it's your Achilles heel grade. When you are a beginner, there is bound to be a huge difference between your best styles, and your most hated techniques. Over the years, make sure you work on all round technique and keep your jingo and wobbly grades, as close as possible. Separately, there is your 'HIGHBALL' grade. This is where the problem is mind blowingly high, and a fall starts to get nasty. This is a completely different game altogether, where mental control is important to control the shaking legs – know as sewing machine legs. Also a high degree of madness is helpful. At this stage, only think of trying highballs at your wobbly grade.

Fairway 4a, a delicate slab that is all balance and technique, and a little dyno for the short. (Tyler Landman)

Marche à pied 4a, slopers with an ingenious rocko-ver, not easy for beginners. (Stow Kelner)

The other nice part with developing your rounded technique, is that you are always using separate muscles, and different parts of the skin on your fingers. After 20 problems of completely different styles, you'll still have skin on the fingers, and your tips won't be bashed into submission. After 4 days, no matter how varied your style is – you will feel trashed and exhausted.

At the end of a good bouldering trip, you can assess your strength and weaknesses. The hardest problem you managed to do, we call your Jingo grade (all strength, brawn, dyno and oomph). But your Wobbly grade eh? That is simply, one grade below – the easiest problem that you failed on. This is the honest and lowly grade that you are confident and technically safe at

Morceau de choix 5a, the highball of the circuit and using pockets, crimps and power, a fully diversified problem. (Tyler Landman)

INTRODUCTION

GIVE-IT-A-GO

IND/BOULDERING

OUT/BOULDERING

IMPROVEMENT

INDOOR SPORT

OUTDOOR SPORT

MULTI-PITCH

VIA FERRATA

WHERE TO GO

INDEX

The very sight of some overhangs and caves, will no doubt scare the timid beginner. However, with nice bouncy crash mats below, you can easily fall off and have a lot of fun. The darker side of caves, is that you can swing around quite easily, but find it almost impossible to make any substantial improvement. This is directly linked with your power to weight ratio, and if you can keep this down during your climbing years. The other equally important part of climbing steep overhangs, is the willingness to train on building muscle power, and the perfect application of technique. On a slab or a wall, you have more room and time to get away with poor technique. On a steep cave, you really have to be quick, and use all the techniques available. The simplest technique is the 'JELLY ROLL,' so amusingly

The Jelly Roll technique: In the top photo, Virginie is simply using an undercut and a jug, note how level the shoulders are. In the lower photo, she has twisted her complete body and thrown out the left leg as a counterbalance - called flagging. Her right shoulder now is a lot higher up and she can easily reach up to another hold. Her left arm is critically still straight. You can do the move by pulling on the left arm - obviously; but this involves a lot more strength.; Virgine Percival, Jingo Wobbly wall

called, because it's the only move that you can make when your arms turn to jelly. You simply hold on with one hand, then with the helping support from the foot, just twist your body onto its side. Simply by making this twist, you can now reach up the wall a good foot higher. So long as the handholds are good enough, you can use this method to climb up most overhanging walls, even when you are pumped solid.

The handy thing with indoor bouldering walls, is that the cave roof's are usually covered in good juggy holds. Outside on real rock, you are rarely so lucky. At least this makes them fun for the majority of climbers, and practically possible for most. You still need to respect the challenge, and make sure you have a good spotter to tip you up the right way if you fall. The photos

Climbing up to a roof of this size can be hard enough in itself, so make sure that you get to the roof nice and fresh, and from a problem you know well. When you have mastered the techniques of crossing the roof, only then begin to add a harder start. In the lower photo, see how Jon starts the roof using a straight arm with the left, maximising energy conservation. (Brunel University - Jon Partridge)

INTRODUCTION

GIVE-IT-A-GO

IND/BOULDERING

OUT/BOULDERING

IMPROVEMENT

INDOOR SPORT

OUTDOOR SPORT

MULTI-PITCH

VIA FERRATA

WHERE TO GO

INDEX

should illustrate the roof spin technique quite well. One of the best tips in climbing overhangs like this, is to keep your arms as straight as possible. Every time you bend your arm on an overhang, you are lifting a lot more weight than usual – energy conservation is the key.

The best way to tackle this sort of roof, is to minimise the amount of time that you are suspended horizontally. You also must use the side vertical walls as much as possible. In the top photo, Jon keeps his foot on the back wall as long as possible. This will be taking a lot of weight off his arms and giving him a chance to conserve strength. When you start to climb across the roof, look for everything to help you. Lower left- Jon has spotted a way to twist his foot between a flake and a jug sticking out. This alone will take some weight and relieve his arms for a moment. Eventually when you feel that you can make it, you release your feet and try to claw a foothold on the other wall, as quickly as possible. Here time is of the essence. You need a good combination of speed, agility, timing, ingenuity and stamina to succeed in caves.

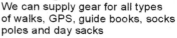

INTRODUCTION

GIVE-IT-A-GO

IND/BOULDERING

OUT/BOULDERING

IMPROVEMENT

INDOOR SPORT

OUTDOOR SPORT

MULTI-PITCH

VIA FERRATA

WHERE TO GO

INDEX

The hardest part for any learning book, is to stay clear and simple for the beginner. There does come a point however, when the subject – bouldering, is in danger of becoming too advanced for the casual climber. If you are comfortable with your leisure climbing, and don't want to get bogged down in super strong – power techniques, then jump forward from this part of the book, into the sport climbing sections. For those of you still with us, we now take quite a different view of bouldering – making it as hard as possible. Warning: Extreme bouldering can lead to all sorts of body and muscle imbalances, so go very carefully and consult a personal physiotherapist, to at least understand your training – to minimise your risk from becoming injured and muscle bound.

An overhanging woodie can be one of the greatest places to both climb and train upon. With soft crash pads, you can push your body in different ways to build strength, but also discover a huge amount about your body dynamics and how to actually move in difficult positions. If you simply repeat the pattern of climbing up 10 jugs on a woody in a straight line, you become a gorilla since the strength gain is huge from repetitive workouts. The disadvantage, is that your muscles only have a small range of movement, and are not going to work well at all when you deviate from that set movement. It's always important to incorporate as many different types of moves with your arms and hands. This way, you build up all round upper body strength. This however, is still pure gymnastics; it's only simple and physical.

Bouldering is all about the complexity of movement, and using your body in the most efficient manner. It certainly isn't meant to be beautiful, but strangely – it often is, when you climb very well. The main part of steep bouldering (steep meaning overhanging), is that you work your body as a suspended triangle. At each corner of the triangle, you have a hook or a pad to stabilise it. We have two hands and two feet, yes four pieces of the anatomy, which can either be hooks or pads. Every movement that you make on a steep wall, can be broken down into static triangles where you are holding on.

A very good way to learn about your ability to hold on to a steep wall, is to pick out a set of handholds that you can reasonably cope with. Next, allow yourself to use any footholds, and therefore make a triangle so that you can easily take one hand off to chalk up. Holding on with two hands is gorilla tactics, holding on with one hand, demands exact and careful foot placement. The resting position you will automatically drop into, is with your feet below and to either side of you. The nearer you have one foot to your centre line, the more unbalance you become – using you hand as a hook, and your feet as pads. What really starts to change the way your triangle works, is when the handhold you have, starts to get sloping and poor. At the extreme end, you hand hold is so poor, it is not a hook anymore, it's just a resting pad. No triangle will stay on the wall with 3 pads, so you have to therefore use one of your toes, as a hook. It makes sense too when you think of it like this, you just have to know how to apply the strength to your hand, foot, and toe hook, in order to stay triangled to the wall.

Every beginner who gets onto a steep wall is going to get stuck, just remember that you should always be able to take one hand off to reach for another hold. If you can't, its because only one of your feet is working in the triangle that keeps you on. Move your feet so they form the triangle with just one hand only, then you can move the other; now, you'll never get stuck again! Well, unless you can't reach the next hold from your little triangle. The answer, is to find another triangle with your feet higher up the wall of course. Unfortunately, that might be an impossible question of strength, then again – that's bouldering.

A very good example of a nice static triangle held by Percy, one foot pushing and the other hooking on the same hold - called a BICYCLE; Percy Bishton - The Edge woodie room

Here Ed has quite a few options to try out. He is resting on a good jug, in a good triangular position. But if he were to move his top hand instead to the right, and took a sloper, then he would almost definitely have to change his left foot from a pad to a hook. Below you can see a very nicely positioned hook for a sloper, in placing the foot sideways, you get a more effective hook on this type of hold.

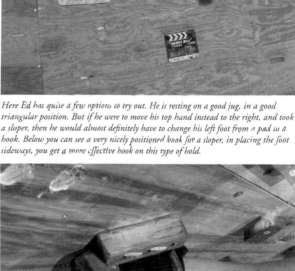

INTRODUCTION | GIVE-IT-A-GO | IND/BOULDERING | OUT/BOULDERING | IMPROVEMENT | INDOOR SPORT | OUTDOOR SPORT | MULTI-PITCH | VIA FERRATA | WHERE TO GO | INDEX

The one thing you should know by now, is that to climb up steep areas, it is easy to bring one hand up to the other and match on a hold, and then think about reaching up again. The disadvantage with this technique, is that it relies on you being able to match on a hold. When you are learning, you spend a lot of time over a many years, getting very good at matching on a hold. There is one lovely technique when the hold is only big enough for 4 fingers, and you have to lift one finger at a time, and replace it with another finger from the other hand. You often get it in sport climbing when you end up with the wrong hand on the wrong hold, and can't simply step back onto the crash pad.

In bouldering, swapping hands is not really done very much, simply because you have the opportunity to stand back and work out the problem from the ground. You can see the obvious finishing holds, and therefore work out the sequence that is going to allow you to end up with your hands in the perfect position. This often means that you have to cross one arm, over the other, in a move that is called a 'CROSSOVER.' You might think this is obvious, and we should

Tobacco Road F6c, Bowles Rocks, Sussex; one of the classic traverses that involves move after move of crossovers. (Miguel Loureiro)

have pointed it out earlier. The main reason for not doing so, is that a crossover is one of the hardest moves in bouldering for a beginner, and certainly on steep rock. All climbers generally find it far easier, to simply shuffle their hands along a ledge. But to be a good boulderer, you want to start making crossover moves wherever you can. You will be amazed at how far you can reach, and how quickly you can get there with a crossover.

A V6 problem at Bone Hill, Dartmoor, Devon; a really nasty sort of problem where the handholds are small and gritty (granite), and the footholds are terrible, so you have to make a lot of distance on every hold; a classic crossover problem. (Dave Henderson)

INTRODUCTION

GIVE-IT-A-GO

IND/BOULDERING

OUT/BOULDERING

IMPROVEMENT

INDOOR SPORT

OUTDOOR SPORT

MULTI-PITCH

VIA FERRATA

WHERE TO GO

INDEX

Ben Moon, one of the world's greatest boulderers, perfectly executing Rosa Negra 7c, Pedra do Urso, Portugal; a problem that involves a perfect sequence of crossovers from the very first hold - until the very last hold.

The whole first half of the climb is done virtually without footholds, and the handholds are only big enough for one set of fingers. There is simply no option but to crossover. This granite is very rough too, so you certainly don't want to be matching your hands and wasting time.

INTRODUCTION

GIVE-IT-A-GO

IND/BOULDERING

OU/-BOULDERING

IMPROVEMENT

INDOOR SPORT

OUTDOOR SPORT

MULTI-P TCH

VIA FERRATA

WHERE TO GO

INDEX

INTRODUCTION

GIVE-IT-A-GO

IND/BOULDERING

OUT/BOULDERING

IMPROVEMENT

INDOOR SPORT

OUTDOOR SPORT

MULTI-PITCH

VIA FERRATA

WHERE TO GO

INDEX

Try to imagine some of the character drawings of ancient Egypt. A usual pose is where a figure seems to be almost dancing and is often squeezed into a rectangle on a long stone tablet. They will have one hand in front of them, flat palm pointing up, and the other hand behind them with the palm facing down. This is where the term in climbing originates. If you try to climb a narrow chimney, this is often the pose you adopt, with each palm flat on either wall.

In bouldering (as opposed to a climbing a trad-style chimney), the term is more influenced by the direction of the feet, than the hands. The term is used when your body is side-on to the wall, and one foot is in front of your, and you are almost sitting on the other. Our photos try to illustrate this clearly. This position is very similar to a move in the closed position that we illustrated earlier, because you are pulling across your body with one hand. You can also do an Egyptian in the open position too, but this is a far weaker move. To climb in the open position on a steep wall as illustrated, would be tremendously hard and demanding. This is the perfect territory to use Egyptians. The most important foothold is the lower one, it can be very small, but it needs to be a horizontal edge. For the higher foothold that you almost sit on , the angle is less important and you can often get away with just a sloping edge. It is without doubt, one of the most beautiful moves in climbing, and the better you get – the more you will start using it.

Here, the steep angle forces Jon to do an Egyptian. Finding a good left hand hold is critical. In this case it is a good sidepull which will enable a lot of height to be gained. Then he gets a good high foothold with the outside edge of his right foot, almost in a sitting position. The body can then pull on the left hand, pivot on the left toe, and take weight on the right foot. Because this is such a strong position and your legs are bent, you can often slightly dyno out of this move to get some extra height. On a vertical wall you can do these moves in an open position with great success.

INTRODUCTION

GIVE-IT-A-GO

IND/BOULDERING

OUT/BOULDERING

IMPROVEMENT

INDOOR SPORT

OUTDOOR SPORT

MULTI-PITCH

VIA FERRATA

WHERE TO GO

INDEX

INTRODUCTION

GIVE-IT-A-GO

IND/BOULDERING

OUT/BOULDERING

IMPROVEMENT

INDOOR SPORT

OUTDOOR SPORT

MULTI-PITCH

VIA FERRATA

WHERE TO GO

INDEX

This is the genuinely silly move of climbing, and a classic. So unless you are into very hard climbing, you certainly will never use it. Even if you can do it perfectly, there aren't many times that you need it. You can often dyno the same distance with a lot more ease. The cute feature of the fig of 4, is that when you do arrive at the hold, you are static and can easily grab the final hold (handy if you have dodgy tendons or poor skin). The name of the move comes from the shape that you make with your forearm placed under your thigh. The principle is that you put one hand on a good hold, and then sit on your wrist quite comfortably! From here you can wave at passers by, or even reach up a long way for another handhold. In practice it doesn't always go like that unfortunately. You rely on several factors.

You have to be supple for a start. A lot of people cannot even hang off a handhold with one hand and throw their leg over easily. Try this move on a vertical wall, and with a spotter for a start. Use the other holds on the wall to get the feel for the whole move. It starts to get difficult when you start eliminating the other holds. The handhold is quite critical since you must have a good hold to support the whole of your weight. You will find that to get your thigh onto your wrist & parallel with the hold, you have to hang below and then

lever your weight up using your forearm; only then do you slide down onto your wrist. The edge of the hold is the effective fulcrum point on your hand, and with the leverage, you get a lot more pressure than just your body weight! Be careful not to pinch muscles and nerves on a sharp edge of rock. You also rely a lot, on your hanging leg to flag and stabilise your body. On a vertical wall the figure of 4 is a fairly easy move, but the moment the rock starts to overhang, you just cannot get the righting-leverage from the hanging leg. This move really sorts out the men from the boys.

Jon, completely static, and easily reaching 1.5 metres with a fig of 4 move; Amersham - The climb

INTRODUCTION

GIVE-IT-A-GO

IND/BOULDERING

OUT/BOULDERING

IMPROVEMENT

INDOOR SPORT

OUTDOOR SPORT

MULTI-PITCH

VIA FERRATA

WHERE TO GO

INDEX

A very popular move in sport climbing is the knee bar. Often you can find a steering wheel sized hole, put your foot on the bottom edge and your knee inside, and then make the top of the knee jam on the upper lip by pressing on the toes and foot. If it is not very overhanging and the jam is good, you can often take your hands completely off and get a fantastic rest. In countries like Greece and Thailand, the limestone caves often present big holes and hanging stalactites to get your knee behind. In those sport climbing areas, the grade of the climb will presume that you are using a knee bar to rest your arms. Your feet naturally will stick to the rock, but the knee is not so robust, so if you know of a route or problem with a knee bar, bring some trousers. Another consideration is that nylon is very poor for friction compared with cotton, so if you are a bit weak in the arm department – pick cotton every time.

You don't often get knee bars in bouldering, but when you do, there is often no other option. You have to be quite careful with them because if they pop out, you are going to fall very awkwardly. You

Arabesque f-7b+, a real classic testpiece problem at Cul de Chien, Fontainebleau. Leaving the ground demands a very confident quick step up, whilst holding a really rounded undercut. One of the hard moves is getting a good knee bar, which allows for a long reach to a very difficult pocket to find. It still remains hard for another 5 desperate moves! (Hjarrand Julsrud & Per Hustad, giving a fine performance)

can get into a knee bar in 2 ways. You either put your knee in first and bring your toes up, or you put your foot on first and then twist the knee in from the side. You certainly get a better knee bar when you twist the leg in, but mostly it is just so you can get a good grip and make the move.

INTRODUCTION

GIVE-IT-A-GO

IND/BOULDERING

OUT/BOULDERING

IMPROVEMENT

INDOOR SPORT

OUTDOOR SPORT

MULTI-PITCH

VIA FERRATA

WHERE TO GO

INDEX

INTRODUCTION

GIVE-IT-A-GO

IND/BOULDERING

OUT/BOULDERING

IMPROVEMENT

INDOOR SPORT

OUTDOOR SPORT

MULTI-PITCH

VIA FERRATA

WHERE TO GO

INDEX

So far, we've worked on all-round technique to cover a broad range of moves and skills. Hopefully, you should by now have a relatively high wobbly grade. There comes a time though, when you want a bit of a lift, something to shout about, and feel that you've achieved something special. This is very much part of anyone's psychology, and it's nothing to feel bad about. The easiest way to achieve this in climbing, is to look at all the techniques which come easily to you; then, pick out the one you want to really develop. By doing this, you can direct yourself to the sort of problem which is going to become your Jingo grade. It's something to make yourself, really powerful on. It also gives you a bit of pride to know that there's at least one style of move that you're really good at, especially when your mates keep coming over and ask you to show them how it's done. Don't view it as a way of showing off, but more of a way to keep your spirits up when you get depressed at failing on lots of other problems. Being strong on one type of move, can be a real lift sometimes, so work at it.

To get good at a particular bouldering move, you need to isolate it, and then train specifically for it. Many climbers, generally quote that the best training for any sort of climbing, is climbing - just doing it. This comes from the pratical reason that climbing is so diversified. For training, you won't often find too many of one type of problem, all gathered together and perfectly lined up for you to work out. There are thankfully, perfectly good other training methods which give spectacular results. In my early climbing days, I found a one handed mantelshelf that defeated me completely. It wasn't rocket science to work out which muscle groups were ineffective, simply the back of the upper arm. With a group of friends, we started to have press-up competitions at the climbing wall, in the hope of improving these muscles. We made the first week a direct competition but were a bit weak, so it was the first to 10. After 2 months, we were having competitions of the 1st to 100 or 200; combining several of these fun head to heads, each night. We returned to the mantelshelf problem 3 months later – it was so easy. We unknowingly got it right on 2 accounts, first to improve our strength, but just as important was to have fun, feel positive, and enjoy the whole training aspect.

Your body - the human frame, has developed to be a walker and runner, and has lost the baboon muscle groups around the arms, fingers and back. There is however one advantage that we have over most other primates, is that we have thumbs to grip with. Always be thankful for your huge amount of extra technical grip with the thumb, and don't underestimate it. Our back is on the other hand, relatively puny. If you're a lightweight, you've got a massive advantage in climbing – you're lucky. The best piece of training advice I ever heard, was to get one of those healthy height-weight charts, and to make sure you were on the lowest, healthy weight for your height. Surprisingly, you do get a few climbers that are a bit on the heavy side and can really climb well of course. But if you are going to specifically begin applied training techniques, then you only want to build the strength that you actually need. In simple and honest terms, your body is weak, joints are weak, tendons are weak, etc. By all means try to strengthen your body, but don't needlessly cause it unnecessary agro it could do without, take real care and respect with your applied training.

I consider applied training, purely as an improvement technique, and importantly – not as a goal orientated training. Anyone who trains in climbing for a particular goal, such as climbing a hard route or a certain grade; is likely to end up very injured, mangled, or even dead. Your body is very often, completely incapable of physically climbing a lot of problems with high grades. Do not even think of trying to copy top climbers, or even attain their levels of physique. They probably have a completely different metabolic rate, bone structure etc. to you. You also don't know the injuries that they may have sustained in getting to the very highest grades of climbing. Applied training is the concept of looking at your own present capabilities, and then working to improve them in a positive manner, and over a reasonable period of time. You, regulate your training ideas; you, monitor your progress; and then eventually you apply your improved strength to different bouldering problems. You may, or may not be successful, but at least you are sensibly training your body within comfortable limits, rather than mindlessly driving it up an insurmountable slope of destruction. Afterwards, analyse your improvement strengths and weaknesses. It is easy to find that the group of muscles you were targeting, might only have got stronger in just one area. The answer then, is to work on a more fluid exercise, which involves more movement than your exercises were providing. Finally, you plan another period of applied training.

There are lots of words used to describe your strength, but the most important word of all is 'POWER.' This is the term in climbing used for explosive strength. You will often hear that a climber is really strong, which means they have good technique, and can often climb very well. The phrase is then followed by "but they've got no power," which means that they have no raw explosive strength. A power move is simply when you have a hold in front of your nose, no footholds worth thinking about, and you have to propel yourself up to another hold. This is 'RAW POWER.' There is one extra element to also

consider, and that is your grip. It's not much use being able to power through the air, and then not be able to hang onto the final hold. A lot of people when they start climbing, have no power at all, it's often something which may or may not develop with your natural climbing. The big advantage, is that training for it is well understood.

To increase your powr, you need to find a pull-up bar for a start. If you can't do a few pull-ups, then go back to the workout gym. A lot of girls don't have the raw oomph to easily cope with pull-ups. Howerver, there is a good machine in exercise gyms that allows you to pull on a bar with adjustable weights on a cable, and by using this over a period of time, you can incrementally increase your strength to do a pull up, plus you'll have a sporty gym trainer to advise you. After this, you are best off progressing quickly onto the campus board. In principle, this is a series of flat holds up a steep wall, and where your feet dangle in space. They come

At Bude climbing wall, there is a very dedicated campus section which gives all different sizes and shapes of campus rungs. (Simon Young)

INTRODUCTION

GIVE-IT-A-GO

IND/BOULDERING

OUT/BOULDERING

IMPROVEMENT

INDOOR SPORT

OUTDOOR SPORT

MULTI-PITCH

VIA FERRATA

WHERE TO GO

INDEX

INTRODUCTION

GIVE-IT-A-GO

IND/BOULDERING

OUT/BOULDERING

IMPROVEMENT

INDOOR SPORT

OUTDOOR SPORT

MULTI-PITCH

VIA FERRATA

WHERE TO GO

INDEX

It's good to have a varied pattern of up and downs. Sometimes miss out rungs, up a small set and then down a large set - think creatively

in many different styles, shapes & angles. To start with, you will need a beginner's campus board. The critical part is the size of the holds. They should be of wood that has low friction, and have rungs that are between 40 & 50mm deep. It doesn't matter how far apart they are, the only thing you want is for them to be a reasonable distance of around 160-170mm minimum. This is because you slap your hand from one to the other, and don't want to crunch your knuckles.

To start with, you simply dead hang on the bottom rung. The idea is to somehow get to the next rung up! You do a pull up – fine! But then you can't take one hand off at all. The answer is to do a pull-up quickly, and just as you reach the top, throw one hand up to the next rung, gripping very quickly. Then see if you can drop your hand back down to the lower rung, you should find this a lot easier, but you will still need good co-ordination to hang on. You need to practise this with both hands and become equally strong on both arms. The next part is to get both hands together on the 2nd rung. You can do this with pure speed of movement, but will find it a lot easier if you do a slight pull-up as you move the lower hand up. From now on, it's easy. You simply go up and down from rung 1-2. Determined progression will soon enable you to go up to the 3rd rung, and then the 4th, etc.

The next challenge for the campus work, is to only use one hand on every rung. This is where the POWER, begins. Now you have to find real power to move between the rungs. There are usually around 8 rungs to a campus board, and if they are close together, you can even start missing some out. A way of gauging your real power, is to hold the bottom rung, then see how high you can grab and hold. The main application of campus boards, is to spend time working the muscle groups in good ranges, rather than to see how dynamic you can be.

Most climbers develop their own routines, depending on their bodyweight and analysing how much they want to do, before any potential strains to their arms develop. Nearly all top climbers use campus boards because on hard climbs, the holds are a long way apart and are mostly without significant footholds. For a lot of moderate and high level bouldering, you just don't need this sort of power.

On a long dyno up, a jump of 3 rungs is a very good standard, also get used to holding on with 3 fingers only, it's often all you can reach.

The other area of applied training that you should consider, is finger workouts. When you take a pull-up bar or even a good hold, the only part you exercise is your arm and back muscles. There are two other areas that you can really build up strength which is likely to be weak. The first area to visit is open hand strength. What you are trying to develop, are the muscle groups for your fingers that are used, when a small hold is at your furthest reach. This is going to always be your downfall, it's no good reaching a hold if you can't pull on it. Stretch you fingers out as far as they go, with just a slight bend at the top joint. This shape of open hand clasp is what you need to train up. Work out a plan of normal pull-ups with your fingers like this for a good exercise. Over a period of months you can very slowly increase from 1 then 2 then 3 etc. pull-ups. It really is an essential grip. The second area is fingertip pressure and body tension. You can train at this on a climbing wall by using very sloping and poor footholds. If you traverse on these, you build up very good fingertip strength and footwork technique. This becomes a real asset in difficult sport climbing.

To sum up, there is quite simply, no shortage of training workout books on the market, development of sports psychology, nutritional physiology, yogic conceptualization, etc, etc. Needless to say, that you're going to find a lot more in them, than our straightforward 4 pages on this subject. On the other hand, keeping things simple is not such a bad thing in the long term. Take a golfer, who sets a ball up on a tee, they can think of a hundred things at the same time, since they've most probably had all the training, psychology etc. They enjoy one lovely privilege that a climber doesn't have, if they drive off into the woods – they simply get another ball out of their bag. If a climber is up on a highball, or in any other dangerous situation, they want to be thinking pretty clearly, and with simplicity plus good judgement. There are also those people who are very good at talking their way

Top: Simon making a 2 handed dyno, almost like swimming butterfly, and as exhausting. It's good for practising your co-ordination too.
Lower: Work on both open hand sessions as well as crimp style.

out of difficult situations. When you're hanging off a hold and getting tired, you only may have a short time to work out what to do. Having a good degree of verbal at this point is irrelevant! Muscle training is important to climbers, but 'clear thinking' and getting on with it, is perhaps more important.

INTRODUCTION

GIVE-IT-A-GO

IND/BOULDERING

OUT/BOULDERING

IMPROVEMENT

INDOOR SPORT

OUTDOOR SPORT

MULTI-PITCH

VIA FERRATA

WHERE TO GO

INDEX

The double slap, is an interesting move that you get at every level of climbing. Usually it is a way of doing a problem when you are short of reach, and you just can't get to the finishing hold. On harder problems, it maybe the only way that is possible to actually do a climb. The qualities of a good double slapper are mostly co-ordination, and the will to think that you are doing the right thing. Most climbers will try to do a move either statically, or with a single dyno. Sometimes it takes courage from a boulderer to admit that they cannot do a problem in one fling, and have to double slap it. You'll find that you use this move a lot when you are climbing arête's. It is a lovely technique, and it can really annoy 'the competitive bunch,' when you double slap your way up a problem. Think of it, as the best sneaky trick in the book.

A lovely close up view of the difficulties on MOON ARÊTE f-7c+, Peninha, Portugal. The angle is diabolical, and with a pretty shoddy landing. The left hand is crimping on just about nothing, and the right hand has to keep slapping up the arête for around 1.6 metres (which at this angle is hideous). Even holding the final slap at this angle is full on 7c+. Get to the gym and practise that double slapping technique.

INTRODUCTION | GIVE-IT-A-GO | IND/BOULDERING | OUT/BOULDERING | IMPROVEMENT | INDOOR SPORT | OUTDOOR SPORT | MULTI-PITCH | VIA FERRATA | WHERE TO GO | INDEX

INTRODUCTION

GIVE-IT-A-GO

IND/BOULDERING

OUT/BOULDERING

IMPROVEMENT

INDOOR SPORT

OUTDOOR SPORT

MULTI-PITCH

VIA FERRATA

WHERE TO GO

INDEX

This is the name given to a problem that is higher than you would like it to be. There isn't a fixed height for any highball, but it is generally given to problems that if you fell off the top, you are very likely to be going straight to hospital! What skills do you need? Lack of brain is the one that springs to mind, yet this is exactly what you do need. You obviously need to be a good climber, and someone with a good level of fitness. You need to practise your downclimbing technique, in particular. Most of all, you need a good level head, and the qualities of someone who does not panic. You need to be a climber with all round technique, and especially mantelshelf skills, since from high up, a mantel going wrong is going to be disastrous. Nobody would ever recommend a highball problem, but you do get a pretty amazing elation when you tick one. Many highball problems are famous and enticing, just go very carefully please. Is there a difference between solo climbing and highball? No.

Wobbly, enjoying the twin cracks of 'Flutings Direct' (f-4a: t-4c), Kyloe in the Wood, Northunberland

Dave Henderson on a true highball with the perfect route name, 'Dont stop now' (f-5b: t-5c: V2), Hay Tor, Dartmoor, Devon.

TSUNAMI s-7a+, Conner Cove, Swanage; Leo Houlding. The summer deep water soloing festival, proving that climbers are completely nuts!

Mark Edwards, nipping up the boulder problem in the sky on 'Demo Route' (f-3b: t-4b), Sennen Cove, Cornwall.

Kings Tor on Dartmoor.

The key components of a free hang dyno, are co-ordination and stomach muscles. From the dead hang, you really need to focus your mind on the 1st slap. The whole move must be done in one quick pull. You let go with your left hand as you are pulling up at speed, and about 75% of the way through the pull. This way, you don't have to actually pull up on one arm, since your momentum is carrying you up. The second trick here, is to hit the slap with the left hand, but as you do, push down on the right at the same time. This spreads your weight between the two hands and you stand a very good chance of holding the dyno, especially if you lock your stomach like steel. A lot of climbers make a 'casual' mistake, and rely on just gripping hard with the upper hand. A single hand will be weak, and usually be in the state of coming off - especially if your co-ordintion is poor, resulting in a very high chance of ripping the palm skin. The 2nd slap is harder - pulling off 2 different holds at different levels, is a lot harder than pulling on two together, it really upsets your dyno direction. So get the simple dyno sorted out first to begin with.

INTRODUCTION

GIVE-IT-A-GO

IND/BOULDERING

OUT/BOULDERING

IMPROVEMENT

INDOOR SPORT

OUTDOOR SPORT

MULTI-PITCH

VIA FERRATA

WHERE TO GO

INDEX

INTRODUCTION

GIVE-IT-A-GO

IND/BOULDERING

OUT/BOULDERING

IMPROVEMENT

INDOOR SPORT

OUTDOOR SPORT

MULTI-PITCH

VIA FERRATA

WHERE TO GO

INDEX

The double dyno is one of the silliest moves in bouldering, but is an essential testpiece for anyone who is intending to make it as a top boulderer. You need all round qualities of strength, agility and co-ordination. You also need to have pretty good landing skills, since you can be missing the final holds a lot of the time, landing thump in the dust. Only bother trying this in earnest when you have mastered all the other bouldering techniques. Getting your leading foot in the right place is crucial. The whole move begins by pulling into the rock with the arms, which initiates the move. Often your trailing foot will have been well placed, starting some momentum before you even put any weight onto your leading foot. Timing is as crucial as the Olympic ski jump. You have to powerfully jump off your foot, to spring you into the air clear of the rock. If you jump too early, all your energy will force you out and away from the rock. Jump too late, and you simply won't reach the finishing hold. However you leap, you are going to arrive at the finishing hold with great speed, and at a glancing angle on this problem. As your hands hit the slopers, your feet must act like buffers and take as much shock out of your body as possible. Often you want a trailing foot to come through a millisecond first, and act as a shock stabiliser. On this problem, you would incorporate a bounce with your feet after hitting, thereby reducing the amount of holding pressure needed for the hands. Because of the oblique angle, if you tried to catch it without a foot bounce, you would simply pivot on your leading foot, and spin off. The best and most demanding double dynos, are the ones which combine angle with distance, and end up on disgusting slopers!

David Perinan leaping through FLOWER POT f7b+, La Tortuga, La Pedriza, Spain. (Photos Luc Percival)

INTRODUCTION

GIVE-IT-A-GO

IND/BOULDERING

OUT/BOULDERING

IMPROVEMENT

INDOOR SPORT

OUTDOOR SPORT

MULTI-PITCH

VIA FERRATA

WHERE TO GO

INDEX

INTRODUCTION

GIVE-IT-A-GO

IND/BOULDERING

OUT/BOULDERING

IMPROVEMENT

INDOOR SPORT

OUTDOOR SPORT

MULTI-PITCH

VIA FERRATA

WHERE TO GO

INDEX

There are perhaps three main questions which you should ask before you go sport climbing; will it kill me, break the piggy bank, and what can I get out of it? Well, thousands of people do it every week and don't die, and a couple of hundred quid will sort you out some equipment that should keep you in one piece. What can you get out of it? Well, a bit of insight will help. The title is a tad misleading, since sport climbing isn't a 'sport' in the slightest. A sport is by nature is a competition governed by rules, and generally played by individuals, focused on pulverising an opposition. Sport climbing on the other hand, is simply climbing for you own, personal satisfaction, in your own time, and to any standard you feel like climbing on the day. There are no exams to pass, no certificates to gain, no time critical kick-offs, and no team mates to upset if you don't feel like busting a gut. It's an activity that enjoys complete freedom, you decide whatever you want to get out of it, when to do it, and however you want to do it. This freedom of self governance certainly attracts many people, who just like getting on with life at their own speed.

To help those just starting out, we've made a diagram with stars, to illustrate 9 different ways to get the most out of sport climbing. Had you thought of all those different aspects, and can you think of any more? Vitally, take on board that there's no regulation on enjoying any of these, so include as few or as many as you want. They are all there to be enjoyed, and it's no-one's prerogative to say that you must partake in any one particular aspect. In your sport climbing lifetime, certainly have a go at all the aspects, but concentrate on which ones you enjoy the most.

The easiest goal to conceptually get a hold of, is to get to the top of the climbing wall. The first time you get there, you will feel a great sense of achievement and pride. It's an undeniable goal, and one that is so easily understood and enjoyed by most beginners. You look up at the towering wall above, some 10 metres high, and highly improbable for you. Placing your hand on that final finishing hold, right at the very top of the wall is magical. You then can progress and become more familiar with climbing movement. You learn to move on rock like a dancer does on stage, seemingly effortless, but controlled and highly skilled. When you climb well, you can feel it in your body, your muscles slowly contract and relax, and your hands just know when to let go if you are perfectly in balance. You get fit enough so that your arms don't tire, easing you up the steepest of overhangs. These are the times that you feel the physical magic. When you are not so fit and don't have the necessary power to do a climb, the wall turns into a chess game, and you're a piece down. Then you have to resort to subtle ways of keeping your energy reserves high, sneaking in little rests where possible, keeping a careful eye on your own internal energy gauge throughout the climb. You can still pull it out of the bag, if you are cool enough not to panic and waste your strength in overgripping when you're stressed. The magic here is getting to the top of a climb that you were not good enough for in reality.

Sometimes a climb is a series of holds set as a puzzle by a fiendish route setter. There may be more holds on it than you need, some may be good and others may be bad. You climb with your wits about you, and know that you are being tested by not only the climb, but by someone else too. Here the magic comes both from getting up the climb, and winning the challenge set down. There are other times when you climb, that you just want to have a really good exercise session and end up completely exhausted. You climb until your arms turn to jelly, and your fingers just uncurl. The best sensation is reserved for wrapping your hot and throbbing hands around a cold glass of beer, the magic is of course, quenching the thirst!

When a climb is too hard for you to get up first go, you have to practise the moves. Eventually you try, time and time again, but can often fail in getting to the last hold. When you do finally get up the climb it is called a 'RED POINT.' You certainly feel the magic of success then. All routes are given a grade which denotes the standard of a climb. The grade sets a good parameter to aim for, and by which you can measure your own climbing standard. For a while, you will find all climbs of a particular grade impossible. It certainly is a magical day when you crack a route of the next grade up. Competing with the rock and set grades is non-combative, but you can enter a climbing competition. These often take place on an

- ☆ CHALLENGE TO GET TO THE TOP
- ☆ PHYSICAL FLOW OF MOVEMENT
- ☆ MENTAL GAME OF CHESS
- ☆ CONTEST OF BEATING THE ROUTE SETTER
- ☆ PHYSICAL EXERTION
- ☆ PRACTISING A RED POINT
- ☆ ACHIEVING A MEASURABLE STANDARD
- ☆ COMPETING AGAINST OTHER CLIMBERS
- ☆ EXHILARATION OF EXPOSURE

Dave Speakman enjoying that magical moment, when you just let you body hang in space; Leeds climbing wall.

overhanging climb that is just about impossible. Here you are measured on how high up you get, and set against how high others get. There are no grades, just competition on the same climb, with the same holds. You don't get to see how the others try, but you certainly hear the crowd cheer, when you reach for the correct hold. There is magic in getting the highest, but also charm in trying your best, since there is only going to be one lucky winner.

The final magical sensation must be the best of all, and that is of the huge exhilaration of exposure that you get when you are high up on a climb. This part of a climb for a complete beginner is where you are generally terrified, but after a while you learn to control that fear, and turn the situation into a positive energy producer. To hang off a single hold on the edge of an overhang high up, and then simply pull up, is truly magical. It's also made especially wonderful since the rope is there to save you if you fall. Sport climbing, it's full of magic.

INTRODUCTION

GIVE-IT-A-GO

IND/BOULDERING

OUT/BOULDERING

IMPROVEMENT

INDOOR SPORT

OUTDOOR SPORT

MULTI-PITCH

VIA FERRATA

WHERE TO GO

INDEX

INTRODUCTION

GIVE-IT-A-GO

IND/BOULDERING

OUT/BOULDERING

IMPROVEMENT

INDOOR SPORT

OUTDOOR SPORT

MULTI-PITCH

VIA FERRATA

WHERE TO GO

INDEX

Earlier in the book, we split climbing into 12 levels of insanity. (IS-scale, p22) This alone illustrated that there are many different styles of climbing, resulting in a cross section of expectations from various types of climbers. Some people will look for a really safe environment, whilst others are very happy in a highly dodgy and unpredictable situation. The word climbing, is intrinsically linked to the word danger, and therefore the words 'Climbing Wall,' should always mean "Danger-Climbing Wall." A climbing wall is simply a man made structure that can be used to climb on. It could on one hand, be designed as 'intentionally highly dangerous,' to replicate dangerous unsupervised climbing (IS-8.9). Or at the other end of the scale, it could be equipped with all the latest safety equipment, to help handicapped people enjoy climbing (IS-3.0). In climbing, you never assume anything. Therefore, if you turn up an unsupervised climbing wall, treat it as the most dangerous and lethal level of (IS-8.9), and leave it only for the use of experienced climbers who accept this high level of danger.

In a practical sense, most indoor climbing is however a lot more friendly and often enjoys a good level of competence – but still never assume anything. To offer any level of safety, an indoor climbing facility must have someone in charge – a manager, who is responsible for communicating to the public, the level of safety measures that the wall management imposes. It is up to you, to read and understand those safety measures, accept them and climb, or not accept them and leave. Every climbing wall in the country is different and has its own management. Some walls may offer highly comprehensive safety and insure the users, others may offer very little safety and not insure the users at all. You must be aware of what the wall management is offering and decide if you are prepared to accept it. The system that nearly every wall uses, is a registration system before even entering the climbing environment. You must read and understand what the wall is offering, what liabilities it will, or will not accept, and then sign in agreement. It is a good and uncomplicated open system, which allows any wall to offer anything it wants to.

Many walls are only designed for very experienced users, and the management will ask you to sign a complete disclaimer that makes you accountable for recognising all possible dangers. This in itself should warn you away from these unless you are highly experienced. When you are in your learning stages of indoor climbing, you don't know what to look for and how to recognise danger. It is certainly worthwhile in looking for a climbing wall that offers a two-sided registration scheme. One that is fair in asking you to accept your responsibility of self inflicted climbing risk, but also states that the wall management makes a reliable effort to offer a high level of safety measures, often undertaking to do daily checks of equipment, and weekly assessment of the wall structure.

Climbing walls are chasms with big vertical distances – 10-20 metres high, and do not want or allow inexperienced people, anywhere near them. They are potentially extremely dangerous places. Any wall management is highly sensible to test people on their knowledge and competence before they are allowed to use a facility. If the wall is offering a good level of safety, then by implication it is undertaking not to allow inexperienced climbers, to pose a hazard to others. Any wall that asks you to pass a strict climbing test before climbing, is doing it for your safety, and for all other users, this is obviously highly commendable.

Your first objective now should be to find a wall that runs beginner's courses for top rope climbing. On this course, you will learn about indoor wall procedures and the equipment involved; such as ropes, harnesses, karabiners etc. An instructor will practically teach you how to tie the correct knots and safeguard each other when climbing. Top roping is when there is always a rope hanging from the top of the wall, just like the give-it-a-go sessions. Only when you have learnt these to use these techniques properly, will you be categorised as a 'low-risk' climber, and allowed on a climbing wall unsupervised. We use the word low-risk on purpose, since in climbing, there is always risk, even from the most experienced and sensible climbers. We can always make a mistake, humans do. Always keep your wits about you.

The first thing you need to know before entering a climbing wall are the potential hazards that you can encounter as an innocent bystander. The major question you need to ask, is who built the wall, and when was it last checked for structural safety. The construction of a major climbing wall is likely to be very well controlled and monitored by any overall construction company. Most walls are built in a similar way to office buildings, in that they consist of a framework of steel girders that are then clad in specialist panelling. Their continual inspection for subsidence problems or anything else, should be monitored and displayed by the climbing wall management. Notwithstanding any of this, you want to start developing a second nature in climbing; always look up and question the likely hood of any structure coming down with a crash, before stepping underneath it.

The more likely hazard is to be hit by a falling object. This can vary from a loose piece of equipment, a hold breaking free, or even an earthbound zooming climber! You should always look up whenever you walk around a climbing wall, and never stand below anyone who is climbing. If somebody drops anything from up high, they often loudly shout a traditional call of 'BELOW or ROCK.' The better and more common word used today is 'WATCH OUT,' which has the benefit

Anything that bolts on - is a possible hazard. (Westway-Entreprises)

A giant steel structure created for building the Westway (Entreprises).

of alerting non-climbers of course. (Attention (F), and Achtung(D) are also worth knowing). Most indoor climbers love the freedom of not having to wear a climbing helmet, and hence you never climb with loose objects in your pockets, and you never drop anything. It's something that is respected worldwide in sport climbing, and is only made possible by excellent self-discipline. If a person on an overhanging climbing wall lets go, they will pendulum out from the wall. This can be a big swing if there are no midway clips to stop them. Beware of flying pendulums! Often at walls, there are big sandbags on the floor which light people can attach themselves to if they are holding the rope of a heavier person. It can be a touch amusing to see people either bump into each other whilst looking up, or to upturn themselves cartoon style, as they trip over a giant sand bag. You simply have just to be a touch on the alert side. Only sit around in an area, that is not either a drop or pendulum zone.

Specific areas marked out for sitting down and leaving rucksacs.

INTRODUCTION

GIVE-IT-A-GO

IND/BOULDERING

OUT/BOULDERING

IMPROVEMENT

INDOOR SPORT

OUTDOOR SPORT

MULTI-PITCH

VIA FERRATA

WHERE TO GO

INDEX

You should not need to buy a rope, prior to going on a beginners, climbing course. I would seriously question any course that asked this from you, and quite simply – what knowledge do you have? On a course, you will properly see how a rope works, and feel its use in practise. A climbing rope is quite different from any other type of rope, and it has special characteristics that are purely designed for climbing. Something to remember is that most big brand names such as; Beal, Edelrid and Mammut; also make caving ropes and mountaineering ropes. These are completely unsuitable for sport climbing, and would be highly dangerous in many situations. Any good instructor should point you in the right direction of where to buy a good climbing rope that is suited for the purpose of sport climbing. This section should serve to refresh your memory, before you go and purchase your lovely new rope. We will leave the technical side of how ropes work, to be covered throughout both sport sections, but here are a few tips that you will find useful about rope choice and care.

Go to a proper specialist climbing shop with a good selection of ropes.

ROPE WEIGHT: This is the most important consideration in sport climbing. At your indoor top rope wall, the rope will go to the top of the wall and hence the full weight of the rope is carried by the top belay karabiner. When you start leading, you have to carry all the weight of the rope yourself – but more importantly, your fingertips have to during the entire length of the climb. One metre of rope can weigh between 57g and 78g – just under the weight of a CD in its case. To go on a 35 metre climb, you could be carrying nearly 3 kilos by the top when your exhausted, or only just 2 kilos with a light rope. The weight of rope that you carry, makes an enormous difference to the enjoyment that you get from lead sport climbing.

ROPE DIAMETER: There's no complicated physics to this one – the thicker ropes are the strongest, most robust, and wear well – just like, a dirty old diesel, chug-a-long. But we are living in the 21st century, where there are a huge range of ropes at our disposal, and great advances have been made technically. Thin sport climbing ropes are a relatively modern invention and must be used properly, but they do make climbing enjoyable and reduce the possibility of tendon and ligament injury. I have actually pulled a tendon, whilst hanging off a one finger pocket, and pulling up the rope to clip a quickdraw; if I had been using a lighter rope with much less weight and drag, I am sure that it would have been different. So how thin can you go!

There are four categories of climbing rope, and only rope classified as 'SINGLE ROPE' is safe for sport climbing. The three other categories to avoid; are half rope, double rope and twin rope. There are various European tests that classify as a 'single rope' strength, and you simply have to believe that they serve your needs. Companies like Beal make a 9.4mm single rope, and there maybe even thinner versions out there. Whilst this is the most lightest end of the spectrum, we all have to think practically and consider what sort of diameter is going to wear well, and withstand a lot of falling off. The maximum you want to consider is 10.5mm, simply because all the good belay devices get horribly awkward to use with ropes bigger than this. Also as a rope gets used, the outer sheath moves and expands – making the rope thicker anyway. If you hardly ever fall off, then definitely get a very thin rope, if you like falling off and do it a lot – get a real thick monster.

HOW MANY ROPES TO BUY: How deep are your pockets? Consider, this is the most important single piece to your climbing equipment and is going to be your number one lifesaver! The standing life of ropes is dictated by the manufacturer on the label – usually around 10 years. With consistent use of ropes, 5 years is an appropriate guideline. You should consider the outlay of buying a new rope each year, I ask - how much do you value your life? I like the ability to have a short, thick rope (30m, 10.5) for the wall; a 50 metre 10.5 for the majority

of steep and short routes; a 70 metre 9.7mm for long routes; and either an 80, 90, 100 metre 9.4mm for places like Verdon Gorge in France. You can of course, buy one rope and use it for everything, but in my experience it is more practical to carry 2 ropes to a cliff, and have the right one for the right route - rather than not having a long enough rope. Buy ropes that suit the length of route you climb, and the style that you climb in. Keep an organised chart of when you buy and use your ropes, it's very easy and quick to do.

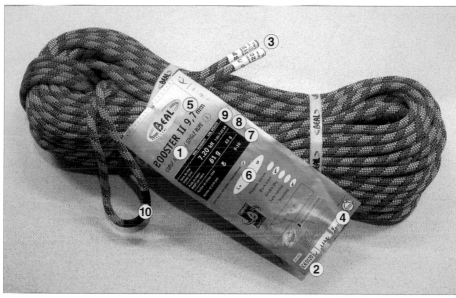

1) - Check it is a *'single'* rope
2 & 3) - Check the CE mark on the label matches ends on rope
4) - Check date of manufacture, and hence retirement date.
5) - Diameter of rope you require - 9.4 - 10.5mm
6)- Length that you really do want 50, 60, 70, 80, 100 metres

7) - Number of falls - higher the better (6 minimum)
8) - Weight per metre - 57g - 73g
9) - Impact force, lower figure is better to put less strain on belayer and anchors. 7.2 - 9.6 Kn
10) - Good substantial middle black mark - 70mm

MODELS AND MARKINGS: You can find alpine ropes that don't absorb water and hence don't freeze up, hardly worth the extra expense for an indoor wall! Special dry treatment does make the rope even slippery'eyr, and will help it to glide through the quickdraws – maybe worth it. You must have a black limit marker on the middle of any rope you ever use. If the rope doesn't have one, you must only put one on with a marker that is stipulated by the rope manufacturer. The label will state an impact force, but this is more of a consideration for traditional/classic climbing. You should inspect

the rope and make sure it has a manufacturers label with the date, and instructions for use, care and lifetime instructions. The ends of the rope must be specially marked with the type of rope, CE markings, length, and must correspond exactly with the label. Ropes degrade over time, but especially in sunlight, so treat with caution any shop that displays ropes for sale, from its windows. Ordering a special bicolour rope that changes colour in the middle by the weave on the sheath, is a good way of getting a guaranteed new rope, and having no confusion over the halfway mark.

INTRODUCTION
GIVE-IT-A-GO
IND/BOULDERING
OUT/BOULDERING
IMPROVEMENT
INDOOR SPORT
OUTDOOR SPORT
MULTI-PITCH
VIA FERRATA
WHERE TO GO
INDEX

INTRODUCTION

GIVE-IT-A-GO

IND/BOULDERING

OUT/BOULDERING

IMPROVEMENT

INDOOR SPORT

OUTDOOR SPORT

MULTI-PITCH

VIA FERRATA

WHERE TO GO

INDEX

There are two big problem areas with ropes – kinks and tangles. When you buy your rope, you then need to prepare it for use. It comes off the weaving machine at the factory, and is fed onto a rotating drum. This puts a circular twist into each turn – each coil of the rope. If you undo the rope by pulling each coil off the rope sideways, you are 'unwrapping' the rope in a totally different manner, and there will be a kink left in every coil. You must uncoil it in an opposite manner to how it was originally coiled. This is done with a friend holding the rope, who uses their hands to act like the factory drum, in a rotating manner. This will give you a kink free rope to start off with. A kink in the rope looks like a small twist, and will catch on any karabiner, they're a complete pain in the rear.

Not surprisingly, we don't coil ropes in sport climbing because that just puts kinks and twists back into the rope. You also find that 70 metres of rope can get into the most humungous tangle that rivals the rubic cube in frustration. The answer is ingeniously simple, a square metre of canvas that you just lay the rope onto. Nearly all rope manufacturers make rope bags, which have a good square of canvas, that can quickly roll up and make a shoulder holdall, or a little carry sac – they are excellent and certainly to be recommended. Start with your uncoiled rope and pick up the top – which will become the bottom end on this occasion. In this, you tie a double figure of 8 knot – as illustrated. It looks a tricky knot at first, but you soon get the hang of it, and can do it in a jiffy. It is also a very safe knot and can be used in virtually any instance in climbing. You then clip a screwgate karabiner into the end loop, and do it fully up. The reason for this is again simple – "IDIOT COMPENSATION MEASURE." There is a great history of experinced climbers who forget about the end of the rope, when they are belaying

The skill with tying this knot, is to take the end and wrap it around the back with your wrist, then use your thumb to poke the end through. It's very quick this way. You can get screwgate karabiners with 10kn cross gate strength for the end, worth the hunt for the extra strength.

their partner, they forget that the rope is not long enough. Unfortunately, the end passes though their hand and of course the belay device too, resulting in death, or if you're lucky – a broken back. Quite simply, a double fig of 8, plus a screwgate krab, ain't gonna go through anything. Then you simply lay the rope, bit by bit on top of itself until you get to the other end. Here you tie another double fig of 8 in this, attach another screwgate krab, clipping it to the canvas sheer. The rope is now ready to come out from the top first, and it won't get tangled, or have any kinks in it. Eventually when you go outdoor sport climbing, you tie on and take the screwgate karabiner with you (even on single pitch climbs), so choose a couple of very lightweight & strong screwgates for this purpose.

A rope should come with a whole range of instructions for care and use, but generally you want to keep it as clean as possible. Any dirt on sand in the outer sheath will wear through your karabiners very quickly. It's very hard for anything to get through the sheath into the core, but if it did, it could then cut away at the rope – hidden from view. Keep your rope out of sunlight, as much as possible, and never lend it to anyone.

Ropes are quite resiliant to wear but what does happen over time, is that they get crushed in all belay devices. By losing their roundness, they will then flatten over an edge. After a lot of use, this really does affect their resistance to being cut over a rock sharp edge. Unlikely, but worth knowing

INTRODUCTION

GIVE-IT-A-GO

IND/BOULDERING

OUT/BOULDERING

IMPROVEMENT

INDOOR SPORT

OUTDOOR SPORT

MULTI-PITCH

VIA FERRATA

WHERE TO GO

INDEX

Any harness that you use on a learning course is likely to be a fully adjustable - one size fits all type. For the purpose of leaning to top rope and belay safely, it should be perfectly adequate. However, when you launch out into the big wide world of sport climbing, the demands of a harness go up ten fold. For a start, you will be taking bigger falls as you get more proficient, which demand greater comfort qualities from the harness. You will need to carry additional equipment on your harness, and be able to get at it confidently and efficiently. The final demand of any harness, is to give you comfortable support at a hanging belay of a multi-pitch sports route. Here you will be sitting in your harness for over 30 mins, and comfort is highly important. Your dilemma is having to buy a harness without experiencing all of these factors at first hand.

When buying your own harness, you have quite a few different options to look for. To get a harness that fits perfectly is vital, this is because

A good example of a well designed modern harness from Petzl. Points to look for are:- A comfortable waist belt, snug but not over tight leg loops, small buckle system which doesn't lift up and dig into your ribs, a good length of tape left over and a system to keep it out of the way, a good clear and big centre loop for abseiling-belaying, 4 gear loops to allow good racking of karabiners. (Do not attach your chalk bag to your harness, have another independent cord for this, which can also double up as a tape spiral for self rescue, p 270-1)

Here you have a good method of support at the back of the harness which allows ventilation, and 3 positions for the leg loop elastic straps.

comfort in the long term is of paramount importance. A big company like Petzl makes usually 4 different styles of sport harnesses in different set sizes. This gives a shop the task of stocking 18 separate items, and that is only one manufacturer! You need to find a good shop that is very well stocked when you go looking for a tailored fitting, sport harness. A lot of shops will sell a single adjustable harness out of practicality, but these always have buckles and extra tape lengths, making them needlessly heavier for you. Alternatively, they can sometimes be more comfortable than a badly fitting, tailored harness. A good harness will cost a reasonable amount, but on the other hand it will last you a good few years, so you want to be influenced by fit, and design quality over cost.

A good shop will have a proper hanging point set up, so you can try on the harness and sit suspended in space to feel it on you. You should take with you your climbing trousers or leggings, depending upon whatever you prefer to climb in. The leg loops of a harness, rub in exactly the same place as a short pair of shorts, and it is why you see most climbers wearing slightly longer shorts. A fully tailored harness will feature shaped leg loops that are not just circular tubes, but well fitted straps that shape themselves around your thighs. You will find that various models are designed for women and others for men. Some girls who climb, are pretty stick like and may suit the men's harnesses better. In the end, go for the harness that fits you the best since they all look the same anyway. You will find that the really comfortable harnesses weigh around 450-480g. They have non adjustable leg loops, and a nice wide belt to support the back and body during a fall. They are also very comfortable whilst on a belay for a long time. The material used can vary, but it is usually nylon webbing with ventilated, breathable material on the inside. You normally get 2 gear loops on either side of the harness. For single pitch sport climbing you only need 2, but when you go onto multi-pitch routes, you will find all 4 very useful.

The buckle system on a harness is down to personal choice. There are about 5 different styles on the market, and some harnesses have a buckle free system. Make sure you fully understand the mechanism that your harness uses, and stick to it You may also come across competition climbing harnesses. These are much lighter and weigh around 300g, and may not even have any gear loops on the side.

On a hanging belay in multi-pitch climbing, you can be literally hanging in your harness for a whole hour as your partner climbs up to join you, and then leads straight up the next pitch. An uncomfortable harness is 'not' an option. Top Tip: In this photo, Jingo has looped the rope over the belay tape (start with big loops and get smaller as you collect the rope). This stops the rope from hanging down the climb in the way of the second climber, but more importantly - stops it blowing around and getting caught in a tree!

Fully utilising the harness loops, with quickdraws on either side, double screwgate quickdraw, belay tube, emergency maillon & screwgate.

INTRODUCTION

GIVE-IT-A-GO

IND/BOULDERING

OUT/BOULDERING

IMPROVEMENT

INDOOR SPORT

OUTDOOR SPORT

MULTI-PITCH

VIA FERRATA

WHERE TO GO

INDEX

INTRODUCTION　GIVE-IT-A-GO　IND/BOULDERING　OUT/BOULDERING　IMPROVEMENT　INDOOR SPORT　OUTDOOR SPORT　MULTI-PITCH　VIA FERRATA　WHERE TO GO　INDEX

You certainly don't see many helmets being worn in sport climbing circles, but you may wonder if there is a reason why this is so. Simply, they are not popular, and most climbers don't like to wear them. It is anybody's own choice to wear, or not wear a helmet. I can certainly point out a few interesting points that you can consider. There are two main reasons for wearing a helmet; protection in the event of a fall, and protection from a falling object.

When you are a beginner, you are likely to be climbing for all the time on a top rope. When you fall, you will drop about a metre onto a cushioned rope. What can happen, is that you climb over to one side and then fall off. You could then pendulum across the climbing wall, since the rope goes directly to the top of the wall. There may be a sharp edge of another part of the wall sticking out, and you could strike your head on it. In this situation, you are likely to hit the wall at the same speed you would walk into a lamp post or crunch your head on a low doorway. Do you wear a helmet to go shopping? This is you likely hazard, and you can make your decision. An instructor, should not put you in a more dangerous position than this.

When you start to take leader falls, you can take some pretty hard thumping whams against the wall. If you learn by increments, you learn how to fall properly, so that you always fall in a controlled manner. You also learn by experience to see the potential of a fall, before you get in the position to take it. **If you lack experience,** and want to go for it, you can easily end up falling and catching the rope around your ankle. In this case, you would tip upside down and quite possibly crack your head on the wall nastily, so a helmet would be suitable. If you are willing to learn slowly and steadily, you are unlikely to need a helmet – just like a gymnast on a high bar. Go at it like a mad idiot, and you are likely to need body armour, gum shield and a very good helmet.

Protection from above! Climbers do have a very high regard for other climber's safety, and it is very rare to ever see anything drop carelessly from another climber. Sport climbing, is an area where you just don't get things falling out of the sky on an everyday basis. Sure things can drop down, just

as pot plants can fall off window ledges onto high streets, or handbags can fall off balconies; just fall asleep at a cricket match with somewone thwacking boundaries – that's highly dangerous. Outdoors, if a rock falls from above, then you need to get out of the way – BIG PRIORITY. You also want to be alert and to watch above.

At slabby cliffs, you will usually hear a rock bouncing down before it comes to you. On the ground it is simple, you step out of the way. When the cliff is overhanging, any rock that comes down will fall out into space away from the foot of the cliff. Whenever you approach a cliff, you must be aware of its 'DROP ZONE,' where you pass through very quickly and look up all the time. The time a helmet is necessary is when you are actually climbing, and cannot physically get out of the way. In this case, it is a lottery as to whether a helmet will save you anyway. If there are stones regularly coming down, I seriously question why you are climbing there. I feel that if you need a helmet, you are in the wrong location, but if you want a helmet, then that's your prerogative. If you see me climbing in a helmet, then you know it's a highly serious place to be, so be warned and watch out.

Jingo in the Kaisergebirge; full on helmet territory.

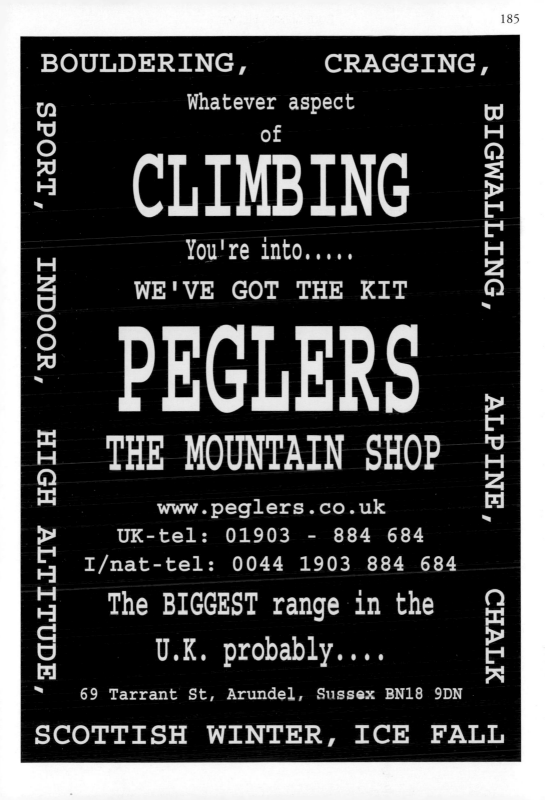

INTRODUCTION
GIVE-IT-A-GO
IND/BOULDERING
OUT/BOULDERING
IMPROVEMENT
INDOOR SPORT
OUTDOOR SPORT
MULTI-PITCH
VIA FERRATA
WHERE TO GO
INDEX

It might be quite useful at this point in the book to explain the wonderful complexity of sport climbing grading. We have touched on it for bouldering, but that is simple by comparison. To grade a single move or even a couple of moves on a problem is relatively easy. But to try and grade a climb that can be anything from 6 metres up to 40 metres – within the same system, is not so straightforward. History will explain a few things. Grades began in the Alps with grand mountaineering. If you had to scramble and actually do a couple of climbing moves, it got grade 1. Grade II was then reserved for continuous climbing on steep rock, but with jug buckets for handholds. Grade III came along for something a bit tricky, where it all started to feel a bit iffy. Real climbing started at grade IV, where you became exposed and had to climb some quite tricky moves on steep rock, and without a real break. Grade V was the big mark for a long time and where you banged in a steel piton to get over a hard bit. This sort grading became the foundation for sport climbing levels. Because everyone from all over Europe climbed in the Alps, you had a highly consistent grade 1-5 everywhere. Then what went wrong was that climbers started to do harder climbs on their home climbing ground. They could hardly say it was harder than the Alps, so they introduced 5a, 5b etc. Eventually people realised that local climbing was different and

they jumped up to 6a after 5c. Because every area in Europe now had developed on its own, they had got out of register, and one area's 5b was the equivalent to another areas grade 6b. You now had (1970's) some areas that were wildly out of sync as it were. What rescued the whole shebang, was the discovery of Buoux in the south of France at the beginning of the 1980's. Here all the best sport climbers in Europe congregated and managed to climb the new high grade of 8a. They then went back to their own climbing areas and could grade all the 8a climbs correctly. Because of this, you now can visit most sport climbing areas of Europe and get consistent 1-5 and grade 8, but the grades in between can vary by about 2-3 grades. You also ended up with some people grading routes by length, so if it was short, it couldn't possibly be hard - or could it. In many areas if you don't know the length of the route, the grade is meaningless. Overall it is a complete hotch-potch. You can make relative grade charts, but they are very hit and miss. The only real way of grading, is to put all the routes at a cliff in order of difficulty, give the easiest the lowest number, and then work your way up. You will find that a lot of indoor walls use that option, so a 5a will vary completely from one wall to another. We use the Fontainebleau colour across all the scales, to give you a quick idea of what you are in for.

A - Artificial climbing is generally covered by A grades; A1, A2, A3 etc. These grades are for big walls and cover all types of aid; they also have new wave which is another way of interpreting the scale!

B - grades for bouldering; used in Yorkshire, Northumberland, North Wales and Annot (France). They are all completely different, so grade 6a is totally different, wherever you go!

C - Czech grades are roman numerals VI, VII, etc; and cover a sport climbing style that is supplemented with knotted rope slings. Falls are big, casualties are not uncommon!

D - German (Deutchland) grades are from 1-11 and are similar to Alpine climbing grades, except that they are harder in the higher grades.

E - English overall grades; these are used for traditional climbs in the UK, where you have to place devices as you go for protection; names such as difficult and severe are used for the lower grades, then E1-E9 for extremes. You also get a supplement of the hardest technical (T) move; i.e. E4,6a

f - Fontainebleau bouldering grades, 1a-8c and are a lot harder than other grades in the 3-5 range.

M - Mixed grades for dry tooling on rock and ice.

P - Point grades used in America, for sport and general climbing 5.1 up to 5.14

S - Sport grades, used across the whole of Europe; except Germany!

SX - Saxon grades used in old East Germany on the sandstone; roman numerals but different to Czech.

T - UK technical grades that represent a hard move, similar to a bouldering move.

U - UIAA, Alpine mountain grades that go from I up to IX, they use roman numerals.

V - V grades, Vermin-the nicknmame of John Sherman, the USA bouldering legend.

International bouldering grades		Sport grades	Technical grades		
Font(F)	V	Sport(S)	GB(T)	D	USA
1-2	-	1-3	1-3	1-3	5.5
3	Vb-	4	4a	4	5.7
4a	Vb	5	4c	5	5.8
4b	V0-	6a	5a	6	5.9
4c	V0	6b	5b	7	5.10b
5a	V1	6c	5c	7+	5.11a
5b	V2	6c	5c	8-	5.11b
5c	V3	7a	6a	8	5.11d
6a	V4	7a+	6a	8+	5.12a
6b	V5	7b	6b	8+	5.12b
6c	V6	7b+	6b	9-	5.12c
7a	V7	7b+	6c	9-	5.12c
7a+	V8	7c	6c	9	5.12d
7b	V8	8a	6c	9+	5.13b
7c	V9	8a+	7a	10-	5.13c
7c+	V10	8b	7a	10	5.13d
8a	V11	8b+	7a	10+	5.14a
8a+	V12	8c	7a	11-	5.14b
8b	V13	8c+	7b	11-	5.14c
8b+	V14	9a	7b	11	5.14d
8c	V15	9a+	7b	11+	5.15a

INTRODUCTION

GIVE-IT-A-GO

IND/BOULDERING

OUT/BOULDERING

IMPROVEMENT

INDOOR SPORT

OUTDOOR SPORT

MULTI-PITCH

VIA FERRATA

WHERE TO GO

INDEX

There are many ways to tie onto the end of a climbing rope. We are only going to suggest one, and that is the double figure of 8 knot. There are three reasons for this. Firstly, simplicity. If every indoor wall uses and recommends this knot, then we can have a very good common standard. Secondly, that it is a knot favoured by many harness makers, who specify this knot to tie into their harness. Thirdly, this knot has a great many safety characteristics, which other knots do not have.

The figure of 8 knot is quite a simple knot that is fairly easy to thread back through itself. It has the great merit of tightening upon itself in many places, so much unfortunately, that it can be a bit difficult to undo after a great big fall. The plus side however for a beginner, is that if you should tie or re-thread it incorrectly, the knot you end up with!!! has a chance of still working. Other knots like the sailor's bowline, rely 100% on being tied correctly. In climbing you never get a second chance, so we like to stack the odds in our favour and use the double figure of 8 knot.

The tying principle, is to tie a single figure of 8 in the rope, then thread the rope through your harness, and retrace the rope back through the knot. So long as you have 30 cm of tail left at the end - and the knot is tightly pulled, that is sufficient. Often a small stopper knot is used to tie up this loose end, but is of no strength or significant importance. It does however add safety for a beginner, in that you need around 30cm to tie the stopper knot, and thereby alerts you if you have forgotten to leave a good end. In a significant fall, the loose end could also flick up and hit you in the face, or maybe bruise your eye, so a long loose end is not what you want.

Taking the top end from the rope bag with a double figure of 8 knot and screwgate karabiner. Keep the krab on your harness, either at the back, or on the main belay loop; this way you won't grab it by mistake for a quick draw.

Measure the length needed for the knot, which is roughly from your shoulder to a fully outstretched arm.

When you have measured the length needed, keep hold of the rope and lift it up to put a sharp bend in it. Then twist the bend away from you to put a twist on the rope, with the long rope end closest to you and looking on top of the short end.

Keeping hold of the loose end with the right hand, and being handy with the fingers of the left hand, twist away again continuing in the same direction, thereby putting another twist in the rope.

The skillful part now, is to keep your left fingers on exactly the same part of the rope, so when you pull tight, the knot is perfectly placed.

Take the loose end and put it through the top loop, going away from you, and pull up tight. You will see the formation of a single, fig-of-8.

INTRODUCTION

GIVE-IT-A-GO

IND/BOULDERING

OUT/BOULDERING

IMPROVEMENT

INDOOR SPORT

OUTDOOR SPORT

MULTI-PITCH

VIA FERRATA

WHERE TO GO

INDEX

INTRODUCTION

GIVE-IT-A-GO

IND/BOULDERING

OUT/BOULDERING

IMPROVEMENT

INDOOR SPORT

OUTDOOR SPORT

MULTI-PITCH

VIA FERRATA

WHERE TO GO

INDEX

Your harness instruction leaflet will show you how to thread your particular harness. Usually in principle, you thread through a loop on the legs and then the waist. The thick tape joining loop, is best left completely separate for arranging an abseil, and to clip directly into a belay, without interfering at all with your knot and rope.

You then simply thread the rope back through the knot, as shown by the photographs. The knot needs to be slightly loose to allow easy re-threading, but try and keep the knot as close to your harness as possible. There are three separate poke throughs, separated by a wrap around each time.

At the end pull tight, and check there is a good end left. In a shocking fall, a knot will easily tighten and pull through around 100mm. Right; you can finish with a stopper knot, wrapping around the rope twice and then poking through both turns, just to keep the end snug.

INTRODUCTION

GIVE-IT-A-GO

IND/BOULDERING

OUT/BOULDERING

IMPROVEMENT

INDOOR SPORT

OUTDOOR SPORT

MULTI-PITCH

VIA FERRATA

WHERE TO GO

INDEX

You should have been to the top of a wall on your give-it-a-go session, now it is your turn to manage the safety aspect of climbing using the protection of a rope from above. Your course instructor should make sure that the belay at the top of the wall is completely safe, and that the ropes you are using are checked on a very regular basis. One person will tie onto the rope with a figure of 8 knot, to be the climber. The other persons job is to hold the rope – called giving a belay. When you belay somebody, you take in, or pay out the rope required by the climber. However, in the event of a fall, you can lock the rope off secure, stopping a falling climber. There are traditional methods of belaying, where you wrap the rope around your body. With the use of a glove too, you can actually hold the weight of a falling climber. This method is very uncomfortable and needless, since we have very simple and efficient little belay devices. Of the many on the market, we

start you with the most simple tube design to get you familiar with the basic principle of belaying. There are other fancy gadgets which work a lot better, but if you ever drop these in the mountains, then you will have to fall back upon the simple tube, so it's best learn the 'emergency method,' from the beginning. (More advanced belay devices are only made for right handed use, so we encourage right handed technique from the start)

To make life simple, pair up with someone of about the same weight, since you would be lifted up in the air by a much heavier partner. You first have to thread the rope through the belay tube. This is quite straightforward, but as a beginner, you will often find the carrying loop getting in the way. This small wire or metal loop is of no strength, it is simply to carry the device, and also stop it sliding down the rope away from you.

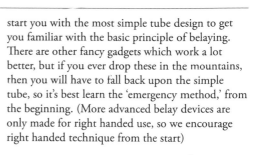

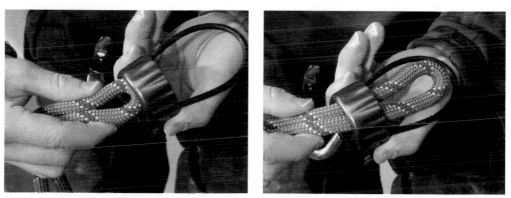

The only type of karabiner that you use in belaying is a totally secure screwgate. I work on the understanding that anything which is a hassle to do up - is not likely to come undone in a hurry. First put the karabiner on your harness loop. Then pick up the rope and put a bend in it (known as a bight). Then you force this through the tube - thick ropes need strong forcing. Then place the loop and carrying wire into the karabiner. Our photo shows a clever plastic device by DMM, that will only close, if the gate is fully screwed up. Top end of rope, should go to the top of the wall.

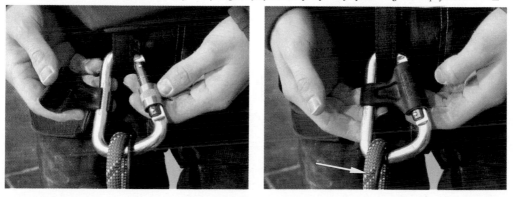

(Note: Nearly all belay tubes are capeable of using of 2 ropes at the same time - hence 2 slots; in sport climbing, you can use either side slot)

INTRODUCTION
GIVE-IT-A-GO
IND/BOULDERING
OUT/BOULDERING
IMPROVEMENT
INDOOR SPORT
OUTDOOR SPORT
MULTI-PITCH
VIA FERRATA
WHERE TO GO
INDEX

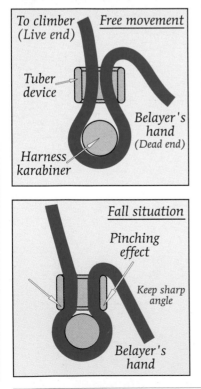

To climber (Live end)   *Free movement*

Tuber device

Harness karabiner

Belayer's hand (Dead end)

Fall situation

Pinching effect

Keep sharp angle

Belayer's hand

When the other person climbs, you ideally want your hands placed apart as in the photo, with your left hand above the tube, and the right hand below. Your hand on the top part does very little, and it is the lower hand that controls the device. If you simply let go of the rope and someone falls off, the rope will quickly zip through the device and they will crash to the floor! Our diagram at the bottom shows the principle of any tube device. The tube is wide enough to allow easy travel of the rope in a free running situation. The tube is also made narrow enough, so that when you pull the lower end of the rope down, it forces the neck of the tube onto the karabiner. When this happens, the edge of the tube will pinch the rope tight against the karabiner and jam completely. Because the rope goes in a S shape, the force actually drags the tube onto the rope and you need very little pressure on the lower rope to hold a fall. What is vitally important, is the angle of the rope to the upper neck of the tube. If the rope fully turns through 180º by coming up from below, then it will jam very well. If the rope only turns through 90 degrees by coming from a hand to the side, you will struggle to make it work. If you need to hold someone, then put both hands below the tube and hold the rope firmly. When you pass the rope through the tube, keep both hands on the rope. To move your hands up the rope, use a hand over hand method on the dead end. The whole process will seem quite cumbersome at first and you will find it tricky. Don't' worry – that's normal, but with practise, it does get a lot more fluid and your hands will end up easily working together.

Common trade names for tube devices: Bug (DMM), ATC - Air traffic controller (BD), Tuber (Lowe)

A good instruction situation at the Westway on a comfortable angled wall, evenly balanced climbers, and an ever attentive instructor.

INTRODUCTION

GIVE-IT-A-GO

IND/BOULDERING

OUT/BOULDERING

IMPROVEMENT

INDOOR SPORT

OUTDOOR SPORT

MULTI-PITCH

VIA FERRATA

WHERE TO GO

INDEX

When someone gets to the top, or they need to come down, you are in control of their descent by feeding the rope through the belay tube - slowly. You have held them by keeping the rope down to your side, but now need to lower them. There are two methods for doing this and I recommend that you learn both. A good instructor will be holding the dead end of the rope to ensure that if you get it wrong and lose control of the rope, then they can take over and control the situation. Lowering off anybody from a climbing wall is exceptionally dangerous. This is principally because they are sitting in their harness and going down backwards, just about the worst position to fall onto the ground at any speed. It is an area where accidents do happen, ranging from broken ankles, to legs, pelvis, and your worst of all – to break your back. Do not try this for the first time without an instructor supervising. You will start by holding the rope with both hands below the belay tube. Slowly let the rope feed through the until your hands get within a few inches of the tube, then stop. Then move each hand individually down the rope. This forms a jerky movement for the climber being lowered of course. You can smooth this out by keeping the rope moving very slowly and walking your hands back down the rope as it feeds through. **At no point do you let the rope slide through your hands using this method.**

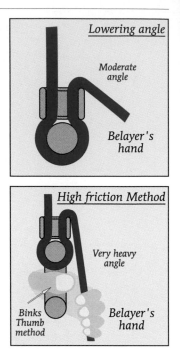

Lowering angle

Moderate angle

Belayer's hand

High friction Method

Very heavy angle

Binks Thumb method

Belayer's hand

There is a second method where you simply let the rope gently slide through your hands. This has a far greater danger of going wrong and is 'not advised' for very new and slippy ropes. The moment a nylon climbing rope starts to move and rub, you get a lot of heat generated. A moving climbing rope is completely impossible for anyone to grip or hold. It will burn straight through your skin in a micro second. This method of letting a rope slip through the plate, works on the control of the angle with the rope to the tube. At a very sharp angle, the tube automatically locks up. So it is a combination of grip on the rope, and the angle that you let the rope feed into the top of the tube. One excellent way of helping to control this method, is with the 'Binks' thumb. You put the thumb on the top hand through the tube screwgate karabiner – and the rest of the hand on the rope. This way you are forced to put a very heavy angle into the way the rope feeds up into the tube, and it generally acts a a very strong break.

Here the girl belaying is using the hand over hand method for a heavy climber, and attached to the floor to prevent being lifted off the ground.

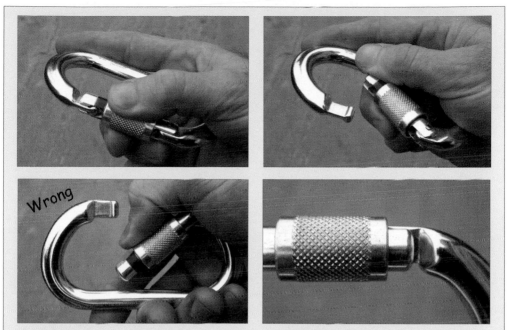

To open any karabiner easily, hold the back in the palm of your hand with the forefinger running to the top. Pull open the gate with the thumb and middle finger, then slide your thumb to the end; this leaves the gate wide open & clear to clip with. Pressing straight down with the thumb just blocks the gate hopelessly. This Petzl karabiner has a very good feature of a red line to warn if the screw is not done up.

INTRODUCTION   GIVE-IT-A-GO   IND/BOULDERING   OUT/BOULDERING   IMPROVEMENT   INDOOR SPORT   OUTDOOR SPORT   MULTI-PITCH   VIA FERRATA   WHERE TO GO   INDEX

The clove hitch is very simple to tie, and it's greatest benefit is with the ease that it can be undone after a heavily loaded fall.
1. You make a twist with the rope by simply holding your left hand still, and twisting the right part towards you. 2. Hold where
the rope has crossed with the left hand and then make another loop, twisting the rope in exactly the same manner. 3. Holding
both loops and bring them together with the 2nd loop going behind the first. 4-5. Put your left forefingers through the loops
together, then scoop into the gate of the karabiner. 6. Then pull both ends at the same time to tighten the knot on the karabiner.
To loosen, simply push both ends into the knot, it undoes easily.

In this instance, Heather is preparing to belay Tom for leading, however, the technique is
exactly the same for top roping. Heather is lighter than Tom and is attaching herself to the bolt
provided, using a double fig of 8 knot, and then a clove hitch on her harness. The belay tube
then goes onto her waist loop for belaying. In this setup, Heather has made enough slack, to
allow her comfortable movement when Tom climbs. When he falls off, she will be lifted off the
ground a short way before the belay goes tight. This will act as a shock absorber for the rope and
the climber. Tom trusts Heather, but still checks that the screwgate and belay are correct.

There are times when you and your climbing partner are different weights, a falling big heavy climber will easily lift the belayer off the ground. When you fall off with a top rope, there is not much energy generated by the actual fall, and most of it is absorbed by the ropes friction over the top belay karabiner. Some walls however, have belays with a pulley wheel at the top of the climbs. This is very good for protecting the rope from wear, but does not absorb any of the fall energy. In this situation, the imbalance of the climber's weight is far more critical. You will soon notice on your learning course how relevant an imbalance is in this situation. The biggest variance is going to be between kids and adults, however there is no reason why a small kid cannot belay an adult with the proper method of a ground belay. In simple terms, the person belaying attaches themselves to

either the ground or a big heavy object; so they are restrained from being dragged up the wall. On a safety issue, the person must always stay in the belay system so that if the ground belay did give way (highly unlikely in a well supervised centre - but not impossible), then at least there is some weight to help cushion the falling climber.

The prepare for this, take the other end of the rope from the rope bag, hopefully with its double fig of 8 in (page 179), and clip this into an anchor on the floor provided by the wall for this purpose, screw up the gate. For simplicity, tie another double fig of 8 in the rope, 1 metre further on, then clip it into your harness loop with another screwgate. With some slack, you might be lifted off the floor in a fall. The figure of 8 knot is very good, and if you make a mistake with one less turn, you end up with an overhand knot – which is still perfectly good but not as kind to the rope. It is a very good method, but getting the correct length to the ground is tricky to judge. A very common and good other way, is to use the clove hitch because this is very easy to adjust the position of the knot when tied. However, if you get this knot wrong, it could either not work at all, or more often, you end up with an alpine hitch, which also doesn't work in this situation. The clove hitch is a knot that you will use a lot in sport climbing, so it really is worth the time to learn it.

INTRODUCTION | GIVE-IT-A-GO | IND/BOULDERING | OUT/BOULDERING | IMPROVEMENT | INDOOR SPORT | OUTDOOR SPORT | MULTI-PITCH | VIA FERRATA | WHERE TO GO | INDEX

INTRODUCTION | GIVE-IT-A-GO | IND/BOULDERING | OUT/BOULDERING | IMPROVEMENT | INDOOR SPORT | OUTDOOR SPORT | MULTI-PITCH | VIA FERRATA | WHERE TO GO | INDEX

In climbing outdoors, you can easily get a situation where you the belayer, cannot see the person climbing. They may have climbed around an arête, or there is a bulge in the rock. You need to communicate with each other by generally shouting. At the wall this is hardly necessary of course, but it is a good idea to know the general 'climbing language.' The funniest term of all is **'Climb when you're ready,'** which sounds a bit draconian and something out of St. Trinian's school days. This is the 'official mountaineering' term used by the belayer to tell the other climber that they are being belayed, and are now safe to climb. At the wall you are far more likely to hear, 'get a move on you lazy bastard,' or 'hurry up, I want to get off to the pub.' By way of reply, the climber says **'climbing.'** This is not to signify that they are climbing, but as a recognition that they are being belayed, and is always said immediately. I never actually start climbing, until I also have checked the whole system again – always from top to bottom, ending up with the final krab: Harness buckle, knot, belayer belaying properly, screwgate done up, knot and karabiner on the end of the rope – every single route, methodically.

When you start to climb slightly overhanging routes, any tension on the rope will pull you off the rock, so you have to watch that your belayer is not too – over enthusiastic. If the rope is too tight, you simply call for **'slack,'** surrounded by any applicable adjectives like, please, a bit of, just a tiny bit. If you feel that the belayer has slightly overcooked the amount of slack given, you ask them to **'take in a bit.'** A very useful call to know about is 'watch me.' These are the words you use to warn the belayer that you are finding it hard and are about to come off, in other words – wake up and pay attention please. It is a nice way of saying it. Often when a section looks particularly blank, you say **'watch me on this bit.'** It's more of a nervous expression, and way of helping your nerves by communicating with your belayer, who usually replies **'don't worry, I've got you,'** meaning that they're still awake, and are in full control of the belaying procedure.

When you get near the top of the wall, it is very difficult for the belayer to judge your proximity to the top belay. So when you do get to the finishing hold, most climbers shout down **'I'm there.'** This signifies to the belayer to hold the climber, and then lower them off. If you just want the belayer to hold you where you are, by locking off the belay tube, you just shout **'take.'**

If you're a very strong boulderer already, you might well up for going onto the harder stuff, pronto. If you fall off the bottom of a very steep section and your rope is only clipped into the top belay, you are going to whizz out backwards, and fly into the central communal area of the wall - highly dangerous. Essentially, if you fall from 5 metres up on a 15 metre wall, the 10 remaining metres of rope is going to have considerable stretch. Your feet are soon going to be around the 2-2.5 metre level. However, as you pendulum out, the swing will take you out in an arc that actually takes you to the lowest point - when you are directly below the belay. This results with your feet travelling with force at high speed, and at eye & neck level – nasty. For this reason, everyone who top ropes overhanging routes at indoor walls, must already have the rope clipped into all the quickdraws on the climb. This restrains any pendulum effect to just the next bolt above them. When you have finished this style of route, you need to reclip each quickdraw for the next climber. Many people struggle with this, but there are a few sneaky tricks that enable you to do this effortlessly. 1) When you are being lowered, push out very gently with your feet to keep a gentle swing going, otherwise you can find the wall, soon out of reach. 2) When you grab the quickdraw to clip, let your body go relaxed and you will find it easy to pull your weight in. You need to shout **'stop,'** to your belayer when the quickdraw maillon is roughly at eye level. 3) Grab the quickdraw at the end, squeezing the end of the karabiner. You need to hold it rigid, since you are going to simply force the rope across the gate, and let it clip itself. 4) Take your other hand and invert it and place it behind your belay knot. The real skill now, is to hold your arm still and create your own little pendulum effect, do this by just swinging your legs out from the wall. As they come back into the wall, your whole body moves towards the quickdraw. With very easy guidance, the lower hand can direct the rope over the gate of the karabiner. Your weight in the pendulum, will simply reclip the rope automatically.

INTRODUCTION

GIVE-IT-A-GO

IND/BOULDERING

OUT/BOULDERING

IMPROVEMENT

INDOOR SPORT

OUTDOOR SPORT

MULTI-PITCH

VIA FERRATA

WHERE TO GO

INDEX

Climbing up first with no rope from above, is called leading. It certainly isn't something you want to even have a go at until you are a good and proficient, top rope climber. The climbing movement of leading is quite straightforward, and certainly not dissimilar to top roping. You clip your rope through karabiners (via quickdraws) attached to bolts on the wall as you go, then also if you fall, the rope held-via your belayer, will hold your weight. There are several huge differences however which our little friend dyno-mite will explain in the diagrams. The most important thing to remember though, is that the 'speed' of events, is a whole lot faster. In top roping when things start to go a bit wrong, an instructor can take the end of the rope and lock it off for you, or the climber might still be able to hang on. When a lead climber falls off, everything happens in an instant, and you are caught unaware. You need good reactions, and all your belaying techniques must be instantaneous, reactive and absolutely perfect. There is often. no room for error at all – that's 'leading.'

Brigit is on a good part of the wall for a new leader with plenty of good holds to use. The quickdraws are set close together, and you only have to move a short distance before being able to clip the next one. Most walls use a very thick - non opening maillon, to secure the quickdraw onto the wall. (Westway Wall)

The up side of leading, is that you are free to climb up without any rope getting in your face. You are free to choose and make all the decisions for yourself, and it's a style of climbing that seems to make everyone feel great. You do need to have confidence to lead, since if you fall off at any time, you will take a short fall that could easily be uncomfortable and hurt you. This is why we recommend that you become a very good boulderer and top rope climber first, it gives you a great deal of confidence, which will allow you to flow nice and freely as a lead climber, and give you enough climbing skill to fall off in control.

In leading climbs, you and your belayer require exactly the same equipment as top roping. In addition, you need some quickdraws, which are two karabiners linked together with a specific short climbing tape loop. Nearly every indoor climbing wall will have these insitu on all their bolts. (If not, refer to our outdoor section for purchasing and use.) We use quickdraws to facilitate the easy running of the rope – simple. You could use a single karabiner on every bolt, but by using a small extension, you cut down rope drag hugely. It won't take you long when you start leading, to feel how desperately tiring and annoying, rope drag can be.

INTRODUCTION

GIVE-IT-A-GO

IND/BOULDERING

OUT/BOULDERING

IMPROVEMENT

INDOOR SPORT

OUTDOOR SPORT

MULTI-PITCH

VIA FERRATA

WHERE TO GO

INDEX

There are three basic elements, which form the backbone theory of lead falling; Gravity, time, and load point. If you can understand the theory of all three and why they are important, then you will have some wonderful knowledge to improve upon your level of risk. Theory of falling is based on pure physics, and gives you an outline of how things work. Importantly, you can see the elements that are required to be working in your favour. After a fall, you can examine all the actual physics of what forces and speeds were involved, yet before a climb, you can't envisage what is going to happen. Consequently, all climbing equipment that we use, is designed for a broad area of use. We are also very lucky to have such advanced items of equipment at our disposal. Fifty years ago there were endless stories of equipment failure, today it is quite unusual. However, any piece of equipment if used incorrectly, can fail.

GRAVITY is invisible, it's a force, but fundamentally it's an accelerating force. It's difficult for a lot of people understand an invisible force, but perhaps a good comparison is to envisage it in money terms. It would be like money entering your bank account, at an ever increasing rate, from an invisible donor – what a dream! When you stop in a climbing fall, it's pay-back time, every last single penny. Option 1, a cheque for the full amount; or option 2, lots of smaller payments that add up to the same.

TIME. What happens in a climbing fall, is that all the force you collect during the fall has to be resolved (paid back). The shortest possible time in theory would be about 0.01 of a second, if you stopped completely in a hundredth of a second. *Basic physics denotes that force = mass x acceleration; and that also force = momentum change divided by time. More complicated maths might loose you, but suffice to say that 80kg (weight) x 10 = 800. In this, case the force needed to stop 800 units, is divided by time.* By stopping your hundreth of a second scenario, you get a figure of 80kn. Karabiners break at 23kn! Statistically you can break just about anything. You therefore have to lengthen the time it takes to slow down. By using a rope that stretches, the payback time is increased and you end up with more reasonable forces. In our example, a payback time of 0.1 second, would involve a force of 8kn

$$MOMENTUM\ CHANGE\ IN\ FALLING$$

$$\text{Force} = \frac{\text{momentum change}}{\text{time}} = \frac{(m \times v) - 0}{t}$$

Dynomite, 80kg = m

Velocity, 10 metres per second = v = $\sqrt{2gh}$

Fall time 0.5 second-ish   Stop time t

5m Fall scenario; giving force involved

Soft stop $\dfrac{80 \times 10}{0.4\ \text{secs}}$ = 2000 (200 kg)

Slow stop $\dfrac{80 \times 10}{0.1\ \text{sec}}$ = 8,000 N = (800 kg)

EN stop $\dfrac{80 \times 10}{0.067\ \text{secs}}$ = 11,940 N = (1200 kg)

Nasty stop $\dfrac{80 \times 10}{0.01\ \text{secs}}$ = 80,000 N = (80 kn)

Note: The value of a kn and a kg are used to represent the same practical value for relative understanding of forces.

and is considered acceptable. You would need to complete a Phd in molecular physics to go into how linear or peaky, the loading was during the 0.1 of a second, on the individual material make up of a particular climbing rope, given any fall situation. Suffice to say, that when ropes are tested, they simply measure the peak load on the rope, during the time that it absorbs the load. You can make a cord that will stretch enormously and lengthen the stopping time. This really lowers the load, and it is called a bungee cord. However, in climbing, you are likely to either hit something else instead or stretch to the ground, resulting in a 0.01 second (80kn) payback! There is a standardised laboratory EU fall test of above/below 2.3 metre fall, which sets out parameters for 'climbing ropes' in a worst case scenario, and gives limits of maximum peak load force (12kn), and maximum stretch – 40% (elongation); with an 80 kg weight. Effectively, all ropes and equipment are made to perform to this test. When making this test on ropes, it is stringent and repeated identically with the rope locked off in exactly the same position to a solid object, until the rope breaks after consecutive falls (5 minimum).

If we look at a fall in real climbing, the theory of acceleration is pure and highly applicable. What is largely variable is the time deceleration factor. Minimum rope out, means minimum stopping time. In the normal case of a climber halfway up a single pitch and falling off, you have plenty of rope out to stretch, lengthen the time and therefore absorb the shock loading. The standard EN test gives a rating on a fall of 4.6m which is representative of a above-below leader fall. On the basis that you purchase a current rope with a rating of 8kn, on 2.6 metres of rope being used, it gives you a stop time of 0.1sec in the above to below 4.6m fall. If you are 11 metres up, then you have 11 metres (4 times) the amount of rope out, and therefore will stop in 4 times as long, and therefore only put 2kn of load on the rope with a completely rigid and static belay in theory. By the time your belayer eases into the wall as the rope goes tight, or they are lifted off the ground as a cushioning effect, the time increases and the force in the rope decreases.

It is in multi-pitch climbing, that you can fall from above to below a belay, and result in a fast slow down rate, similar to the EN fall test. This test is highly destructive in having so little rope out, and also forces the rope to nearly go through a right angle over a karabiner edge! Any rope manufacturer will advise the retirement of a rope that has held, just a single, above/below fall. Whenever you are climbing near a belay on a multi-pitch climb, it is crucial to clip a bolts as soon as possible, even if it means pulling on a bolt up to it. It is crucial, not to fall in this area with so little rope in the system. In 'fall theory,' if you were falling and wanted to stop by lassoing a spike with a short sling as you passed, there would be so little stretch available in the short sling, that the force of stopping in your 0.01 sec instant, and simply break the sling. The more distance you fall, the faster you go, but the more rope there is to act as a decelerator. The maths of a longer fall mean that your fall of 20 metres above to below is 4 times bigger, but the force spread over 4 times the length of rope is 4 times longer, and is actually lower at around 5,7kn. Also remember, the your acceleration is the same rate, as the acceleration of the rope being paid out. A proper climbing rope will therefore cancel out your increased force.

What we can effect in belaying, is the time factor – or the force absorption rate. Simply by moving

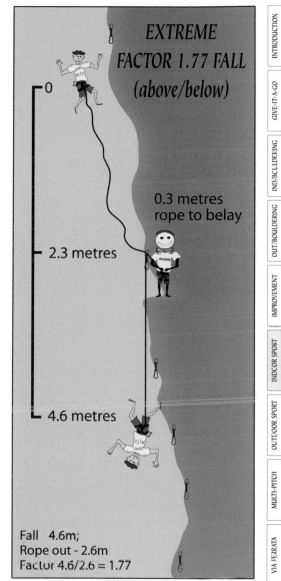

EXTREME
FACTOR 1.77 FALL
(above/below)

0.3 metres
rope to belay

0

2.3 metres

4.6 metres

Fall 4.6m;
Rope out - 2.6m
Factor 4.6/2.6 = 1.77

An example of a very extreme fall similar to the EN test fall.

your body into the rope as it goes tight, will have a wonderful cushioning effect. There have been a great many tests which show that ropes slipping through belay devices before locking up, naturally lengthen the time to stop and therefore reduce the force on the system. A lighter climber belaying may get lifted off the ground a metre, and that has is an incredible cushioning effect.

INTRODUCTION
GIVE-IT-A-GO
IND/BOULDERING
OUT/BOULDERING
IMPROVEMENT
INDOOR SPORT
OUTDOOR SPORT
MULTI-PITCH
VIA FERRATA
WHERE TO GO
INDEX

INTRODUCTION

GIVE-IT-A-GO

IND/BOULDERING

OUT/BOULDERING

IMPROVEMENT

INDOOR SPORT

OUTDOOR SPORT

MULTI-PITCH

VIA FERRATA

WHERE TO GO

INDEX

The LOAD POINT, is the highest runner that you have clipped and which takes the full force of the fall. In theoretical physics, this is twice the actual force (Max EN 12kn up to 24kn). In practical real life, there is rope movement and friction generated at this point, and you end up with the 'theoretical practical' highest values of around 20kn with current EN testing situations. This is simply why in general, all sport climbing gear is manufactured to this rating. In real life terms it's about the weight of 4 grand pianos, a heck of a lot! In real life you have ropes in everyday use that have supremely better force control statistics than the maximum allowed. You can do tests with different belay devices in different situations on the load point, but all these are purely dependent upon the dynamic qualities of absorption and elongation of the individual rope in use.

Technically speaking, you would be very unlucky to have a rope actually break, whilst falling off. I'm not saying it couldn't happen, but your average top sport climber will take hundreds of small falls each year on the same rope, and be fine. You simply don't hear of ropes breaking in normal use. You also have to use a bit of common sense, and appreciate that the more you use and fall on your rope, then the more wear you give it and the sooner you

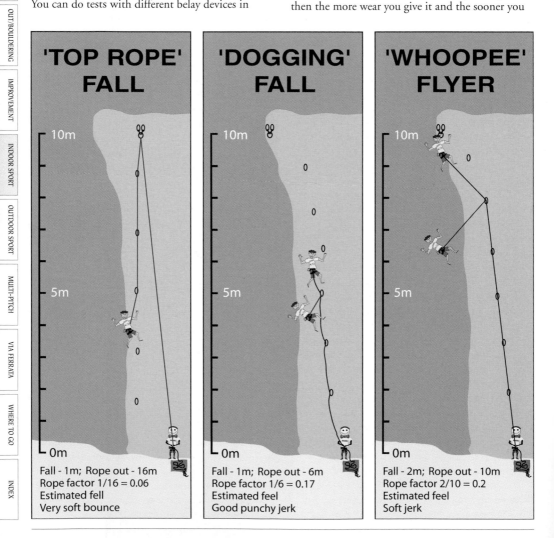

'TOP ROPE' FALL

10m

5m

0m

Fall - 1m; Rope out - 16m
Rope factor 1/16 = 0.06
Estimated fell
Very soft bounce

'DOGGING' FALL

10m

5m

0m

Fall - 1m; Rope out - 6m
Rope factor 1/6 = 0.17
Estimated feel
Good punchy jerk

'WHOOPEE' FLYER

10m

5m

0m

Fall - 2m; Rope out - 10m
Rope factor 2/10 = 0.2
Estimated feel
Soft jerk

should retire it. When a route is equipped, it should be done in a manner that will both protect the climber, and the rope. It is normal for the first bolt to be placed at 2.5-3 metres high, so that you can comfortably boulder up to clip it. The next 2 bolts need to be placed at single metre intervals in order to prevent you from hitting the ground if you fall at this time. I would estimate that clipping the 2nd bolt on any sport climb, to be the most dangerous position you are ever in. Here you are high enough to fall and damage yourself, and if you fall whilst clipping the rope into the quickdraw, there may be enough slack in the system, so that you would hit the deck. This is where the belayer must make the decision whether or not to let go of the belay tube and spot, or to be quick enough to belay and spot only if necessary. Fortunately most route setters know of this danger and will make indoor climbs very easy until the 3rd bolt. Outdoors you may not be so lucky!

Good belay and rope management is essential in leading and will serve to cushion your fall, and also prolong the life of your nice, groovy new rope. A rope is very robust from end to end, but it gets hammered in the cross section when you fall off. It obviously goes through 180° over the quickdraw karabiner, and will flatten out and damage the internal fibres microscopically. If a rope is held perfectly static, then all the force will be concentrated at one precise point, the 'load point' at the apex of the fall. If the rope is allowed to move during the fall, then this load is spread along the short rubbing distance, and the squashing effect is minimalised. If the climber is high up on a route, then there is plenty of rope to generally absorb the fall energy. At this point the belayer will hardly feel the impact of the fall at the belay tube. You still have to remember though, that the impact force of a 5 metre fall is still generated. Should the rope jam anywhere on the quickdraws, or get stuck under an overhang for instance, then although the belayer would not feel anything, you might still end up with a damaging fall and have to retire your rope. A badly zig zagging line of quickdraws will also place a lot of friction on the rope and prevent it from taking load over its entire length. Small points, but ones to have in your intelligencia.

Overhangs are a menace in many ways, especially ones with right angled corners. What used to be great fun in bouldering can present a dangerous problem for the sport leader. Your most vital concern is that if you fall off, you can pendulum back into the face supporting the roof. What often happens, is that you clip all the bolts leading up to the roof, but don't often find any quickdraws under the roof since they would impede the rope from running, by making a dog leg in the rope. A leader will therefore seek to climb all the way out to the lip before clipping. If you fall here, gravity drags you vertically down, but the taught rope pendulums you straight back into the wall. The 'obvious' thing to do, is normally to clip a quickdraw under the roof to protect you, whilst you make it out to the lip. Then when you have the lip clipped, you simply unclip the intermediary quickdraw. In the nasty event of a badly planned pendulum fall, the belayer must literally run to the wall and jump up high. This effectively adds instantly another 2 metres to the fall, and negates as much as possible, the pendulum effect.

Because of the high stretch factor of climbing ropes, when you fall off very high up and go a 'very long way,' you are going to keep going & going, some way after the rope takes up tension. On indoor walls, it is usually compulsory to clip every single quickdraw on a climb, so this will never happen. What you find outside, is that after the steep and hard initial part of a route, there are less bolts and you find the top part easy. Height is something that is very easy to misjudge! It is surprising how you can find yourself at that critical point, whereby if you fell off, even though the last bolt is above halfway, the stretch in the rope, would mean that you hit the ground. At 19 metres high and with a stretch of 38% on a high speed fall, you could end up with 7 extra metres. A bolt at 12 or even 13 metres might not protect you, especially combined with your belayer being asleep - and commonly just paying you out slack on easier ground. You can see that in this situation, having a belayer attached to a bolt on the ground might prove life saving, but alternatively on our roof scenario, you would want to be free completely. These are just two instances which illustrate perfectly, why there just isn't a single or even correct way to do things in climbing.

INTRODUCTION
GIVE-IT-A-GO
IND/BOULDERING
OUT/BOULDERING
IMPROVEMENT
INDOOR SPORT
OUTDOOR SPORT
MULTI-PITCH
VIA FERRATA
WHERE TO GO
INDEX

Everything must be completely assessed for every individual climb. You have to determine between the 'leader and belayer,' what leading methods you are going to use, what belaying techniques are required for the route, and if you have the suitable rope, harness and quickdraws for the climb. Only when you know all the leading and falling theory inside out, should you attempt to lead your first climb.

A web site run by the UIAA (Union Internationale des Associations d'Alpinisme) at www.uiaa.ch includes tests of alpine ropes carried out by various organisations, and is always a good source to keep up to date with general rope technology. You can see for yourself, tests carried out around Europe to look into climbing rope technology. Rope company websites are also very good sources of current technology advances.

! *DYNO-MITE CAUTION* ☠

Try to belay directly beneath the 1st quickdraw, and make sure that the angle of the rope going through the 1st quickdraw, is around 11 o'clock. If the angle is sharper (9-10), you massively increase the likeliness that the bolt may pull out, or a karabiner may twist and break.

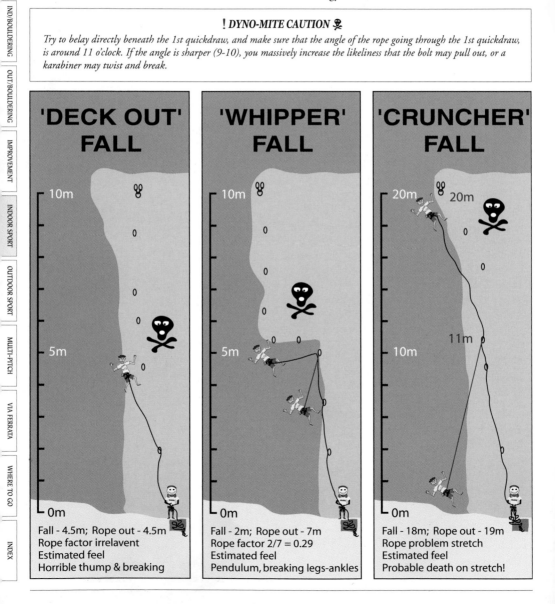

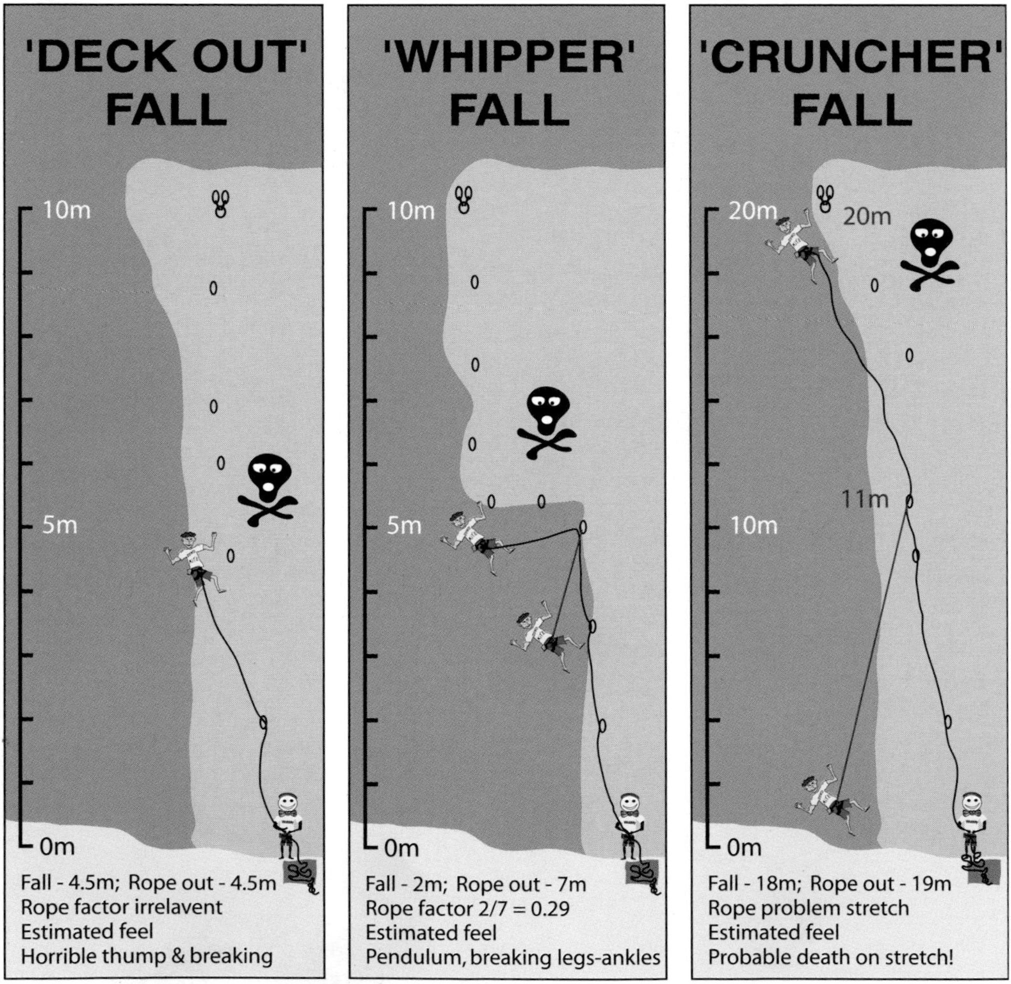
'DECK OUT' FALL
10m
5m
0m
Fall - 4.5m; Rope out - 4.5m
Rope factor irrelavent
Estimated feel
Horrible thump & breaking
'WHIPPER' FALL
10m
5m
0m
Fall - 2m; Rope out - 7m
Rope factor 2/7 = 0.29
Estimated feel
Pendulum, breaking legs-ankles
'CRUNCHER' FALL
20m
20m
11m
10m
0m
Fall - 18m; Rope out - 19m
Rope problem stretch
Estimated feel
Probable death on stretch!

INTRODUCTION

GIVE-IT-A-GO

IND/BOULDERING

OUT/BOULDERING

IMPROVEMENT

INDOOR SPORT

OUTDOOR SPORT

MULTI-PITCH

VIA FERRATA

WHERE TO GO

INDEX

The first thing that you really need when you start to lead, is a good experienced belayer, who definitely knows how to 'clip' up a route (clipping your rope into each quickdraw on a lead), and can keep a good, watchful eye on you during the climb. Clipping a rope into a karabiner is easy enough; but when you fall off, the rope can also unclip itself – result –aagh! Clipping into a line of quickdraws on a wall isn't rocket science, but it's incredibly easy to get your clipping wrong when you start, and put yourself in a needlessly dangerous position. Climbing on lead, and clipping your rope into open gate karabiners, is dangerous at the best of times, since there are inherent weaknesses in the whole concept. It is only by knowing about all these weaknesses, and how to minimise them, that you can achieve any level of reliance.

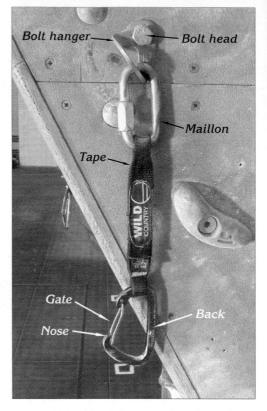

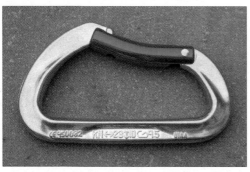

A highly technical and strong karabiner from Petzl. The thick inside section, leading to a thinner outer edge, gives high strength for the open gate situation for relatively little weight. Measurements are in KN, kilo-newtons which in 'easy speak' mean 23 = 2300 kilos. (4 pianos)

We use open gate – spring loaded karabiners, for ease of clipping and simplicity. They will always be the weakest part of a quickdraw in 'good' condition. On the side of every karabiner, you find stamped, 3 different strength ratings denoting full and complete strength, a sideways pull, and a pull with the gate purposely held open. All karabiners work wonderfully, when they make a complete loop, and is not the vital concern. It is always the weakest link in a belay system that you have to look for and analyse. On the nose of the karabiner, there is a lock mechanism, but this only comes into play when you weight is more than a person. This is so that you can hang from a krab, and still clip in and out. If you try to pull a karabiner apart, you will see it flex quite easily – alarming, not really. Above your body weight, the catch or ball in the nose, grabs the gate and securely locks the karabiner tight. If you pick up a karabiner and thump the back of it into the palm of your hand, you will hear a click. This is the gate opening and closing. If the karabiner hits the wall at the same time as it is loaded, it too clicks, and the full force is put on an open gate. There are many different karabiners on the market offering wire gates for less inertia, heavier spring loading, etc, and it is down to personal preference. It is wise to understand that all snap karabiners can open, and must be valued at their weakest strengths. In the past there have been known failures around

5kn for sure. Today with companies like Petzl and DMM offering open gate strengths of 9.5 and 10kn respectively, it would seem silly to settle for less.

The next 'disaster' scenario, is for the rope to unclip itself from the quickdraw. This might seem absurd, but it really is quite likely if you get things wrong. There is lip on the nose of the karabiner to enable easy clipping, but this could easily work against you if you get it wrong. My approach is that nothing is impossible in a fall situation. However, just try to unclip a completely free hanging quickdraw, it's virtually impossible. The karabiners weight is generally lighter than the action of the spring loaded gate. It simply moves out of the path of the rope. On the other hand, if you trap a karabiner against the rock, you can flick a rope in or out of it, as easy as pie. For this reason, the quickdraw should always be able to move as freely as possible to reduce this risk. If the rope gets twisted around a quickdraw, the likelihood of it unclipping rises dramatically. Alternatively, if the rope comes up from one side, and then goes off to the other, the falling climbers rope would not cross the gate and reduce the risk considerably. In the end, leading on quickdraws is risky. All indoor walls insist that you clip every quickdraw, you can now perhaps see why.

On an indoor wall quickdraw, you have a lower karabiner with a bent gate, attached to the wall via a non-opening maillon onto the bolt hanger. The bolt itself, usually will have a minimal breaking strain of 2200kg – those 4 pianos again, and may indeed be stronger than the structure it is actually in, or attached to. The integral strength of any bolt hanger is from the bolt at the core. Many of the bolts we use today are so thick, that they are pretty strong, even if the hanger can slightly move. However, they are only tested for strength when they are fully tightened up! Changes in temperature and structural movement can easily cause a bolt hanger to loosen, so if a bolt hanger is spinning, do not use it. Alert the wall management immediately. The inside edge section of the hanger, is a sharp 90 degrees, and will carve into the soft aluminium or a karabiner very quickly. Hence on indoor walls, you will generally find that the quickdraws are joined to the wall by a solid steel link called a maillon. The joining maillon is of exceptional breaking

strain, and is very tough. Next you have the tape of the quickdraw. There have been incidents when these have broken! Any respectable wall will have a general policy of checking and replacement, but importantly - no wall management has the staff or resources to check every quickdraw, after every climb. It's down to your sensibility to check every quickdraw before use, it's your life remember. Also think about the consequence of a quickdraw failing, or the rope actually flicking out of the karabiner, look at the reality of what will happen, and climb back down if you don't like it. What is comforting however, is that most indoor climbing walls are often over equipped with bolts to clip, and generally speaking, if a quickdraw did fail in any way, then there should be another one just below to save you. It's why you always clip, every possible quickdraw.

A rope must always come up the wall from behind the quickdraw, and out towards you. We call this term 'coming up from behind.' When you look directly at the quickdraw, the rope must go directly from your waist, into the karabiner and then run down nearest or touching the wall. It's very simple,

INTRODUCTION

GIVE-IT-A-GO

IND/BOULDERING

OUT/BOULDERING

IMPROVEMENT

INDOOR SPORT

OUTDOOR SPORT

MULTI-PITCH

VIA FERRATA

WHERE TO GO

INDEX

INTRODUCTION   GIVE-IT-A-GO   IND/BOULDERING   OUT/BOULDERING   IMPROVEMENT   INDOOR SPORT   OUTDOOR SPORT   MULTI-PITCH   VIA FERRATA   WHERE TO GO   INDEX

if you fall, then the rope behind the karabiner should not unclip itself. If your rope was going around the back of the karabiner, and into it, then a sharp tug as in a fall, would twist the karabiner around, and could unclip the karabiner!

Trying to clip a rope into a quickdraw, is the equivalent of taking hand off to wave at someone - not something you usually have time to do on the crux of a boulder problem. The first part of making a clip, is getting yourself into a good position so that you can take one hand off, and still be in a relaxed manner. It's a new style of climbing move, since it doesn't help you go up at all, and is something that you would never do in bouldering – unless you're a groovy kind of 'wavy person.' On easy climbs for beginners, you generally find a nice big jug next to a bolt with two good footholds nicely positioned below, so taking a hand off to clip, doesn't present too much of a problem. The moment you go onto more difficult climbs, you have to include special clipping moves – bouldering moves in themselves, in order to get yourself into a good position to clip from.

Belayer

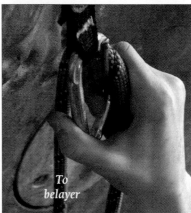

To belayer

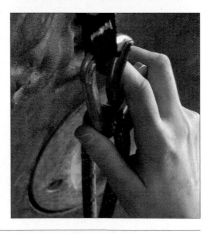

BARREL CLIP

CHECK IT!

CHECK IT!

To belayer

There are two different ways to clip your rope into a karabiner 'quickly and efficiently,' and you will need to practice both of these for each hand. These 4 options will enable you to clip from either hand, and from just about any position. Choosing when to use either method, or either hand, depends on the route you are on, and the way you are choosing to climb it. There are no rules as to how you can clip a quickdraw, and you have many options that will become clear. When a quickdraw hangs, the gate of the lower karabiner will generally face left or right. It is very confusing to explain in words, as either hand can be used. Our photos hopefully should do the trick. Basically, you have the option to either stroke the rope across the gate with the 'BARREL' clip, or to rest your middle finger on the bottom of the krab, and flip (buck) the rope over the nose of the gate with your thumb, as in the 'RODEO' clip. Both styles are very good and there really isn't anything to choose between them, it's mostly how the gate is positioned in relation to where your body is, and which hand you can free up to make the clip.

RODEO CLIP

To belayer

To belayer

To belayer

Heather nicely demonstrating both styles of clip for leading. In the barrel clip she is quite near the ground, so picking up a good length of slack is quite easy since there is no weight in the rope. In this case, the position of the left hand hold forces her to keep a bent arm, but there is a good bridging rest for her feet. Critically the next blue hold up and left is a horrible rounded lump, so she wants to get the quickdraw clipped before the difficult move begins. The rope is laid across the gate, and then with the thumb stopping the krab from moving, it simply pops into the karabiner. Note that the rope end to belayer is against the back wall, and is coming up from behind the krab. In the Rodeo example, she is forced to hold on with the left hand, and cross over with the right to make the clip. Using her middle finger, and then her forefinger to stabilise the krab, her thumb is then nicely able to flip the rope over the gate. The sheer weight of the rope going down the wall behind will normally open the gate of the krab automatically.

Right Hand Rodeo Clip   *Right Hand Barrel Clip*

INTRODUCTION · GIVE-IT-A-GO · IND/BOULDERING · OUT/BOULDERING · IMPROVEMENT · INDOOR SPORT · OUTDOOR SPORT · MULTI-PITCH · VIA FERRATA · WHERE TO GO · INDEX

INTRODUCTION

GIVE-IT-A-GO

IND/BOULDERING

OUT/BOULDERING

IMPROVEMENT

INDOOR SPORT

OUTDOOR SPORT

MULTI-PITCH

VIA FERRATA

WHERE TO GO

INDEX

Dave Reeve arrives at the lip on this overhang and clips the quickdraw at the first opportunity. Clipping level or above the bolt would be easier, but the fall could be substantial, resulting in a semi-pendulum onto the wall below.

good hold that you have chosen is below the karabiner, then you won't be able to make the clip from a straight arm. You still however want to conserve energy, and can do this by preparing for the clip whilst straight hanging from the good hold. Only when you have the rope in your hand and prepared to clip, do you make the final pull up to do the clip, then you return to the straight arm rest. Keeping your balance is also another problem when making a clip if you only have one foothold, and it is directly below the good handhold. In this situation you can use the technique of flagging. Here you simply put one leg out to the side, almost like sticking out a flag. This can stop your body from swinging around and flicking you off the hold.

Chris here is using a sidepull with the right hand, and is stood on a small pebble style foothold. His position is perfectly comfortable due to the counterbalance and flagging of the left foot. He can easily reach for slack rope in order to make the clip.

When you approach a quickdraw, the most important thing you are looking for is a good hold to make the clip from, invariably you will choose the biggest jug in the close vicinity. This might be a bad decision if it's not perfectly situated. The most energy efficient way of clipping a quickdraw, is hanging from a completely straight arm. This way, you only use your finger and hand muscles, and let the arm and back muscles have a good rest. You will often see beginners really pulling in hard whilst they try to make the clip, bad move! A good hold to clip from is one that is level or slightly above a quickdraw, then you can hang off a straight arm and easily do a barrel clip. If the

Pulling up rope slack to make the clip at the bottom of the climb, and is totally different from pulling it up at the top part of a route. As your tie in knot is well below your shoulder when you reach straight down, you only get about a foot of slack rope. By holding your arm out to the side and letting the rope slide through your hand, you can get a full arms reach of slack rope. This is easy at the bottom of a climb when there is no real weight in the rope. When you are halfway up a climb, you have around 1 kilo of weight, and a huge amount of friction being generated by the rubbing of the quickdraw karabiners. The muscles that hold your arm out to the side are very weak and tire easily, so it is far easier to do a two stage pull, directly from between your legs. You take the first foot of slack and grip the rope with your teeth, then you slide your hand down the rope to get another foot of rope and have enough to make the clip easily. If you should fall off during the middle of this, shout aaaghh for a start; don't bite whatever you do – unless you want to loose all your teeth! The best way of all to make any clip high up, is when your waist is slightly above the quickdraw.

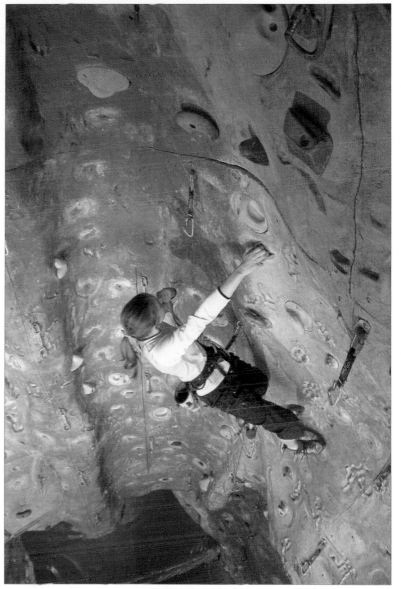

Clipping at this height, always means gripping the rope with your teeth.

This way, you don't have to waste any energy at all pulling up slack, and can very quickly and easily flick the rope into the clip. The obvious disadvantage, is that you have to make the move past the bolt before clipping. Falling on a vertical climbing wall is pretty horrible, especially with biggish holds sticking out, clip a bolt as soon as possible.

INTRODUCTION

GIVE-IT-A-GO

IND/BOULDERING

OUT/BOULDERING

IMPROVEMENT

INDOOR SPORT

OUTDOOR SPORT

MULTI-PITCH

VIA FERRATA

WHERE TO GO

INDEX

INTRODUCTION

GIVE-IT-A-GO

IND/BOULDERING

OUT/BOULDERING

IMPROVEMENT

INDOOR SPORT

OUTDOOR SPORT

MULTI-PITCH

VIA FERRATA

WHERE TO GO

INDEX

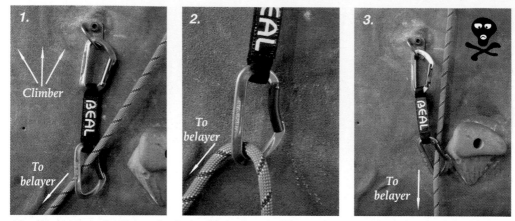

A lot of karabiner manuals will quote, that the gate of the karabiner should be away from the direction of the climber, and not be trapped inside as in photo 1. In 99% of climbing, you don't know where you're going and can just as easily end up going right or left. You often cannot predict the preferred side. On most walls, you cannot change the direction of the gate anyway, and even if you fall off as in photo 2, the karabiner should work well. The major thing to worry about though is if you clip the rope from the front. As you can see in photo 3, if the climber above fell out and away from the wall, the rope wall automatically fall across the gate and could easily unclip. Make sure you never clip as in photo 3.

The most awkward clip for a leader, is the 'behind the head clip' on an overhang. You will have got used to clipping the rope up from behind all the time by now. However, if you are below and inside an overhang, and look out into space to see a quickdraw, clipping from behind (as from your position), will put the rope coming up from the wrong way once you go past it. In this case, you need to twist the karabiner around before clipping; or put your hand ahead of the quickdraw and put your middle finger in it. This is so that as you climb past the quickdraw, it is then flowing up from behind. It looks complicated and feels a bit odd, but as soon as you pass the quickdraw, you will see immediately if you have done everything correctly.

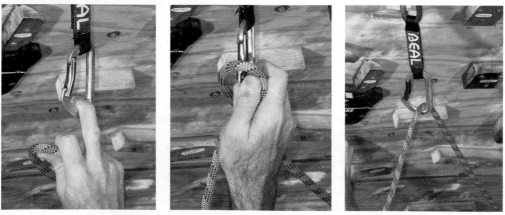

INTRODUCTION

GIVE-IT-A-GO

IND/BOULDERING

OUT/BOULDERING

IMPROVEMENT

INDOOR SPORT

OUTDOOR SPORT

MULTI-PITCH

VIA FERRATA

WHERE TO GO

INDEX

On steep and overhanging routes where you just fall into cosy space, you have the luxury of enjoying the movement to climb past the bolt before clipping it. When you do get to a difficult part and don't like the prospect of falling off, then don't take stupid risks. At this point, you can simply grab the quickdraw for safety, why take a crunching fall and hurt yourself for no reason at all. There are good and bad ways to grab a quickdraw which need to be remembered in the heat of the moment. Grabbing the karabiner is to be avoided at all costs. They are awkward to hold for a start, especially around the

outside with the gate opening. If you put your hand through the karabiner and hang off it, you simply crush any part of your hand at the bottom of the neck, and can end up with horrible tendon and ligament injuries. You need to grab the quickdraw on the tape, and facing away from you, just like you do if you have to lower off a climb and re-clip with the top rope (page 201). This is a relatively comfortable grip, but most importantly of all, allows the gate of the karabiner to be completely free for the other hand to clip your rope into it.

Chris Cubit, demonstratng a smooth and relaxed falling pose. Even with a short fall, a good belayer will let you go a few metres if there is clean space below you. This takes shock out of the system as they move into the wall when you fall. Another good reason for a 10.5mm thick dogging rope on steep routes, is that you can get a far easier grip with your fingers around it, to pull yourself up, time and time again.

Taking a fall in sport climbing can be either great fun, or a nasty experience when the wall curves in and you hit a slabby area. If you are going to fall off on an indoor wall, make sure that you are going to fall into clean air, and not down onto a flat wall. On the easy climbs, you get holds that are often big and stick out as nasty lumps. It's very easy to hit or glance a big hold and really hurt yourself. Top level climbers comfortably fall off steep climbs all day long into mid air, don't try the same thing on easy climbs and expect to get away with it. When you climb outside it's different, since a lot of the holds are hidden pockets in the rock, and you generally slide down. Your harness will work in most directions, but is best when fall into it with a sitting position and your hands together above your head. This way the rope will pull equally on both the leg loops and the waist belt of the harness. You need to relax your legs, so if they do hit a hold, they bend and move over it. It is always worth reminding your belayer that you are finding a section difficult

and to be aware that you might be coming off. They should always be ready of course, but it is worth communicating at all times. A good belayer can tell from watching a lead climber, usually 'exactly' when they are about to come off. When you have finally stopped because the belayer has held you, choose to either carry on, or just be lowered off. The standard way to go back up to your high point is to pull up on the rope going down to the belayer. This is popular since most climbers can do this quite easily and it saves fingertip strength. (Outdoors it saves fingertip skin also.) When you fall off several times at a single bolt, you resemble a dog whizzing around on a lead, hence this style of climbing is called 'dogging.'

A more realistic fall for Chris after trying an 8a+ version of a disgustingly overhanging route at the Westway in London. His clipping style is cool and effecient, in using a straight arm on a giant hold - well, for him it is! The skill is to be really tense and full on in your climbing, but then to relax if you do fall off.

INTRODUCTION

GIVE-IT-A-GO

IND/BOULDERING

OUT/BOULDERING

IMPROVEMENT

INDOOR SPORT

OUTDOOR SPORT

MULTI-PITCH

VIA FERRATA

WHERE TO GO

INDEX

INTRODUCTION

GIVE-IT-A-GO

IND/BOULDERING

OUT/BOULDERING

IMPROVEMENT

INDOOR SPORT

OUTDOOR SPORT

MULTI-PITCH

VIA FERRATA

WHERE TO GO

INDEX

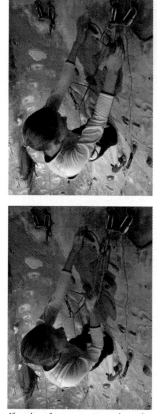

If you have forgotten to tie your knot, this method of still keeping a hold whist you weight the rope, may save your life!

Communicate with your belayer

Finishing a sport route is one of the most dangerous moments that you are going to get, or more to the point, it's where you get some nasty accidents, because of 'preventable,' mistaken communications between leader and belayer. Your first challenge at the top of a route, is to get your rope into the final karabiner. Sometimes there is a spring loaded gate, and other belays have a screwgate karabiner. For simple lowering off that is done perfectly smoothly and carefully, the spring loaded gate can be used, but if a twist got in the rope and travelled up to this mechanism – who's to say that it couldn't unclip. I am extremely careful and vigilant when using a spring loaded mechanism. My preferable choice would be a screwgate system of course. At this point, you try to open the gate of the karabiner and

it is stuck solid! If this happens, take the screwgate from your harness, (remember, the one that was on the end of the rope before you went to tie into it), and put it through the karabiner and then clip your rope into that and do it up. Now put one hand on the other rope and sit into your harness slowly. You transfer the other hand to the rope and hold yourself on the belay. You are presuming that your belayer has fallen asleap, and is not concentrating. You then utter the appropriate words to your belayer if the rope does not go tight and hold you securely in place. Only when you are totally confident that your belayer has got you, do you take both hands off the rope. Your belayer must hold you completely still before you let go. Some leaders simply jump off at the top of climbs and expect

If you've developed your bouldering skills, you will know the advantages of 'knowing how to do a problem,' and know the difference that practising can achieve. A sport route is simply 20-50 boulder problems in a row, so the complexity and difficulty is compounded. The harder you push yourself into the higher grades, the more the routes will seem like non-stop, continuous boulder problems. What makes sport climbing attractive, is the challenge to crack all of these problems first go. Ultimately, there are two styles of sport climbing; 'Onsight,' where you start at the bottom and pull out every stop to get up a climb first go, and 'Redpoint,' where you might even practise a route endlessly, and then try to lead it in 'one complete go.' Redpoint climbing at your indoor wall is uncommon, simply because you have bouldering areas for your power training, and therefore you don't need to hog the routes – having respect for other climbers wanting to have a go. Climbing onsight is pure and challenging, with most walls regularly changing the routes, so that there are always new and different climbs to onsight. Your leading is dependent upon your bouldering grade of course, but you can sometimes find that a very long route, might have a relatively low bouldering level, but is very sustained all the way through. With experience, you do learn to look at the holds on a route from below and spot all the big ones - in relationship to the footholds around them. You will naturally see places to rest. Climbing onsight, is not a full-on sprint, it's calculated small sprints between rests. A good way to start, is to plan your route and break it down into lots of boulder problems and small flowing sections. You should be always looking 2 clips ahead, to make sure you arrive at them, with the best hand to clip in the easiest manner. Work out a section from the rest at the end, or where you make the clip. You will quickly see that definite techniques and holds are needed, and work it backwards to your position. This often means that you have to start your intended sequence with some difficult, tricky moves. Cunningly, you are far better attempting this when you are fresh, than getting to the end of the section tired and in a muddle, not knowing how to get out of your pickle. Really examine what is over the lips of overhangs, since they will be invisible when you are on the climb. Finally, inspect as best you can, the end up to the top belay. You will be exhausted by then, so really work out somewhere to finally rest as best you can. A small amount of planning is worthwhile, and it really can make onsight climbing, more intellectually challenging.

Sometimes you get a situation of 2 ropes going to the same belay. They must never touch each other, and each rope must have its very own separate maillon or karabiner. Any moving rope will generate heat, and simply melt and cut through a stationary other rope! You can tie the ends together of an insitu rope, then pull the whole rope through, to check any rope before use, if you are safety concious and concerned.

their belayer to be alert – sometimes they are not, it's your life remember! Now with your full weight on the rope, you will most probably be able to undo the wall screwgate. It jams because aluminium karabiners stretch under load, and if done up tightly under load by the last climber, the thread is squeezed and can only be undone in the same manner. Your weight now enables you undo the top screwgate and retrieve your own. When you finally do up the top screwgate, do it up fully, but then loosen it a couple of millimetres. Your belayer will then lower you down nice and slowly to the ground. To retrieve your rope at a busy wall, pull it back through to the belay. This way the rope is supported all the way down by each quickdraw, and it doesn't come down with a great thump on everyone's heads.

INTRODUCTION

GIVE-IT-A-GO

IND/BOULDERING

OUT/BOULDERING

IMPROVEMENT

INDOOR SPORT

OUTDOOR SPORT

MULTI-PITCH

VIA FERRATA

WHERE TO GO

INDEX

INTRODUCTION

GIVE-IT-A-GO

IND/BOULDERING

OUT/BOULDERING

IMPROVEMENT

INDOOR SPORT

OUTDOOR SPORT

MULTI-PITCH

VIA FERRATA

WHERE TO GO

INDEX

There is a huge difference between outdoor and indoor sport climbing, do not underestimate the difference in danger, techniques, and consequences between them. The merits, highs, and exposure can be incredible with outdoor sport climbing. However, they don't come with any level of safety comparable to that of an indoor climbing wall. Outdoor sport climbing can be highly dangerous, and deserve a severe health warning in itself. That aside, if you are careful you can have some of the greatest days of your life on cliffs outdoors. Indoor climbing is almost like draughts, where you don't have to think very much and can leapfrog from hold to hold since they're all pretty similar. Outdoor sport climbing is like chess, where you have to **think** all the time. Half of your mind is thinking about the climbing, and the other half is thinking about trying to stay alive if you fall off. If you ever stop thinking, you can easily hurt or kill yourself. If you have an attitude that doesn't like thinking very much, stick to bouldering, you'll live a lot longer. There is no quick way around the fact, "all outdoor climbs, are definitely not bolted for your safety." They are nearly always bolted for the safety of the first ascentionist, who may be a considerably better climber than you, and is only concerned about their own safety. Be warned, some climbers are not even that thoughtful of their own safety! When you embark upon anybody else's sport climb, there has never ever been any planning for 'your' safety. You must learn to look after yourself and recognise any possible danger, and know what to do in every circumstance. Take this caution with you, and climb with your wits about you at all times.

We give outdoor sport climbing a full grade 5 on the insanity scale (p.22), and it fully deserves its high rating; a whole 2 grades more dangerous than indoor sport climbing. Your first practicality, is that the whole environment is unstable, the term 'solid as a rock' is really only applicable to something that lands on your head at great speed from above. Every year, I visit cliffs where completely bolted up sections have fallen down; yes fallen down, and sometimes millions of tons of rock as in the Dachstein mountains! Our natural environment is surprisingly unstable. You are wise to remember, that just because some nerd has put some bolts is a piece of rock, it doesn't mean that it is likely to stay up for very long. This applies to the whole of Europe, and just about any cliff that I can think of. The falls you are likely to take at an indoor wall are only every likely to be small and of little impact on the rope. Outdoors you can easily get into situations where you have very high fall factors. With care and appropriate equipment, you can be precautious, but you have no room for error and really must know what you are doing. Learning this entire book, is simply the beginning, it's only a small part of a sound climbers education. If this page does anything, it simply says watch out, and never relax your guard when you are outdoor sport climbing.

The plus side of outdoor climbing is the wonderful complexity of climbing on real rock, where every hold is different, and knowledge and technique are as important as pure strength. There are different types of rock, much more so than in bouldering, and this gives a vast diversity of problems, testing you across the whole of your climbing repertoire. Outdoor sport climbing becomes a far more psychological test. Coping with height and exposure is really tested when you start getting up to 30 metre heights, and with a 1000 metre drop beneath you. It is something that you can learn to enjoy; or quiver and run. Happily there are a huge array of cliffs to go sport climbing on, and in different locations; some with sunny aspects, others behind gnarly factories. You have the choice to go wherever you want, but choose wisely for your ability. Eventually you can progress onto multi-pitch outdoor sport routes. Here you visit completely wild locations and really commit yourself to a whole day on a cliff face. This without doubt is a crank up in the stakes to an insanity level of grade 6. The feeling and rewards are incredible for this style of climbing, but the risks have increased enormously. You will have to be a very confident and safety conscious person to continue living, whilst enjoying multi-pitch sport climbing. Outdoor sport climbing is a thinking persons game, are you a thinking person?

> *ATTENTION: If you have any climbing accident - anywhere outside the UK in Europe, you could be rescued by professional mountian rescue that use helicopters. You will be liable for the cost of this expensive rescue and are extremely advised to have insurance for this.*

LE FRANCO SUISSE s-6b, Lechaux, Cluses, Savoie, France; Wobbly

INTRODUCTION

GIVE-IT-A-GO

IND/BOULDERING

OUT/BOULDERING

IMPROVEMENT

INDOOR SPORT

OUTDOOR SPORT

MULTI-PITCH

VIA FERRATA

WHERE TO GO

INDEX

There's nothing to really stop you, from learning to climb in an outdoor environment. However, it's a tough place to learn, and if anything, can put more people off climbing than attract them into it. This is simply because natural rock just doesn't offer that many holds. You really do have to become quite a proficient climber to even get off the ground. That said, if you can find an easy climb – which your instructor can often do, you can have just as much fun outside, as inside. Why not, if it's a beautiful summers evening. Top roping is the natural way to begin outdoors, and observe what is going on in that wild, outdoor climbing environment. Well, it ain't so wild as you may think, far from it. Areas for top roping beginners have become very popular over the past 20 years, so much today, that erosion is now a big problem and has to be taken very seriously. At an indoor wall, you simply bolt on a new section of rock or give it a coat of paint. On an outdoor cliff made of soft sandstone, you can cause irreparable damage to the rock and surroundings. Undergrowth, plants and trees tend to be exceptionally resilient, but rock itself has taken millions of years to form, and if worn away, certainly won't come back in a hurry! We therefore have a big obligation to protect the environment in the way we use the rock, and the methods we use to organise a belay and work out the running paths of ropes. With good thought and careful planning, you can protect the rock and still have a very reliable means of rope protection.

The first and very important thing to learn about cliff environment, is that land slips. It doesn't take long for a steep path to disintegrate, and push the soil down the hill if it is not supported. As a climber, you will soon realise that a nice terrace at the bottom of the cliff is wonderful for sheep to munch the lovely grass, and you to have a very comfortable day on the green carpet - blissful harmony. As a climber, when you approach an outdoor cliff, always think about the footpath and soil erosion that you are participating in. Often, local climbing clubs will have worked out with nature conservancy groups, the best way to minimalise soil erosion and organise set footpaths to cliffs. These will contour – traverse in sideways to the base of the cliff, and come up or down at a slight angle. This reduces erosion to a minimum.

You can also be taken through zig zag paths in woods to gain height, you may lose the wonderful view for a while, but the trees will bind all the soil together, and the footpath will have a very minor effect on erosion because of the tree roots. As a climber and someone who is wanting to enjoy the outdoor environment, you must always use these special footpaths and always think considerately about your tramping across the countryside.

We also have to share our climbing cliffs with birds and plants. We can't always live in complete harmony, but we can certainly make a very good effort to allow birds to nest when they want to. Many cliffs in England and Wales are the happy nesting grounds of many birds. They can nest in cracks, crevices, in little pockets and on big ledges. February to the beginning of August is the popular time and you will see many climbing signs up for voluntary climbing bans during these times at particular cliffs. An interesting example is at Riglos in Spain, is where there are 4 huge cliffs, and lots of Vultures. Climbing is agreed on 3 of the cliffs, but not the 4th cliff. This has sustained the healthy Griffin Vulture colony, but reduced it to a manageable size. Farmers can graze their sheep without non-stop devastating attacks from the heavens! Farmers, climbers and wildlife enthusiasts all benefit together, oophs - and theh vultures. A huge amount of work and good will goes into organising these voluntary bans, so please respect them, even if you just want to do some quiet top roping. At many cliffs in Europe, you are expected to use your discretion. If you are climbing and start get alarming fly-pasts from a bird, just back down because you are getting near the nest, leave the birds in peace. At the Saussois cliffs south of Paris, every spring the bird watchers look out for nesting peregrines, and then place little signs at the bottom of the climbs where they are nesting. The climbers can easily respect this and leave these climbs alone for the early season. In the Pfalz in Germany, it is exceptionally well organised, with long lists placed everywhere to designate when nesting birds have flown. Some German restrictions are not voluntary, they are compulsory with fines up to 250,000 euros!

SCHELLNECKWAND cliff, near Regensburg. One of the finest cliffs in Germany, but definitely out of bound during the nesting season of 1/2-30/6.

Setting up a top rope on an outdoor cliff is quite easy, but you must protect any rock surface from moving ropes. Any rope that moves across rock, will cut into the rock with a sawing action and erode it. If you are on granite, you will find that although the rock erodes, your rope actually erodes about 10,000 times quicker, making it a very expensive pastime! On a rock like sandstone, the rock is always softer than the rope, just a minutes, you will have a serious groove cut in the surface crust. In a few weeks you can completely destroy a sandstone outcrop! You have to be exceptionally caring and preventative to look after soft rock. There can be signs to warn you, but you should be able to recognise soft rock and act accordingly without prompting.

You need additional technology for setting up a top rope belay on soft rock, and it is a good idea to implement this procedure into any sort of top rope belay. You first of all need to locate the climb that you are doing from above, making sure that your access to the top of the cliff, does not cause unnecessary erosion. A gully to the side of a cliff may be fragile, so use an easier angled path that may take a bit longer. On your top rope belay, the karabiner must be completely free hanging, allowing the climbing rope to come through it, without touching the rock at all. This allows free running of the moving action of the rope, when taking in and then lowering off, and will never rub the rock. In some cases, the rope touching the rock may be unavoidable, so you should then certainly consider not climbing. Climbing ropes stretch (p179), and you must always use a good 'stretchy' climbing, single rope for top roping. However, you must not on any occasion use this sort of rope for a top rope belay. You must only use caving static rope. It is nearly always white in colour, and with black flecks in it, and can be easily recognised as non-leading rope. The basic reason for this, is that you tie this to something immovable, which we can call a 'belay post,' and then suspend from it the top running karabiner. Then if someone falls off, the rope going over the edge just goes tight, and there isn't a sawing action that you would get from a normal climbing rope, which just stretches back and forth. However, caving rope stretches a bit, and especially if a knot is not fully tight. There are extra precautions that you can make to protect the rock. You can buy flat climbing tapes that are 32mm wide. These will spread any load onto a flat & wide area, which has a very minimal cutting action, as opposed to the bottom circumference area of a single 10mm rope; these tape slings are nearly always non-stretch. By using several slings together, it is even better.

Finding a good anchor-belay post at the top of a cliff is essential. Some areas are purposefully set up for top rope climbing, and have twin giant bolts placed at the top of routes for this. These bolts are not guaranteed and you will have to judge whether or not they are safe to use. This is an inherent danger to climbing outside. So how do you make that judgement? Well, anything has to be very solid for me to trust my life on it. Visual inspection is important, you must consider if the bolts could have rusted just under the surface and out of view? If you are not happy with the state of the bolts, walk away and do not climb. If there are no bolts at the top of routes, you have to find a natural lump of something to belay to. Trees are very good belay posts – well, big ones are. You have to judge that for yourself, but going for one about 1 metre back from the edge is a good move, and generally over 30 cm in diameter is a good bet. You can attach to a tree in several methods. A long sling looped round is the best idea, and by threading it through itself, you make it tight, and this is referred to as a 'Larks Foot.' If you are using a caving rope, then there are 2 options. You can use the same method as tying into your harness, with a re-threaded fig of 8. A more practical way, is to use the bowline knot. It is very quick, and much easier to get the correct length of rope worked out. The huge disadvantage of a bowline, it that tied incorrectly, it will fail! It is an exceptionally useful, but exceptionally dangerous knot. Just about all experienced climbers will use it. Ask your instructor to teach you how to tie it, and know exactly when it is tied incorrectly. When you join the rope to the tape at the edge of the cliff, always use a screwgate karabiner, and then you can use a figure of 8 knot to link up. You can also use a giant boulder to tie a rope around and use as a belay post, you find these often at the top of many gritstone outcrops in Derbyshire and Yorkshire. Sometimes you can use traditional climbing protection devices such as nuts, wallnuts, and Cams; seek further instruction on this, as it is very complicated.

INTRODUCTION

GIVE-IT-A-GO

IND/BOULDERING

OUT/BOULDERING

IMPROVEMENT

INDOOR SPORT

OUTDOOR SPORT

MULTI-PITCH

VIA FERRATA

WHERE TO GO

INDEX

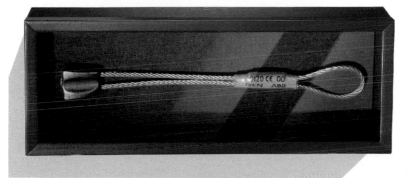

Ideally, you want the tape that goes over the edge, to go through a 90° bend and downwards. This puts a good amount of force, directly onto the rock, and thereby relieve strain on the belay post.

If you are using a post of a tree a long way back, the you can tie the caving rope to within half a metre of the edge, then use a sling to finally run over the edge and suspend the belay karabiner. Protecting the edge with a carpet is even better. An excellent protection comes from a tube made with nylon sail material, which can be knocked up on a simple domestic sewing machine. This sail material is very slippy, and will encourage movement between itself and the sling, and really help to prevent rock damage. The belay running karabiner should be a typical normal screwgate. A lot of climbers use a traditional steel karabiner for this purpose. It has the advantage of being very hard wearing, and also very heavy, which keeps the belay in place as the climber gets near, and eventually climbs above it and over the top.

MOONLIGHT ARETE 4b, Harrisons Rocks, East Sussex; Shyama Ruffell

A good long tape extension used to protect the rock from rope abrasion

Your responsibility as a climber does not end with the belay set up. If the rock in an area is soft, then use it gently, and certainly do not abseil on it. On most soft sandstone you are asked to walk around the side to get down, rather than lowering off. This is simply to minimise any wear to the rock, where possible. Sandstone also is a rock that absorbs moisture and therefore becomes weaker when wet. You should obviously refrain from climbing when this type of rock is wet.

Static rope used to exactly position a sling over a rock edge, and ninimise erosion.

A larks foot, helping to protects the bark

INTRODUCTION   GIVE-IT-A-GO   IND/BOULDERING   OUT/BOULDERING   IMPROVEMENT   INDOOR SPORT   OUTDOOR SPORT   MULTI-PITCH   VIA FERRATA   WHERE TO GO   INDEX

It is best getting used to tying the sport bowline from one side first. We illustrate the right handed method. You start by grabbing the live end going with your right hand, then twisting away from you. (Grabbed like this you can only turn one way, and end up with the correct twist). 3) Then you pick up the short end with your right hand and pass it up through the loop. 4) Take the end between the ground and the live end, 5) then arround the back and into the loop you can from. 6) Pull it snug and taught but not tight at this stage - this is a loose normal bowline.

7) By pulling with the left hand and pushing with the right, you can alter the position of the knot.[You can also see how easy it undoes without the sporting finish]. 8) By now pulling the dead end out and over 9) the knot, you can thread the end back through and follow the live end out - 10.

SPORTING FINISH

INTRODUCTION

GIVE-IT-A-GO

IND/BOULDERING

OUT/BOULDERING

IMPROVEMENT

INDOOR SPORT

OUTDOOR SPORT

MULTI-PITCH

VIA FERRATA

WHERE TO GO

INDEX

INTRODUCTION   GIVE-IT-A-GO   IND/BOULDERING   OUT/BOULDERING   IMPROVEMENT   INDOOR SPORT   OUTDOOR SPORT   MULTI-PITCH   VIA FERRATA   WHERE TO GO   INDEX

A normal set of equipment needed for single pitch, simple leisure sport climbing, 12 quickdraws, 1 double safety quickdraw with locking screwgates at both ends, belay tube and a tape sling.

The real bonus with sport climbing, is the small amount of extra equipment that you need to buy. You will definitely need a longer rope. For the majority of steep hard climbs of 6c upwards, a 50 meter rope is perfectly adequate, but on most European 5a-6b routes, you will find a 70 meter rope essential. You will need a set of quickdraws. This is a very personal choice, with each style of karabiner presenting a different feel to it. A sport quickdraw is removable, but is not double ended. The top end, is quite different from the bottom end. For the top, you need a karabiner with a straight gate, and a way to identify it as the top karabiner. On the bottom end, you need a krab with a bent gate that enables the rope to clip itself easily, and should also be quickly identified. The tape in the middle should be sewn together, right up to the ends, which traps the krabs. Having both gate noses the same way, is only personal. The top karabiner will get really gnarled up inside, as it rubs on the edge of the bolt hanger, if your rope runs through this end – you will rip through the outer sheath of the rope in hours! Keep the bent gate end, really smooth and free running.

I would personally, always choose a claw free karabiner on the top end. Some older makes of karabiner have a claw to hold the gate shut; which is purely to stop wire nuts falling off them easily in traditional-classic climbing. You will find that this claw gets caught, time and time again on your harness loops and bolt hangers when you are clipping, and is a complete pain. There are many different claw free karabiners on the market, and as long as they have an open gate strength of 9kn and above, try them out. I visually inspect my karabiners quite often, and find that they need replacing every 5 years, about 5000 routes. On the other hand, I always use immaculately clean ropes, so there is very little wear from grit etc. Karabiners are only strength tested when they are new, not when 1mm of metal has been worn away! I would also advise that you buy a few different types of krab to start with, to get the feel and see what you are comfortable with. Invariably you will be teaming up with someone else, so you don't need a full rack of 15 quickdraws to start with either. It's a very expensive mistake to buy 30 karabiners that you end up, not

Top karabiner at the bolt clipping end, fully cut up by hangers.

Botton karabiner with the rope end, fully polished and smooth.

liking! I love karabiners that fit together nicely so you can handle them 2 at a time, this means that you can rack up your harness twice as quickly. Keep an eye out too on all the karabiner manufacturers, they will always be trying something new and whizzy to make your life easier, and hopefully safer. Some karabiners will also come with a little control sheet, that gives storage and maintenance notes applicable to that particular karabiner.

It doesn't matter which way around you organise the quickdraw gates, some people like them with gates on both sides, other climbers like them on opposite sides.

This DMM karabiner has a special captive nose without a claw.

These PETZL spirit karabiners, can easily be opened together.

On an outdoor sport climbing cliff, you rely on man made bolts for security. In this situation, anything has the capacity to go wrong. Bolts can be badly corroded - internally or externally, they can be placed in suspect and fragile rock, they could have been incorrectly inserted at the wrong angle, they even may have been damaged before insertion; the glue holding them in could have been incorrectly mixed – or past its sell-by date. The scope for bad or dangerous bolts in enormous, and you need to be well aware of this. There are times when I trust a single bolt; however, I certainly don't expect anyone else to. I know that to get what I want out of sport climbing, I am prepared to risk my life on a single bolt, and a bolt that I don't know any history or anything about. On the other hand, I look very carefully at every bolt I use, and question the strength that it may have. I cannot remotely suggest in this book, what is, or what is not, a safe bolt. I can only illustrate a few different types of bolt, and describe the few precautions that I sometimes carry out before using one.

There are literally hundreds of different types of bolts, but they generally fall into 2 categories, expansion, or glued. There are pros and cons of each, and neither is necessarily better than the other. Expansion bolts come in many different diameters, and are relatively simple. The normal diameter of a regular bolt is a 12mm diameter and 100mm long. When it is usually inserted, there is 80mm of bolt in the rock. A hole is drilled into the rock, which obviously wider than the bolt, but only just. When the bolt is inserted into the hole, the nipples on the sleeve of the collar stick, and the bolt has to be forced into the hole. When a nut is placed on the bolt, it drags the shaft outwards. The taper on the end, then pushes out and forces the sleeve to wedge on all the sides of the hole. The force of expansion, is around 70mm in from the surface of the rock. Most bolts are made from mild steel and are anodised or galvanised to protect against rust. I have seen many of these bolts lying around for years, and the expansion sleeves, do start to rust. With the hole being larger than the bolt, there will always be ways for water and air to creep down the shaft of the bolt and continue this rusting process. When the sleeve does finally rust through, the bolt will often be held in place by a gungee residue. A sharp

A standard 12mm expansion bolt placed in good solid limestone, with a stainless steel hanger. You can just make out an old hole to the left, where there would have been an original 8mm expansion bolt.

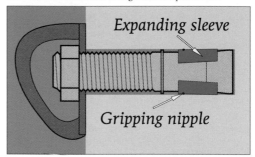

A cross section through a typical expansion bolt, showing how it works. It relies on a very tight and smooth circular hole being drilled. Any deviation by the drill will act as a lever and make the expansion sleeve unable to grip. The sign of this is a big stud sticking out from the nut, so act cautiously when you come across big studs!

pull directly away from the rock will simply pluck the bolt out! When you normally fall onto a bolt, all the force is at 90 degrees to the popping out action, and consequently, even a bolt without a sleeve could actually hold a fall – but I certainly wouldn't try it. However, if the bolt is upside down in the roof of an overhang, you must be exceptionally wary of anything, especially an expansion bolt. They are also very quick to place and are known as 'single fix fittings.' This means a climber can abseil down, drill a hole and then place the bolt all in one go. You can also climb on them immediately, which is a bonus at times. Their disadvantages are:- they rust and corrode relatively quickly, the nuts can come loose (15mm often are fitted with vibration nuts), nuts can be removed and the hanger can be stolen, they are the quick fix for amateurs so are more likely to be placed irresponsibly, the hangers are sharp edged and can cut you in a fall, the bolt and nut head get in the way when you are trying to clip the hanger. You might think crikey! Is there anything good about them? They are a good short term solution in many places, but have been nicely superseded by resin bolts. You can find stainless steel expansion bolts, and some are extra long with 2 stages of expansion sleeves, but these are very specialist, and you are not very likely to come across them. You can recognise stainless steel, since the hangers are usually made out of this, and it is a dull but shiny brushed steel colour. Expansion bolts are used in high mountains when routes seldom get done, and bolting resources are absolutely minimal.

Most resin bolts are 12-15mm in diameter and of incredible strength. Above is a normal galvanised version, with a stainless steel version to the left. The stainless steel style here has the added advantage of being large enough, to accept 2 karabiners in it, if necessary.

All modern bolting is done with resin anchors that vary from area to area, and suit the demands of the local rock and sea salt conditions. For a resin anchor, the whole operation is a lot more in depth, and time consuming. The bolts themselves can either be of galvanised steel or stainless steel, the latter being better lasting but considerably more expensive. A clearance hole is first drilled and must be cleaned out immaculately, to give a very pure and clean internal surface. Then the hole is filled

with a 2-part resin that is suitable for gluing to the rock in question. This will usually have a characteristic of setting in a few hours, so all the bolts must be placed in relatively quick succession once the two parts of the resin are mixed together (epoxy can take 8 days to cure). Then the bolt is simply twisted into the hole, which in turn exudes the surplus resin. By twisting the bolt in, spiral channels are created by the retaining indents. This adds a retaining asset, even if the metal was to part company with the resin. It would literally have to spiral out, to get out

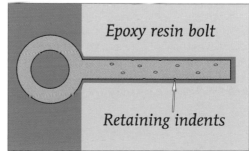

Epoxy resin bolt

Retaining indents

INTRODUCTION
GIVE-IT-A-GO
IND/BOULDERING
OUT/BOULDERING
IMPROVEMENT
INDOOR SPORT
OUTDOOR SPORT
MULTI-PITCH
VIA FERRATA
WHERE TO GO
INDEX

of the hole. You can also find staple style bolts that cannot be twisted in. These will also have retaining indents on them, but rely on gravity to drag the resin down into these to prevent a straight pop out (highly debated by some people). The resin mix should match the expansion and contraction of the particular metal it was being used for. You will also find that most professional bolters will recess the heads of the bolts. This makes them exceptionally strong, and a far smaller lump to hit in a fall.

It is very difficult to assess the quality of any resin bolt by simple visual inspection. You simply have to go on your instincts. If there is cracking between the resin and the rock, this is a weakness, but may only be on the outer surface. The advantage of resin bolts, is that the inside of the hole will be glued up, and the resin can soak into the surface of the rock. This actually bonds all the area together and re-inforces the local rock around it. An expansion bolt will always put pressure onto the local rock, and can weaken it in the case of hollows or flaws of the nearby rock. In many areas of central Europe, you will find old steel pegs that are cemented into the rock. These have often been around for a good many years, and are still strong. You just have to assess at the time, if you think they are 'safe-ish!'

Your other major consideration with bolts in the outdoor world, is their actual positioning. Here there are 2 important factors. Firstly you must assess whether or not, the entire lump of rock with the bolt in, is likely to give way in a major fall. This will have 2 consequences. Firstly, you won't stop of course, but more importantly, you don't want a falling giant block being attached to your rope. Natural rock often has cracks and flaws all over it, and some bolters are living in cloud cuckoo land, when they put the bolts in. A big loose block falling down the cliff will kill anyone in its path, and if it is attached to the rope, it is almost certain to kill both you and your belayer. I consider it responsible, not to clip my rope into a loose block that will endanger my belayer – they didn't ask, or expect me to do that. Some climbers have an attitude, well its there so I'd better clip it just in case. 'Wake up' – climbing is about making real decisions all of the time, and examining the consequences of everything you do, all of the time. Secondly, you have to look seriously

at the landing area if you fall off. What are the consequences of falling and being clipped into the last bolt. Sometimes you can be in a situation where if you don't clip a bolt, you will take a 10 meter fall into space. Alternatively, you could otherwise clip a bolt, and be impaled on a rock spike. It's always worth considering, the merits of do, or don't I clip a bolt – they're not always placed sensibly.

Well inserted resin bolts, certainly do not come out very easily, so it's crucial that they are placed in exactly the right place. Across Europe, most cliffs are looked after by the local climbing club, who are in charge of a cliffs 'bolting up.' Many cliffs have developed over the years and seem to have different types of bolts all over the place. It's more common now for the local authorities and tourist boards to get together with climbers, and sort out the whole bolting issue in a sensible and organised manner. They will organise that all the routes be done on a top rope first, by lots of different climbers of different heights and abilities, to suggest suitable bolt placement positions. Then, experienced climbing bolting technicians will ascertain, where there are good places to structurally support a bolt, as well as a good hold to clip the bolt from. Then finally, the cliff will be drilled, then resin placements done, and curing time monitored. In some areas, you can offer to help out with the bolting up of cliffs. Help is usually accepted, but you will have to go on a proper course to make sure that your bolting knowledge and skills are very good, reliable, and up to standard. In England and Wales, there are a lot of cliffs with bolts on, but there are also a lot of other cliffs, where bolts are not used. Nobody is going to thank you, if you start bolting areas where there are no bolts, especially if there has been a tradition of bolt free climbing on beautiful natural rock shapes, such as fine our gritsone edges. It's obvious that many cliffs in the future will get bolted in the UK, but please give your support to professional bolters, rather than making a mess of it yourself.

A fine route REGGAE NIGHT 7b+, Remigny, Côte d'Or, France. Mathieu Midonet, climber, first ascentionist and bolter. The route is so overhanging, that even temporary expansion bolts had to be placed for the driller to get close into the cliff and place all the resin bolts. Mathieu beforehand, worked out the entire climb for both short and tall climbers. Bolts were then placed so they did not interrupt free flowing climbing moves with having to clip bolts. Note also: a straight line for the rope was designed to give hardly any rope drag.

INTRODUCTION

GIVE-IT-A-GO

IND/BOULDERING

OUT/BOULDERING

IMPROVEMENT

INDOOR SPORT

OUTDOOR SPORT

MULTI-PITCH

VIA FERRATA

WHERE TO GO

INDEX

When you get to the top of an outdoor sport route, there are 2 essential differences to your indoor wall; reliability of the belay, and no karabiner to clip. Reliability of a belay is not straightforward, and you sometimes have to make some awkward decisions. At the wall, there will be well qualified people to check the safety of all the top belays, and you are very likely to find that they are over engineered enormously, especially for just a soft, top rope fall. Now you are putting yourself in the position of 'chief safety inspector,' and the belay you have arrived at may be scheming to catch you out! There could be sneaky rust under the head of a bolt, there might be a crack in the back of the bolt hanger. I've known climbers to trust rusty old single pegs or bolts, and then they fail with disastrous consequences. If you don't like the belay, you can always climb back down. If you quit by lowering off, try to maximise your safety. Use a karabiner of your own clipped straight into a bolt hanger and lower off. You can also clip your rope through a quickdraw on the last clip as a full back up. Discarding karabiners is better than your life. Also consider, that when you lower off a climb and retrieve your quickdraws, that you are effectively removing any backup from the entire belay system, and transferring all your reliance onto the top belay. By doing this, you must be completely confident with its strength and reliability.

When you get to the top of a climb, also consider what you are doing in terms of reliance and responsibility. If you are going to lower off, and immediately retrieve all your quickdraws on the way down, and then move onto another climb, 'you,' are fine. But very often, the leader is usually a better climber, and will in turn, happily belay their partner for top roping the climb. In this situation, the partner will start climbing and remove the quickdraws as they go. When they unclip the last quickdraw, they are only protected by the belay at the top; **they have never seen it**, or examined it. You are entirely responsible for their well being, and that is a huge responsibility. A fair and good way around this, is for when you lower off, to unclip the top 2 quickdraws from 'their rope end,' and clip them into the rope coming from your harness, the end that you are lowering from. This way, they will be protected by 2 quickdraws when they arrive

A very typical top belay that you are likely to find. Both bolts are expansion style with hangers. A chain is used to link them that is relatively taught, if the bottom bolt failed, you need to minimise the shock on the top bolt. The maillon at the bottom is quite thin, but adequate for smooth and gentle lowering off.

at the belay, and can then make for themselves, the decision to trust the belay and retrieve the quickdraws on the way down. It may protect you legally, but it's worth doing anyway, since how can you tell that the belay is perfect? It is one of the very few situations in sport climbing where you are very involved with another climbers safety. When you lower off a climb and remove the quickdraws, it's called 'stripping a route.' If your leader shouts down, "dodgy belay here, shall I strip the route," the answer is "yes," and let them sort it all out.

The other pleasantry of outdoor climbing, is not having a convenient karabiner to easily clip and lower off. Usually there is a big maillon or ring at the top of a climb, and you have to thread the rope through this to lower off. No prizes for guessing, you have to untie from the rope, thread it through the maillon, and then re-tie back on; and yes, it's a friggin dangerous time. You need to sort out your own procedure, we illustrate the Jingo Wobbly method, that we do approximately 1000 times a year! There are quicker ways to untie and re-tie, there are more thorough and stronger ways to untie and re-tie, you have to choose your own method.

When you get to the top of a climb, grab the centre part of the chain with one hand, just above the lower bolt for comfort and stability.

First clip a quickdraw into the belay maillon. Then take another one and clip it into your harness loop.

Then clip them together by holding the quickdraw on your harness, it is easier to locate the free hanging quickdraw that way. Sit back, phew!

By using 2 quickdraws (keeping smooth ends together), this will generally put you a comfortable distance from the belay. Now ask for slack.

INTRODUCTION

GIVE-IT-A-GO

IND/BOULDERING

OUT/BOULDERING

IMPROVEMENT

INDOOR SPORT

OUTDOOR SPORT

MULTI-PITCH

VIA FE-RATA

WHERE TO GO

INDEX

INTRODUCTION

GIVE-IT-A-GO

IND/BOULDERING

OUT/BOULDERING

IMPROVEMENT

INDOOR SPORT

OUTDOOR SPORT

MULTI-PITCH

VIA FERRATA

WHERE TO GO

INDEX

You first need to pull up around 2 metres of slack rope. Your belayer, must keep you on belay all the time, during this procedure.

Then tie a double figure of 8 knot into the rope, just over a metre from the end tied into your harness.

Use the spare screwgate to then clip this knot into your harness loop. This procedure keeps you in the belay system when you untie; in case of the belay failing, or you accidentally become unclipped, or dropping the rope by mistake! If you fell onto this krab, it is possible that the strain could be across the gate, so choose a krab with a high cross gate strength. As you are at the top of the system near the last clip, and with plenty of rope to stretch, the force onto the krab should be quite low. When you are learning, check to see if the rope is long enough to reach the maillon, before untying.

Untie from your lead end and take out the single figure of 8 knot left in the rope. Thread the maillon up from behind

Re-tie back onto the end of the rope now it is threaded. Make sure to get the knot in the right place, and tight into your harness.

When you have re-tied your figure of 8 knot to the harness, make sure you still have a good end of the rope left away from the knot. Now you can undo the temporary double fig of 8 knot, and put the screwgate karabiner on the back of your harness.

Ask your belayer to take in the 2 meters of slack that you used to tie the knot. Then pull the other end of the rope, and pull yourself up on the rope into the belay. By doing this you test everything before you finally unclip the quickdraws. Then ask to be lowered off slowly.

INTRODUCTION

GIVE-IT-A-GO

IND/BOULDERING

OUT/BOULDERING

IMPROVEMENT

INDOOR SPORT

OUTDOOR SPORT

MULTI-PITCH

VIA FERRATA

WHERE TO GO

INDEX

INTRODUCTION

GIVE-IT-A-GO

IND/BOULDERING

OUT/BOULDERING

IMPROVEMENT

INDOOR SPORT

OUTDOOR SPORT

MULTI-PTICH

VIA FERRATA

WHERE TO GO

INDEX

When you start climbing outdoors, you really need to learn how to abseil. It's a simple method of sliding down a rope, and is quite easy to learn if you are already an experienced indoor wall belayer and climber. The principle is almost identical to belaying with a tuber, but instead of the rope moving, you move instead. Setting up a belay is by far the most dangerous part, and just like an outdoor top rope belay, there is no little safety team to check it for you. Accidents can happen in abseiling because people choose an inadequate anchor. If you are learning to abseil, there is no reason at all for choosing anything other than an incredibly strong and reliable anchor. Since climbers use an abseil as a way of travel, you need to be able to retrieve your rope when you are at the bottom. There are knots which could be used so that you could abseil on one end of the rope, and then pull the other end which automatically undid the knot, and it all dropped to the ground. The knot method suffers from 3 deficiencies. If you pulled or abseiled on the wrong end, it would go spectacularly wrong! When you are abseiling, you often need to use every inch of the rope to descend as far as possible, and don't want to waste any of it in knots. Getting a rope down after you have abseiled is tricky anyway, and the last thing you want is a stuck knot.

To set up a 'simple learning' abseil, you simply thread the rope through a maillon or ring at the belay, then pull the rope through until the halfway mark is at the maillon. You can let the mark rest just to one side of the maillon, since the ink makes it very stiff at the mark. You then need to make sure that both ends of the rope have reached the bottom. An excellent way to achieve this is to have someone actually holding the ends of the rope at the bottom (consider wearing a helmet for this job). They can also act as a safety break in case of emergency, simply by pulling on both ends of the rope hard, this jams the tube abseil device on the rope in a normal setup. By looping the rope through the maillon without any securing knot, you need to abseil down both ends at the same time, putting an even amount of weight to both sides, which keeps the marker knot at the maillon. By putting each strand of the rope through either side of the tube, and into the main screwgate karabiner, you equally load the rope and have relatively the same friction generated by either side of the tube. With your weight on the rope too, there is considerable friction on the belay maillon, and it becomes quite difficult to even move the centre mark of the rope. Just like in belaying another climber, you attach the main screwgate karabiner into your harness belay loop and fully do up the screwgate. It is practical to learn abseiling right handed, just like belaying, if you hold the slack end of the rope down at a sharp angle, the tube will lock up. As you will have practised belaying a lot, you should be very familiar with controlling friction.

You will often abseil off a single bolt on big mountain routes. It is risky, but is a normal part of climbing in the high mountains. If you are learning, then choose a substantial belay as below, one that is fully backed up by a second bolt and a substantial, taught chain.

Wherever you set up your ab-point, the rope will hang over the edge and its own weight will keep it pretty tight. A good tip is to bring up a few handfulls of slack and put your foot on the rope. Then you can thread the rope into the tube without is constantly being dragged out of your hand. Make a bend in a strand and then push it through the bottom first, then do the same for the top hole. It is best to keep the karabiner on your harness, ready to clip the ends and tube retaining loop. You must remember to do up the screwgate on the karabiner. It must remain done up at all times when you abseil. You want to keep the ropes nice and separate, and smooth flowing. The live rope ends go to the ab-point should effectively be at the top, and the dead ends beneath, ready to go straight down between your legs.

INTRODUCTION

GIVE-IT-A-GO

IND/BOULDERING

OUT/BOULDERING

IMPROVEMENT

INDOOR SPORT

OUTDOOR SPORT

MULTI-PITCH

VIA FERRATA

WHERE TO GO

INDEX

INTRODUCTION

GIVE-IT-A-GO

IND/BOULDERING

OUT/BOULDERING

IMPROVEMENT

INDOOR SPORT

OUTDOOR SPORT

MULTI-P'TICH

VIA FERRATA

WHERE TO GO

INDEX

Walk backwards to the edge, feel the tube working, but then stop before you go too far. (Note: a left handed abseil here, learn both sides)

Now you must always keep the hand on the dead rope, but use the other hand on the rock to keep steady as you step down

The big difference between belaying and abseiling, is that now you have 2 strands of rope in the belay tube, and twice as much friction. You soon realise that you don't go anywhere because of the massive friction. At the top of an abseil, it's bloomin awkward to even move, but as soon as you move a couple of feet down the abseil, you will find that the friction generated by the tube is about perfect. As you descend, the weight of the rope beneath the tube decreases, and you find that you need to grip harder on the rope with your hand. Nearing the bottom of an abseil, you will be having to grip considerably, to slow down. I find that a leather glove is a very useful addition to my belaying and abseiling kit, and would definitely recommend that you get one for outside climbing. I don't use a glove all the time, but choose when to use it, for comfort and a higher level of security. Simply, if a rope starts to move too quickly, it instantly melts your skin and you cannot hold the rope, or stop it at all. A leather glove can absorb the heat generated and you will have a terrific chance of getting the rope back under control. So if I'm using a new rope, or a thinnish one, I will invariably use a leather glove. When you belay, you tip your head back to look up. When you

abseil you generally look down between your legs, consequently any long hair has a great trick of going into the belay tube – a hair band is essential.

Going over the top is always disgustingly awkward in abseiling, any instructor worth anything will try to get your abseil belay, as high as possible for your first learning abseil, hopefully! In real life, you need to learn how to cope with a low ab point. I see time and time again, instructors asking people to step back and lean outwards, then as they go over the top edge; thwack, as they plop down or spin out of control. To go over the top edge when abseiling, you simply sit on the edge like you would on a wall, and slither over it, keeping your hand firmly on the dead side of the rope. If possible, you actually climb down over the edge, keeping yourself taught on the rope. As soon as your waist is 6 inches below the edge – stop. At this point, look for a few footholds to stand on. Then with one hand on the live ends of the rope, you can lift them up - ever so slightly, to move them left or right. You can also see the path of the rope back to the belay maillon for any dangerous sharp edges. Simply by lifting the rope with the live hand and moving your feet, you can move

Now in this position you can feel the edge for sharpness, and because the rope is not heavily weighted, you can move it along the top edge

the position of the abseil rope, so it runs over part of the rock that is smooth and rounded. You will often see plenty of V grooves, have a nice 10mm scoop at their base, which is where other climbers have pulled their ropes through afterwards, and it has worn. With a static load of an abseil, it's pretty difficult to cut through a climbing rope. Something to remember however, is if your ab-point is 5 metres back from the edge, there would be a good few inches stretch between the ab-point, and the edge where the rope is going over. If then you stopped halfway down an abseil, and bounced around for a few minutes, the rope would be going back and forth across the edge in a very abrasive manner. If the edge is sharp, it will certainly can cut through the rope! You are not likely to do this, but as it has actually happened – I wanted to warn you. So make sure for a start, that your rope is running over a nice and smooth edge.

When you begin abseiling, let the rope feed nice and smoothly through the tube. Don't bounce around or stop suddenly, why put unnecessary loads onto the belay system. The more you descend on the abseil, the less weight you have on the dead

rope end. Eventually it becomes quite difficult to control your abseil, especially on new and thin ropes. I find that wrapping a rope around your leg once, puts just about the right amount of extra drag on the rope to make controlling it, nice and easy. When you are making quite a big abseil, it is often simple and easy to have both hands on the dead end of the rope for extra security. If you let go of the rope completely with your hands, you will go zooming down the rope uncontrollably. You will not be able to stop or grab the rope with your bare hand, more to the point, you would be going so fast and being knocked around so much, you would be unlikely to even grab the rope with a leather glove on. Never let go of the dead end of the rope! Your only chance with a disaster scenario, would be if someone pulled the bottom of the rope, completely tight. This would lock up the belay tube for you. It's good practise and knowledge for beginners to stop someone on an abseil, then in the case of an emergency, you will know exactly what to do. We cover more advanced abseil techniques in multi-pitch sport climbing.

Here the dead rope goes between the legs and then goes around the right leg to add extra friction for the abseil.

You don't find that many grade 4 climbs at climbing walls, and the ones that you do are generally very easy. In the outside world it's different. Grade 4 is a comfortable climbing grade and is to be well respected. It's also a great grade to start leading on. Finding sport routes of grade 4 in the UK is almost impossible, but if you go anywhere else in Europe, there are a huge wealth of superb grade 4 climbs. When you climb indoors, by the very nature of using bright coloured holds, means that everything is obvious and straightforward. When you tackle an outdoor sport route for the first time, you will see how different and confusing it all becomes. By starting on a grade 4, you can ease yourself into route finding and clipping gear gently. Most people will enjoy a good handful of grade 4 routes before progressing up onto grade 5. You are best off, choosing a climbing area with a few cliffs that have plenty of grade 4 and 5 routes for your first climbing trip. Grade 6a on many outdoor cliffs around Europe, is quite a stiff number. Just because you romp up 6a on an indoor wall, don't think for a minute that you will do the same outdoors. I hope you do well of course, but certainly don't be disappointed if you find outside climbs harder, it's just the way it is.

Work out how many clips you will need. Count the bolts and add a couple more for clipping into the top belay and threading. You always want a couple more than you need anyway. With more experience you will spot in advance which hand will clip them onto the bolt, and which side of your harness they should be. Equally distribute them on each side of your harness for now.

You can either clip the quickdraws on your harness up like this, or down with the nose facing in. It's personal preference, but this way, your thumb is in a good position to easily push to open the gate when you need to get at the quickdraw.

Grade 2 and 3 climbs in the high mountains are full standard climbing which can be on vertical rock, but don't have what you would call 'difficult moves.' What gives grade 4 it's status, is that there should be at least one or two moves that need thinking about, and are difficult, i.e. you could fall off them. It's no joking matter, they may be quite easy climbs, but you will need your belaying and clipping to be perfectly up to standard, since you could easily be relying on it. A grade 4 won't be relentlessly vertical, but then again, you often won't find the handholds so generous on outside rock. You need to find with the help of a local guidebook, some friendly grade 4's to start with. Principally because this grade is often used for beginners, there should be an ample supply of bolts on the route. You definitely want to walk away from a grade 4 with hardly any bolts, you can top rope those routes and they might just be intended for top roping anyway. You should find bolts going the whole way up and generally spaced 1.5-2 metres apart. Anything more distantly spaced is scary, and not the norm. A lot of cliffs around Europe are used by local schools for teaching climbing etc, so you will often find nice picnic areas nearby in the forests. You might also get swamped by kids if a school group does arrive of course.

If you suspect a brittle flake of rock, tap it with the fingers joined, the noise will ring if it's solid, or a dull thud if its cracked or loose.

You will often find an old thread of rope through a natural hole in the rock, hardly brilliant but still worth clipping.

Looking for footholds will be your biggest problem since they are now disguised in the rock. Rely on the bouldering techniqes you learnt.

Try to read the rock in advance, here it is an obvious left hand clip with the bolt to the left of the good jug. Remember to clip from behind.

INTRODUCTION   GIVE-IT-A-GO   IND/BOULDERING   OUT/BOULDERING   IMPROVEMENT   INDOOR SPORT   OUTDOOR SPORT   MULTI-PITCH   VIA FERRATA   WHERE TO GO   INDEX

You will often find terribly placed bolts in ridiculous positions. Here we have a perfect example of an incorrectly placed bolt. Everyone knows the typical length of a quickdraw, yet this bolt is positioned so the lower karabiner will just hit the prominent lower ledge. A sharp fall on this could easily cause whiplash and open the gate. Wobbly simply grins and crosses her fingers, there's not a lot else you can do.

Remember all those push down techniques, they are used a huge amount in mountain limestone routes.

Control your fear by concentrating on the job in hand. You will always find a foothold in the right place if you look long enough.

Grab the chain, enjoy the moment but don't stop concentrating. Route - CLARK GAYBEUL 4b, Courmes, Alpes Maritimes, France; Wobbly

INTRODUCTION

GIVE-IT-A-GO

IND/BOULDERING

OUT/BOULDERING

IMPROVEMENT

INDOOR SPORT

OUTDOOR SPORT

MULTI-PITCH

VIA FERRATA

WHERE TO GO

INDEX

you need strong fingers, it gets propelled into grade 6. A grade 5 can be exceptionally difficult bridging and smearing on your feet. You are also now going to find out that you actually have to climb! I mean that you will not be able to get to the next bolt unless you climb there. You will now become aware that when outdoor rock is blank, it really is blank. Sure enough, there maybe 2 ways to do a grade 5, but in most cases the second way will be around 6b or 6c. So if you can't do the move, you're stuck. You will now discover the real world of dogging, and hang off a bolt with a gazed stare at the blank rock in front of you. Climbing has just become a lot more interesting and challenging. No longer is it a pure physical workout.

Photographing a typical grade 5 climb is very difficult, since most grade 5's often have very good holds that just don't look difficult to get a grip of. These photos are of a classic route at Courmes which is a corner-diedre called DISCO PATHIE 5c. It is so typical of grade 5 it's lovely, an unsuspecting corner of modest steepness and slightly undercut at the bottom. All the perfect ingredients for an almighty puzzle-struggle.

Not an obvious move at all, you begin completely to one side so that you can get established above the little overhang. Tip: Bolts are usually in the right place, but you don't neccesserily climb directly up to them.

At least of grade 5's, you are likely to find a bolt well placed above the very hard moves. The problem here being a complete lack of handholds.

Your first grade 5 climb could either be a straightforward jug pulling experience, or a technical nightmare. It really does depend where you end up and on what style of rock. There are many areas of Europe that don't use the grade 5 very much and climbing begins at grade 6. In most parts of France, you are likely for a full-on treat at grade 5, and better have got out of bed the right side. A helpful clue, is that some areas, you get grade 5 and then 5+, which is an older grading method. Here you are likely for a soft touch. The moment you come across 5a, 5b and 5c as separate grades, expect a full-on approach. In saying this, you can get some absolutely cracking routes at grade 5 which are all time classics, and will have you thinking and sweating all the way. You will also find that if you do a grade 4 climb on a top rope, you won't end up thinking that much, because it is the lead above the bolts that is the thinking part. I can promise that even on a top rope, an outdoor grade 5 will give you a lot to think about. In many cases, you don't have to be hugely fit or powerful, you just have to be able to use your feet very well. The moment a route demands that

A real mother of a move, keeping your feet perfectly still on sloping and smooth footholds, crossing the hands so the left hand can go directly up to the slot, and leaving the right free for the next clip, highly technical.

INTRODUCTION

GIVE-IT-A-GO

IND/BOULDERING

OUT/BOULDERING

IMPROVEMENT

INDOOR SPORT

OUTDOOR SPORT

MULTI-PITCH

VIA FERRATA

WHERE TO GO

INDEX

INTRODUCTION

GIVE-IT-A-GO

IND/BOULDERING

OUT/BOULDERING

IMPROVEMENT

INDOOR SPORT

OUTDOOR SPORT

MULTI-PITCH

VIA FERRATA

WHERE TO GO

INDEX

Anyone by now who has spent a considerable time at their local climbing wall or on a sport cliff, will have seen a multitude of belay devices that seem to do the same thing as a tube device. They are generally simple bits of metal that put friction on the rope. There is one belay device however that has revolutionised the world of sport climbing, and that is called the Gri Gri, and is made by Petzl. In simple terms, you will find that 80-90% of outdoor sport climbers will use this to belay with. I personally would never do a sport route without one, end of story. The bottom line in climbing, is not how well things work, or if they are easy to use; but how good they work when things go wrong. If you are using a belay tube to lower or hold a fall, and you accidentally let go of the rope, then it is hospital or worse for the leader. If you are using a Gri Gri, it has a very good chance of locking on its own. This automatic system however, can be prevented from working, if you use very thin and slippery (i.e. new) ropes. But solemnly remember, that the tube belay, won't have any chance of working at all if you mishandle the rope! I prefer to stack as many odds in my favour since we are all human and will make a mistake, sooner or later. I fell off once and surprised my belayer, who was flung into the roof of a cave where they were belaying. They accidentally (I hope!) dropped the belay rope, however the Gri Gri saved my life, by locking up completely on its own.

When you buy any piece of climbing equipment, you are then in charge of how you use it for your own safety. This applies to ropes, harnesses and hardware. There is always the standard use as recommended by the manufacturer on the instructions that are supplied. You also can have an advanced use which may conflict with the wishes of the manufacturer, then it's completely down to you of course. The Gri Gri sits into two categories of use; manufacturers, and advanced use, because just about anyone you see at a cliff, will have their own advanced way of using a Gri Gri. You will often visit a cliff to see climbers belaying, whilst eating their lunch, lighting up a cigarette, pouring coffee, sunbathing - all with both hands off the rope. I can't recommend this, and must of course say that this is ever so terrible, just for the record. But if I'm to be realistic, that's sport climbing culture, just see for yourself. Another important thing to know about a Gri Gri, is that it works on friction between the rope and a spring-loaded cam. Petzl have done their utmost best to make the device grip wherever possible, but a brand new thin rope that is highly slippery, will not generate friction, and can defeat the device by pure and simple physics. Without enough friction, the cam will not jam. When your rope is used a bit, you will find that the problem is more about getting a Gri Gri to un-jam, than actually be worried about them locking up.

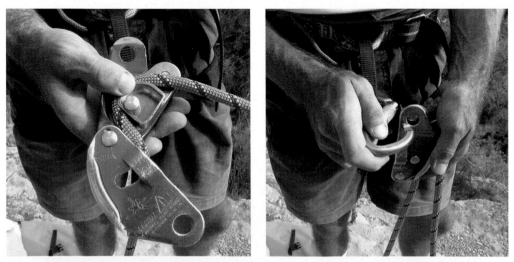

Start with the karabiner on the harness with the gate nose on the top left. Put the leaders rope through the Gri Gri as illustrated on the device. Clip the Gri Gri into the karabiner as shown with the lead rope being at the top. Swap hands to take the Gri Gri in the right hand.

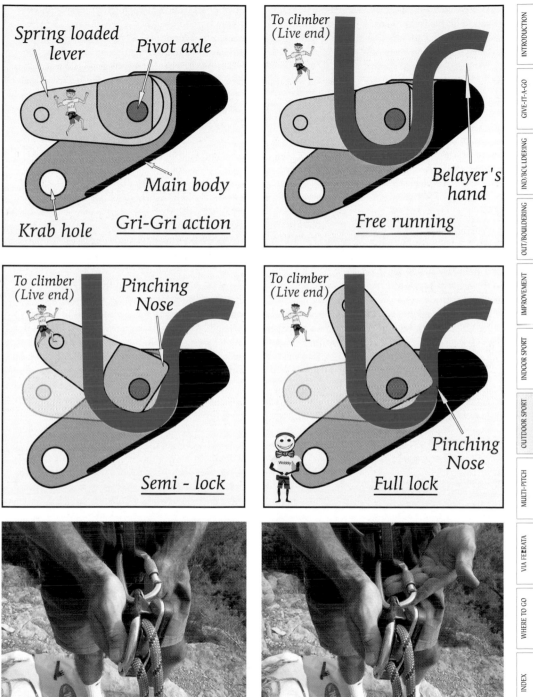

Spring loaded lever

Pivot axle

Main body

Krab hole

Gri-Gri action

To climber (Live end)

Belayer's hand

Free running

To climber (Live end)

Pinching Nose

Semi - lock

To climber (Live end)

Wobbly

Pinching Nose

Full lock

Graphic to illustrate the action of the cam, do not use in an open position

Simply draw your left hand up, starting with your thumb on the gate, and then your fingers. By the end of the draw, the gate should be done up.

INTRODUCTION

GIVE-IT-A-GO

IND/BOULDERING

OUT/BOULDERING

IMPROVEMENT

INDOOR SPORT

OUTDOOR SPORT

MULTI-PITCH

VIA FERRATA

WHERE TO GO

INDEX

INTRODUCTION

GIVE-IT-A-GO

IND/BOULDERING

OUT/BOULDERING

IMPROVEMENT

INDOOR SPORT

OUTDOOR SPORT

MULTI-PITCH

VIA FERRATA

WHERE TO GO

INDEX

By comparison, Grand Prix drivers spin their cars to get back on the track, hardly recommended in any driving manuals eh! Advanced climber's use a Gri Gri in a different way called the 'quickfire method,' and is totally against the wishes of the manufacturers, hence you won't find it in their instruction manuals! It would be ridiculous to ignore this method, since just about everyone who uses a Gri Gri at top level, uses it in the quickfire way. We include it so you know why other climbers belay like this, and will know how switched on and quick you have to be to use it. The belayer feeds the rope in and out, similar to a normal tube belay. But to pay out rope quickly, a rope simply jams up the device, especially when you are using your thick old dogging 10.5mm rope. The only practical way to quickly pay out slack for a good leader, is to purposely prevent the Gri Gri from locking, with your right hand clasped under and around the spring lever mechanism. By doing this, you accept that you are preventing the Gri Gri from working properly. Only a very experienced climber should ever use this method, since they will be watching the leader and know exactly where and when they are going to be falling. They will certainly not be gripping the spring lever during a falling time. You have to be very quick and very skilled to use this method.

A good and correct way of handling a Gri Gri.

Note: An inexperienced climber is likely to freeze when the leader falls, and just grip tight – hence the tube belay is good for beginners. With the quickfire method, you have to be relaxed, and think accurately in a fall situation. Some climbers alternatively put their left thumb on the spring lever to stop it jamming. I prefer the hand underneath since if you only grip lightly, a fall tends to rip the spring lever out of your fingers, and you simply slide your right hand onto the dead end of the rope. If the lever mechanism in the Gri Gri stopped working, then it would not lock up and the device would act like a normal friction belay device. If you put the rope into it the wrong way round, it wouldn't lock up either. Because of this, I always treat it as a normal belay device and often wear a leather glove.

The Gri Gri can be conviemiently held for right handed advanced use; note the very sneaky middle finger used to free the Gri Gri from locking.

Lowering somebody off with a Gri Gri is much smoother than a tube device, but I fully recommend that you wear a glove. First you take the dead end of the rope firmly in your right hand. I control the descent of the climber, completely through the grip on the rope through a glove. There is a black release lever on the spring lever which folds out. In wearing a thick glove, you can let the rope slide through your hand in control with superb smoothness. By pulling the black lever fully back, you can completely unlock the cam and then control the descent with your hand. If at any point you want to stop, release the black lever on the spring arm. It is possible to use the black lever as a variable friction control, but I find the cam is so aggressive, that it is immensely difficult to get this right. If you got it wrong without enough friction, the climber would plummet to the ground instantly.

A Gri Gri fully locked off with the spring lever vertical.

The Gri Gri with the black release handle fully pulled back and released in the main photo. Partial pinching adjustment (inset), is stupidly tricky and unnecessary when you wear a glove. All pinching of a rope will soften the rope-core, you do not want this. Soft old ropes, give bad rope drag.

Partial pinching!

INTRODUCTION

GIVE-IT-A-GO

IND/BOULDERING

OUT/BOULDERING

IMPROVEMENT

INDOOR SPORT

OUTDOOR SPORT

MULTI-PITCH

VIA FERRATA

WHERE TO GO

INDEX

INTRODUCTION
GIVE-IT-A-GO
IND/BOULDERING
OUT/BOULDERING
IMPROVEMENT
INDOOR SPORT
OUTDOOR SPORT
MULTI-PTICH
VIA FERRATA
WHERE TO GO
INDEX

Welcome to difficult climbing. Although grade 6 may be at the bottom end of a grading chart, it certainly isn't easy, and outdoors it's going to look pretty daunting. On sport routes, the grade is to represent the overall difficulty of the climb, rather than any one particular move. However, since bouldering has now developed with the Font and V scales, you are going to see more sport climbs with an overall grade, and perhaps a bouldering grade for the hardest move, subject to local variance & interpretation. A typical outdoor 6a climb would be vertical the whole way, with at least one section of fingertip climbing that would be way beyond the scope of an energetic, and sporty newcomer – and that's just on a top rope. That section would be normally up to 3 metres of which, two would be above the bolt. You seriously do need to be able to boulder font 4b (UK t-5a) onsight, to sensibly go on a 6a climb. If you can, then you are in for a great time. A lot of climbers can cope with the lower grades quite well, and don't often fall off. There seems a lot of people who start cranking up flying time as soon as they move into 6a climbing, a few tips!

Limestone is formed by sediments being laid down in oceans, and then compressed over millions of years. You get layers formed that vary in density and consistency. When you look at a cliff, these

are often apparent and you can see horizontal lines giving lots of good holds, then blank areas of highly compressed limestone. It's the blank areas where your going to come across the 6a moves, but at least the highly dense limestone will take a good and substantial bolt placement. If you get a band of this on the lower part of the cliff, you can have a 3 metre, 6a section, with only one bolt for protection. If you fall here and your rope unclips from the quickdraw, you can smash yourself up pretty badly. There are 3 methods that we use in this situation. The quickest and simplest is to clip the quickdraw and rope as normal, then invert the lower karabiner in the sling. With both gate noses being at the top ends, you have reduced the risk of the rope unclipping itself. The next level up of precaution, is to use 2 quickdraws back to back, with gates facing opposite ways on the same bolt. Anything is possible, but for the rope to unclip from this would be extraordinary. However, you often find bolts with small eyes, so that you can't get 2 karabiners into them. Here you are best off using a quickdraw with a screwgate karabiner on both ends. With this in place, you will feel a lot more confident of taking that risk on just a single bolt.

You also must think really carefully, what would be the consequences of that single bolt failing, and can it be avoided. Many climbs in the 6a-6b grade are

Flipping the lower krab; twin clips on the same bolt.

The wonderful expansive world of 6a - LES SOULIERS DE TCHOU 6a, Gréolières, Alpes Maritimes, France; Wobbly

INTRODUCTION

GIVE-IT-A-GO

IND/BOULDERING

OUT/BOULDERING

IMPROVEMENT

INDOOR SPORT

OUTDOOR SPORT

MULTI-PITCH

VIA FERRATA

WHERE TO GO

INDEX

equipped by 7c level climbers for their level of safety, so they're not going to be falling where you are. You must always remember that it is your level you are thinking about, and be realistic about your competence, don't take unnecessary risks. Another tip, is to arrange for a high clip to be in-situ, especially when you are making that jump from 6a-6b-6c, Usually, you get a lot of these grade of climbs together on a cliff. When you pull a rope through a clipped up route, it usually falls back through every runner except the last one. If you pull the rope with 'only' the bottom three bolts clipped, the weight of the rope when it falls, will generally carry most of it straight down, and the 3 low three clips will remain clipped. So simply by transferring the bottom 3 clips on your climb to the next one, you can at least set up a preventative measure of possibly busting a few bones, making the first few clips. You might eventually get to the top of a route after many falls. You think wow, let's top rope that to get some training in. There's no problem with that, considered that you're not route hogging, but please be aware that top roping, really does wear through metal. Do not use a lower off karabiner, or top bolt, for top roping on. Use your own screwgate karabiner instead. Placing chemical resin bolts is a long job, so why needlessly wear away other peoples good work. (Always back up a single bolt too!)

Now that you are living in 6a-6c cliffs, the tops will often be directly above your head. Remember that any loose stone knocked by a goat or sheep, is going to fall directly down onto you without any warning at all. If you are looking up and belaying you will see it of course. But if you are just hanging around the cliff, hang around a bit away from it and always try to keep out of a possible drop zone. Belaying on a grade 6 becomes a lot more skilful, since they are routes where you can hit something if you fall off. You need to pay out slack when it is asked for, but you really do have to be attentive. The 6's are with-

Special easy-thread lower offs - soon show dangerous signs of wear.

out doubt the hardest grades to belay, since leaders are right on the edge a lot of the time, and don't have the incredible stamina of the grade 7 climbers. Too much slack and you could easily add a couple of broken bones to their fall. The most important thing of all on grade 6's, if you are not happy with the bolting for your ability, back off, because it certainly could be totally unsafe for you.

A real tell tale sign on a route, is a maillon on a quickdraw! This is where a vast majority of climbers get to, and then can't get any further. Rather than leave a karabiner, someone will leave a 6mm maillon and lower off. They are like little warning signs all over the cliff, you know that you're in for a hard time, above one of these. A lot of climbers carry a few spare 6mm maillons, in case it happens to them. They are 'not' belay points or top roping points; and remember, if you took a belay on one, then your partner would be taking a maximum fall, on the hardest part of the route, something exceptionally stupid. If you are stuck, please don't simply thread the bolt and lower off, remember they wear out. Either place a maillon or karabiner to lower off, or thread the bolt and then abseil off. Pulling the rope without any person's weight on it, through a bolt will hardly wear it at all. Tip: karabiners with a T section bar, allow you to thread a rope through a small bolt eye at the same time, you can't do this with round section karabiners.

Heading towards grade 7, and you won't find many climber's using the fig-of-8 to tie in any longer. Most higher level climbers graduate up the sport climbers bowline. The more you fall off onto a fig-of-8 knot, the tighter it gets and becomes a real bugger to undo. The sport bowline is a far better choice of knot since it is easy to undo after repeated loading, which you give it whilst dogging. You must learn to tie it correctly since if you don't, then it won't stand a chance of holding you (See page 229 for tying method). The knot is a normal bowline, but then you thread the loose end back through the knot. This simple extra turn and thread uses up a minimal amount of rope, and keeps the end out of the centre on your harness. It also means that you can tie in completely tight, and get the knot right into your harness which in turn has enormous benefits when bouncing about. For a start, it gets you the highest possible when you rest on a quickdraw, and it gives you the maximum pull when you have to do a 'Jingo' pull. When you are lowering off, you will be conveniently nice and tight into the rock for easy unclipping.

Here you can see illustrated the normal bowline knot, very tight into the harness and closing the tie-in loops together.

The finished sport bowline; a knot that is still quite easy to undo after some really energetic jingo pulls.

First Wobbly jumps up in the air and takes in, ending belaying 1.5 metres up. Then the Jingo pulls up with a dyno pull on the rope, because he is so strong he goes zooming up.

Dynamic Jingo-pull

The momentum of the pull will leave Jingo in the air for a split second, and Wobbly falls back to the ground taking the slack in before Jingo heads back to earth.

FLAGRANT DELIRE 7a, Gréolières, Alpes Maritimes, France; mon ami. Superb, but highly technical and wonderfully sustained.

If you're a beginner, then these grades might feel a long way off, but don't feel it's an impossible grade, you could get there in a couple of years if you make it click. Actually getting up an easy grade 7 on a top rope, is the majority of climbers full ambition after many years of climbing. Climbing an outdoor technical 7a route on-sight, is something which seems about 100 grades harder. At this level, everything seems to be coming at you incredibly fast, and you have to make decisions on where to put your feet, and which configuration to use your hands in an instant. There are grade 7 routes that are simply overhanging staircases like you find at the indoor wall, and these are regarded as great fun outings by most climbers. When you graunch up a gorilla climb, there is very little elation in getting to the top, but when you onsight a fiendish technical 7a wall, the sense of achievement will stick with you for many years to come. Climbing at this level requires good bouldering skill, excellent fingertip and forearm stamina, and a high level of experience to read the moves. Most importantly of all however, is to keep a cool head throughout, and 'flow' up the climb. When you watch all good 'sport route' climbers, they seem to flow across the rock.

At this level you are also likely to start getting injuries, because of the hard nature of climbing combined with your sheer determination to succeed. Many climbers become fixated about a grade or a particular route, but whilst this gives them a goal, it more often than not, leads them to nasty injuries. No climber is the same, so it is impossible to gauge an improvement programme. But good rest between days climbing is essential, and doing a lot of easy warm up climbs during a day is paramount. I find that my 6,7,8th routes of the day are around my top level, and I spend routes 1-5, going up a grade or a half grade each time. One of the easiest types of injury is a clipping injury. At grade 7, you often have pockets or small holds to clip from and they are unsuitable, so because of the strain you are in – combined with anxiety and rope drag, you over crank to clip and pull a muscle. A good rule of thumb at this level, is to only ever clip from a good jug, or clip when you have passed the bolt.

You will also find that your fingertips start to get a real hammering in these grades, especially on semi-steep routes. Taping up the skin can really work well, and also has a wonderful but slightly cheating effect on sharp crozzley limestone. All the sharp crystals dig into the tape and grip superbly, you hardly have to grip with your muscles at all! The tape also does a huge amount to prevent your joints from being damaged by Goutes d'Eau, water droplet pockets.

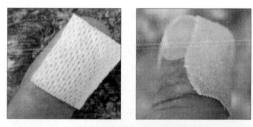

Always use an undertape on the soft fingerprint. Start taping across the nail to get a good grip, then work back up the finger to the second joint.

These sort of flutings are beautiful to look at, and to climb on, but you must respect the sharp edges. Good footwork saves rubber too.

INTRODUCTION

GIVE-IT-A-GO

IND/BOULDERING

OUT/BOULDERING

IMPROVEMENT

INDOOR SPORT

OUTDOOR SPORT

MULTI-PITCH

VIA FERRATA

WHERE TO GO

INDEX

There are lots of different ways to improve at sport climbing. For sure, time spent on your bouldering technique and skills is well worth it. If you can't even do the moves on a route, then your not in with a hope. Secondly - variety, you really need to climb on lots of different types of rock to learn all the different climbing techniques. The third and highly crucial part of improving, is confidence in your own ability. A good way to build confidence, is to climb with other people and exchange ideas on problems, work out different moves together, egg each other on, and set yourselves a few fun challenges. A lot of people when they are beginners, find things a bit difficult and remain very shy, they keep out of the way of 'expert boulderers' on the wall. Ironically, most good boulderers are more than happy to give a few minutes to help you as a beginner work out a problem and get on the right track, we were all there once upon a time. If you do want to improve – fast track, then seriously consider some help from a climbing coach. A climbing instructor, is somebody who specialises in teaching beginners the safety aspects of climbing and basic skills, and doesn't need more than a basic competence at safe climbing. A climbing mountain guide on the other hand, is someone who is a highly competent mountain climber and can actively guide 'and' look after clients in the mountains. A climbing coach is entirely different from either of these. They are someone who is personally very skilled at bouldering and sport climbing, and are often expert at analysing your climbing weaknesses. They can help you enormously both short term and long term, especially if your work doesn't allow you so much time to get out with other climbers of your ability. Climbing coaches also run special coaching holidays, enabling you to team up with other climbers of the same ability. You get a superb motivation from the coach, and normally go to a good climbing location. With the ratio of pupil to coach being so much higher, they will be very cost effective ways of getting top level coaching. Some very top level 'Climbers' run single day events called a Masterclass. This day, is entirely up to the Master giving the class. If you seek a top climber, famous for wild achievements – think, you might be in for a 'wild class.' The classes are usually practical sessions where you can participate with a top level climber for a few hours, and get an insight into the climbing mind of the Masterclass teacher.

A lucky group of girls, seducing an expert boulderer for tips and tricks; Jerry Moffatt, an incredible wealth of climbing knowledge and ability.

Going up through the climbing grades is fun and rewarding, you start climbing on steeper rock and in more impressive scenery. So why do the numbers keep on going up? It's as simple as bouldering, where the holds get smaller, and you get progressively more tired on longer and longer routes. It's very difficult to talk sensibly about the higher grades because it is more down to individual body mechanics, rather than any simple climbing principles. At grade 7a, you have to climb superbly, with all the perfect techniques and skills. Above that, you don't really have to know any more, or be a 'better climber,' you simply need to have more

BLANCHES FESSES 7c, Céüse, France; this stunning cliff has 200 routes of 7b & above.

fingertip strength, power and stamina. If you want to be tested as a pure climber, then 7a is just about as far as you need to go. There is one enticing thing though that gets to you, and that is rock architecture and scenery. You can get a 7a climb that is outrageously steep and 'out there,' but invariably you don't find them. The majority of 7a climbs are very steep, technical and have small holds. Sure they're impressive, but they're not wow impressive! When you get a big steep and leaning cliff, the routes just don't come that easy. It seems to be the natural

way of the world that 7b is the operating grade for most steep, 25m sections of rock (7c for 35m). The nooks and crannies, finger holds, toe edges etc, seem to demand constant *f*-6a and *f*-6b moves. It just naturally happens that 7b is the grade which gives climbing in the most constant, dramatic scenery. Above this grade, it just gets progressively harder with smaller holds and far harder bouldering moves. If you can get fit and strong, and work on your stamina enough to climb 7b, then the world is your oyster, enjoy it.

Nanette Raybaud resting happily on AVEC VUE SUR LA MER 7c, Sugiton, Marseille, France (1st ever, Women's world competition champion)

INTRODUCTION

GIVE-IT-A-GO

IND/BOULDERING

OUT/BOULDERING

IMPROVEMENT

INDOOR SPORT

OUTDOOR SPORT

MULTI-PITCH

VIA FERRATA

WHERE TO GO

INDEX

On 7b routes, getting the clips out is a problem in itself, requiring a multitude of techniques and giant swings; Ben Moon & Jerry Moffatt.

INTRODUCTION | GIVE-IT-A-GO | IND/BOULDERING | OUT/BOULDERING | IMPROVEMENT | INDOOR SPORT | OUTDOOR SPORT | MULTI-PITCH | VIA FERRATA | WHERE TO GO | INDEX

Just in case the photo of the Verdon Gorge doesn't say danger, then I should remind you that multi-pitch sport climbing is up another grade in the insanity chart to level 6, the highest we go in this book. It is a full grade more dangerous than general sport climbing, and please don't ever underestimate this. I would also like to make you aware that this sort of exposure can really freak some people out the first time they experience it. Exposure is what it's all about on multi-pitch, and it's not necessarily your cup of tea. Alternatively, some climbers get a real high from big drops and wonderful views, and end up climbing far better because of it. You certainly won't know how you'll react until you give it a go. I would suggest that you fully become acquainted with outdoor sport climbing for several years, before attempting anything super huge like the Verdon Gorge. On the other hand, there are many smaller multi-pitch climbs that you will be able to try, and become accustomed to the whole bigger environment.

We have laid out this section for anyone visiting a big area like the Verdon, so it can be used as a refresher-reminder before your trip. I have to again state, that whilst all climbing knowledge is useful, it is your decisions in making the right choice from your options at the time of climbing, that is the real key to sound climbing. Only you can decide if the weather is calm enough to attempt a climb that takes many hours, or how strong any of the belays are, or if you want to use a particular knot or abseil technique. Don't use outdoor multi-pitch climbing, for an experiment.

The first part of multi-pitch climbing, is environment assessment. You have a list of events that can happen, and you need to know how that will affect you. Time is critical, since you are now planning something that you simply can't just lower off when it starts to rain. Before you even go on a multi-pitch climb, take a record of timings for you to lead a normal 30-40 metre pitch. Then time how long your partner takes to second the climb. Since most climbers are a bit cautious when they begin multi-pitch climbs, you would be well advised to add 10 mins for a belay between pitches; sorting out your quickdraws and finding somewhere to hang comfortably. You can easily come up with 3-4 hours on a 3 pitch climb if you find it a bit tricky. During this time, you most probably will have a drink, maybe a chocolate bar, or even a fag - pending legislation of course, etc, etc. You'll probably have to put some sun tan cream on, and perhaps some lip salve as winds notoriously scream down river gorges. How many times do you put a jumper on and off, and how cold do you get if the sun goes in and stays in. These all point to the fact, that you want to damm well know what the weather is going to be doing, for the next 4 hours. The big problem in mountain areas, is that weather patterns are very local, and also can be changeable. You soon end up opting for, I'll take this just in case. A good multi-pitch climber, is someone who climbs in an area first and gets to know the local weather patterns as much as possible, before getting committed on anything more than a 2 pitch route. During this apprenticeship, you also find ways to make the weather work for you. You calculate when the sun will come onto a wall, and how it will affect you. Generally you will try to do the hardest parts of a route in the shade, then enjoy the sun on the easier sections.

There becomes a point however, when the weather is not comfort related, but life threatening. This is with lightning storms. In the UK, we don't have 'real' lightning storms - that I can promise you. In the Alpine areas of Central Europe, there are the most amazing and ferocious storms, which are simply beyond imagination. They're just like a cinema surround sound gone completely berzerk, with someone emptying full buckets of water on your head at the same time. You also have massive electric charges flashing down to earth that kill people. You, as a point sticking out from a big, flat, rockwall are like an attractive beacon to be incineratorarily zapped. If there is any possibility of lightning, you want to be out of there at least 2 hours beforehand. All across the Alps during summer on lovely hot days, you get cloud build up. Crescendo is around 4-5pm with amazing storms; they can come early or later, or fizzle out to nothing. You can also be on the lee side of a giant rock wall and not even see them building. Anybody still on a rockface in the Alps after 3 in the afternoon, is simply suicidal or has incredible visionary powers. This alone explains why a mountain guide in multi-pitch climbing, is superbly helpful, and especially so on your first visit to an area.

The sector Dalle Grises of the Verdon Gorge in France. One of the most perfect multi-pitch areas in the world, with lot of grade s-5/6b routes.

In sport climbing you always lower off, so generally 35-40 metres is the maximum length of pitch you are likely to find. In traditional-classic style climbing, you can get 50 metre pitches since there may be no natural belays at 35 metres and you just keep on going. On some cliffs, you get a mixture of classic and sport routes. What you have to remember, is that if you only have a 70 metre rope, then you only have 35 metres of abseil. Not a big issue on a bolted slab, but a complete pain if you are abseiling into free space. Without doubt, you do want to buy a local guidebook to a multi-pitch cliff that illustrates all the ab-points, so you can work out before hand, the rope length you are going to need. Sometimes ab-points are set at 50 metres apart, so you need 100 metres of rope, although the newer trend is to get this down to 40 metres.

There are 2 other types of rope that you can buy, double rope and twin rope. Double rope is specifically designed for trad-classic climbing, and works on the principle of 2 separate ropes going up in parallel as you climb. In trad climbing this is useful to cut down rope drag, but you might rely on just one of the ropes holding you in a fall, hence they are thick (if you're sensible) and will weigh around 50g a metre. If you were to take 2 of these on a route, they would weigh you down 5 kilos plus drag of perhaps another 5 kilos at the end of a 50 metre pitch! Try doing a font 6a move with 10 extra kilos when you're tired, a completely, ridiculous concept. The next option is to go for twin ropes that are used together as one, but allow you the double abseil length. These come at around 7.6 mm and weigh around 38g; immediately a saving of some 1.2 kilos plus a lot less drag. I prefer the option of going for a 100 metre, single rope and would choose a low diameter one of around 9.4 mm of 57g/p/m The advantage of this is at the end of a 50 metre pitch you only have 2.85 kilos of weight and extremely low drag. You can actually still enjoy climbing during the entire pitch and feel fantastic. Yes! It does get a bit boring having to pull all the extra rope through to the belay after the lead, but if it's the sport climbing that you enjoy, this is the one for you. For sure, the best compromise is an 80 meter 9.4 since you can nearly always find ab-points at 40 metre intervals. (Smaller dia. belay tube is essential).

Wobbly, abseiling down the Pichenibule headwall in the Verdon Gorges; knowing where you are going is crucial.

Dealing with abseiling in multi-pitch sport climbing, is a whole different issue to some fun abseiling at the indoor gym. There isn't any room for error, and you can be in wild situations, with some possible awful pickles awaiting you. Many climbers have their own abseil systems, and you can read many different opinions on how to approach this subject. There is no definitive way to abseil since you can never definitively say what is most dangerous part in abseiling. We show you the Dyno-mite method, which reduces equipment to an absolute minimum, and which gives me a safety back up system that I like, it is very quick and simple to use.

You first set up an abseil by threading your rope through a metal maillon or screwgate karabiner. Often you will come across giant rings to abseil from also. As soon as you thread one end through

In well developed areas like the Verdon, each sector is marked at the top, so you know where you are the first time you visit the cliff. Study the topo well to find the best descent for your chosen route.

the ring, tie a double figure-of-8 knot in the end. This has 2 objectives, primarily that you now have a complete ring of rope, and even if you drop it, then it won't disappear off to the bottom of the gorge. The knot has the added benefit of stopping you, should you try to abseil off the end of the rope into space! It does however, have the big disadvantage of getting stuck in anything that is going. Often you get high winds in gorges, your abseil knot can blow in the wind and get stuck in a tree some 20 metres to one side. On windy days like this, I always take around 12 loops of the end of the rope and with a quickdraw, make a quick release clip (similar to rope laying p.174). This bulk in the rope will weight it down, and carry it straight down in the line of the intended abseil. I would always recommend that you climb with a single length of rope, and do not tie 2 ropes together. Two ropes tied together gives you a knot that will jam all over the place. If you do decide to use 2 twin ropes, then follow the instructions for joining them together that come with the ropes and are given by the actual rope manufacturer, they may have special characteristics in their ropes.

On multi-pitch climbing, you will often use the rope that you are climbing with to tie into the belays. On an abseil descent, you need several tape slings for this instead. The most useful way it to have a double length

Many routes have specific ab-in points, like Wall of Woodoo; handy to know that you're abseiling into an 8a+!!!!

sling that you thread into your harness tie in loop, and which is often referred to as a cows tail. You can wrap it around your waist to take up the slack when you abseil. By having a double length sling, you have the option of using it single or double, to exactly control your comfort position at the belay. You make sure that the rope halfway mark is at the ab-point, before you attach your abseil tube. (See page 240 for general abseil threading.) I always clip immediately into my tube, so that if I need to reclip any quickdraws, I can do this straight in front of myself. Some climbers use extensions, but this gives you all sorts of headaches on big overhangs. After you have attached yourself to the rope for an abseil, you could descend, however, I find it far more comforting to have a backup system, since a belay tube does not lock up in the event of losing control. I use something called a 'tape spiral knot.' For this

You often have a choice of abseil points. Look for ones that have good slippery edges near them, which will assist you when trying to pull the rope down. The more points you thread, the harder it is to pull the rope through, you choose your own level of safety. At the top where they are set back, they are particularly difficult to pull through. Always, choose a left and a right rope end, and keep them separated at all times. Trying to pull through a rope that is twisted can prove impossible. Thinner ropes have less drag, and are easier to pull through, but remember to use a smaller version of a belay tube.

An early morning sunrise in the Verdon Gorges

INTRODUCTION
GIVE-IT-A-GO
IND/BOULDERING
OUT/BOULDERING
IMPROVEMENT
INDOOR SPORT
OUTDOOR SPORT
MULTI-PITCH
VIA FERRATA
WHERE TO GO
INDEX

INTRODUCTION

GIVE-IT-A-GO

IND/BOULDERING

OUT/BOULDERING

IMPROVEMENT

INDOOR SPORT

OUTDOOR SPORT

MULTI-PITCH

VIA FERRATA

WHERE TO GO

INDEX

Start with left hand and around 3 inches off the rope, then make 1 spiral around and down, then a 2nd and a 3rd. On the 4th pull around take the long end and pass it through the top loop. It is best to make the tape go fully tight on the top loop before pulling the long end back towards you. It is a knot that you might need to adjust to work perfectly every time. Note: Other types of gripping knot used with circular cord, do not work on new slippery ropes, so you should try out your method on your own rope and be satisfied with it per- sonally. To undo the knot, simply reverse as in photo 5, then pull the long end and it will unravel itself automatically and quickly.

I use a thin 12mm climbing tape of the short length. This spirals around the rope 4 times, and then goes up through a top loop and back down to a separate screwgate on the harness loop. You may need to adjust the number of turns according to your ropes. You then can have this knot in your left hand as you abseil, only 10cm above the tube. Any further away, it simply locks solid on the rope. I start to abseil without my hand on this spiral knot, just to make sure it is working. Then you have one last check to see that your 2 screwgate karabiners are done up, before unclipping yourself from the top belay.

When you abseil, always go down slowly and really survey the cliff as you go. You don't always want to look at the climb you are going to do, but you do want to know where other belays are. You must always keep an eye out for roofs and where the rope is hanging. If you come to a small roof, then bend your legs to go past it, otherwise your feet will simply go under it, and you will pendulum straight into the sharp

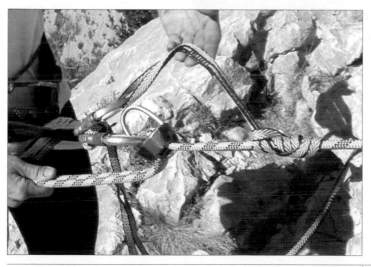

You always check that the spiral tape knot is working on the rope before abseiling. To release the spiral knot, simply pull up the rope with the left hand between the belay tube and the spiral knot, then lock off the tube with your right hand. You only need a few inches to release the knot and it is a very simple technique. If you cannot pull your body in with one arm, what on earth are you doing abseiling into a place like this! If you ever get into trouble, you can climb a rope using 2 of these knots.

! DYNO-MITE CAUTION ☠

If there are any loose stones around, seriously consider wearing a helmet.

INTRODUCTION

GIVE-IT-A-GO

IND/BOULDERING

OUT/BOULDERING

IMPROVEMENT

INDOOR SPORT

OUTDOOR SPORT

MULTI-PITCH

VIA FERRATA

WHERE TO GO

INDEX

Abseil technique: Feet slightly apart with the rope going down between the legs, left hand on the spiral tape knot easing it down; going slowly.

edge of the roof with your face! If you are abseiling an overhanging pitch, then you definitely need to clip into some of the bolts as you abseil. You must keep swinging in and out, so that you don't just end up dangling in space. If the abseil is slightly overhanging, you can easily control the rope with the right hand, then clip the quickdraws with the left hand. If the angle gets really silly and you need 2 hands, then the tape spiral will jam up, and you can put several turns around your thigh to make sure you don't go down the rope at all.

Since you have already put a double fig-of-8 in the end of the rope, you won't abseil off the end. There is one very slight benefit of the tape spiral above the abseil tube, in tests above a crash pad, I found it to lock automatically onto the end of the rope, if I abseiled off the end. It tended to grip with about 4 inches of rope left! I couldn't recommend this at all, but at least it could give you the slimmest of hope, if you made the double disaster of forgetting to tie a knot, and then abseiling off the end by mistake!

You also have to consider movement at a belay. If a rock falls from above, you need to pendulum out of the way. I always rely on a single point where I can easily pivot, but will often have this point backed up with another bolt. Only when you are belaying in a factor 2 situation, do you trap yourself in an equalising position on 2 bolts for that brief period. The procedure at the belay is set. First you add a tape sling with 2 karabiners to join any bolts together. Then you clip your main cows tail into one and let it take your full weight. Then you remove the spiral tape knot, and use that sling as a second back up sling. Only then do you take off your abseil tube. On a multi pitch abseil you would be then joined by your partner. I have a very strict method of pulling the rope through. You untie the ends of the rope, pass one through the abseil maillon, and then tie a double figure-of-8, three metres down the rope, and clip it into your harness tie-in loop. Then you can pull the rope through and it doesn't matter if you lose the end by mistake. When the other end comes down, you scoop it up and can tie the both ends together since you have enough slack. Then you have your loop to equalise out and get the centre mark at the maillon.

Always have a sling and 2 screwgates per climber.

Make sure to get your feet taking as much of your weight as possible.

INTRODUCTION
GIVE-IT-A-GO
IND/BOULDERING
OUT/BOULDERING
IMPROVEMENT
INDOOR SPORT
OUTDOOR SPORT
MULTI-PITCH
VIA FERRATA
WHERE TO GO
INDEX

There are times on a multi-pitch excursion when you may have to carry your own rope. Especially if there are group of you, and you can all utilise a common abseil descent to a terrace on a big wall. If you are setting up a common abseil with a spare rope, tie it fully into the belay ring so that it remains fixed. Then you will also have the possibility of ascending the rope if necessary. You don't want the faff with then having to carry a rope bag, also you also will have a considerable amount of rope to carry in an 80m or 100m rope. There are 2 convenient ways of organising a rope to be carried. We call it coiling a rope, but coiling is definitely not what you do, since that would put awful twists into it. I never ever, coil a rope. The principle is that you simply lay the rope

Make each loop about 2 ft. You need to start wrapping the rope around itself when there is about 8ft left. Wrap the rope around for 5-6 tight turns. Pull a double loop through the centre top, and then thread the remaining 5ft tails through it. These tails then can come over your shoulders, back around the rope crossing sides, then back in front of you. Here you can tie them together with a simple reef knot.

in short loops over your hand, going one way and then the other. When you palm becomes too small, you can transfer the loops to your neck. At the end, you can tie a variety of knots to stop the loops becoming undone. If you leave ends of around 2 metres, you can strap the rope quite easily to your back for an abseil. With a shorter rope, it is often easier to use the 'Spaghetti' method. This looks bizarre but is superb for setting up a top rope, since when you need to undo it, you simply clip the centre loop in the karabiner, and it will undo itself automatically under its own weight – no promises though! Again, if you leave long tails you can carry it easily.

> **! DYNO-MITE CAUTION**
> *Thieves target any cars left at the top of known abseil cliffs - don't leave anything in your car, and only leave water at the cliff top.*

The Spaghetti methodoni; you start with both tail ends of the rope together. At about 6 ft. you make several twists in the rope, then take a small amount of rope from the long end, and make another loop through. You keep doing this to give you a chain effect that simply undoes. When you get to the end (centre point), poke it through the last loop. Then take one of the tails and collect the centre loop, again with this tail thread it through the remaining rope as you half it. Continue to do this until you have a small bundle. Then tie both ends together with a reef knot. You can then tie it on your back in the same manner as opposite.

INTRODUCTION
GIVE-IT-A-GO
IND/BOULDERING
OUT/BOULDERING
IMPROVEMENT
INDOOR SPORT
OUTDOOR SPORT
MULTI-PITCH
VIA FERRATA
WHERE TO GO
INDEX

There are more names for this knot than any other knot (Italian being popular), but it is a hitch used in the Alps – simple. It is a superb concept, and when used, gives friction similar to that of the belay tube. You can even abseil on a single rope using this knot. You may pull a block off, knock out your belayer, who then slumps onto a locked Gri Gri! You can tie the rope off to a quickdraw, and abseil down the rope using this knot. You can also use it to belay a climber, should you ever drop your belay tube down the gorge! With our rope system, you will always have a screwgate karabiner with you on any sport route, which means you can use the Alpine hitch, to set up belay wherever, and whenever you want to. This knot was used before belay devices were invented. It's still used a lot in mountains because it is so quick. If you need to be moving very quickly in the Alps on a relatively easy route, you simply arrive at a belay ring & put a clove hitch on; then take in, put an Alpine hitch on, and the second climber starts to climb. You can do all of this instantly, and with gloves on. It's disadvan-

Clip a screwgate into the ring first, then slip on a clove hitch. Then hold the pear belay krab with your right hand little finger; then make a twist ending up behind the main rope; then scoop up the main rope with your thumb. You now have the karabiner quickly to hand and can clip it into the loop and then the belay. Do the screw up and you have belayed your partner.

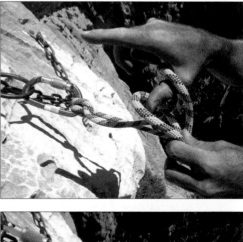

tages: It has a turn on the rope, that sits on one side of the karabiner. To change from taking in rope, to paying out rope, this turn has to flick through the karabiner and is really awkward – especially if you are needing to help someone with a bit of a tug seconding a hard section. Having a pear shaped karabiner helps you get the turn through the krab, (when you buy a krab for your belay tube, get a pear shaped one). You can abseil both single and double rope with the hitch, but it doesn't nicely separate the ropes like a belay tube. Note: there is a device called an eight-descender which is used for abseiling. It can be used, but also twists the rope like the Italian hitch, and is needless extra weight to carry.

These are a pair of river walking shoes. This Lizard model is extremely lightweight and comfortable. They are perfect for walking descents and fold flat against the back of your harness, an essential addition for M-P.

A wonderful twisted tree. Be extremely careful to avoid these, becasue they will catch your rope, and it is impossible to pull the rope out!

If you end up seconding a climb, you may get stuck under an overhang, and then swing out into space. Lowering off on a big cliff is not an option. Here you can use your short tape. Attach it as you would during an abseil to the rope in front of you and clip it into your harness loop with a screwgate, pull up tight. Now you use the long tape you have as a foot loop. Take it from your harness and attach it to the rope with a tape spiral knot – above the main harness one. (You can never remember which way around – but it soon becomes obvious). You can now put one foot in the long tape loop – that is

Alain Guinet smiling, when Wobbly asked him about length. (The Verdon guides use a 200 metre static rope, so clients can abseil directly down to the Jardin des Écureuils in one easy go.)

only attached to the rope, and stand up. It is then easy to just slide the main spiral up the rope. If you do anything wrong in this situation, you are still tied on anyway.

! DYNO-MITE CAUTION ☠

Be cautious when walking about the tops of cliffs since they are favourite sunbathing spots for snakes!

INTRODUCTION | GIVE-IT-A-GO | IND/BOULDERING | OUT/BOULDERING | IMPROVEMENT | INDOOR SPORT | OUTDOOR SPORT | MULTI-PITCH | VIA FERRATA | WHERE TO GO | INDEX

Going off to the Alpine areas of Europe should be an impressive holiday, especially for anyone living in the UK with it's diddy little hills. Welcome to the grand mountains of Europe that soar up to 3000 metres and even higher. The whole concept of Via Ferrata's are superb, you can swiftly skip up a mountain track, and then be hanging off vertical rock in the most wild places without any faffing of ropes and quickdraws. For the enthusiastic climber, the only drawback is that they are a bit soft and easy if you're a 7a rockspider. They are usually graded from 1-5, but on a sport climbing scale, grade 5 is about equal to 3a – plus you have a cable to pull on anyway. You climb a Via Ferrata more for the scenery than the technical difficulty of the actual climbing. It's also something nice and different to do, especially when the weather could be slightly fickle. When you get into multi-pitch routes in the big mountains, you will soon realise that if the sun goes in, you can really get frozen on a route and find it pretty ghastly. On a Via Ferrata, you keep moving and warm, you are often up and down quite quickly, and have time to enjoy some stunning vertical scenery.

As an ardent climber by now, you also may go off on summer holiday with your families and friends who aren't committed rockies. Introducing them to a Via Ferrata can be a fabulous day out for you all, so long as you all know what you are doing, and can operate with a good level of knowledge and equipment. Because of the rise in popularity of Via Ferrata routes, you can often rent a harness with special Via Ferrata lanyards, and a helmet. You should also make sure that you are all insured at the same time, since if there is an accident, the rescue will be highly expensive. Insurance can be obtained by a variety of different specialist companies, but often by joining a club like the Austrian Alpine Club, a basic insurance is included for general climbing, Via Ferrata and Skiing rescues. In France, the national F.F.M.E. is likely to offer similar options.

Mountain areas are generally run by quite sensible authorities, and you rarely get a conflict of activities. When you have wonderful cliffs with clean sweeping sections of nice rock, they see this as perfect sport climbing terrain, and reserve it as such. When you get an area with a lot of loose rock but a few solid sections, they put a Via Ferrata up the solid sections since, there won't be anyone going up the loose areas!

The dangers of climbing Via Ferrata's is mixed, but must be regarded as highly dangerous. You have a bad concoction of circumstances, very high mountains, lightning storms, treacherous ground around the routes, loose rock, and the area being full of novices! High alpine via ferrata's, deserves a full rating of 6 on our insanity scale. The nice part however, it is relatively simple to contain the danger level with quite basic and easy precautions. It is an activity that is objectively dangerous, but at no time do you really need to take silly risks like the higher levels of climbing.

Cloud on the Tofana Mezzo, making the routes a miserable proposition; maybe time for a Via Ferrata

Wobbly tackling the SOSAT via ferrata, grade 2 (B), Brenta Dolomits, Italy. (Crozzon di Brenta 3115m, in the background)

INTRODUCTION
GIVE-IT-A-GO
IND/BOULDERING
OUT/BOULDERING
IMPROVEMENT
INDOOR SPORT
OUTDOOR SPORT
MULTI-PITCH
VIA FERRATA
WHERE TO GO
INDEX

Wherever you go in Europe, you will find different styles of protection on Via Ferrata routes. They follow the basic principle where there is a thick wire cable, running up steep ground that you climb. At certain points along the cable, it will be attached to the rock face. That is it – end of story. It is up to you the climber how you use this cable, and how much you trust in the cable. You have both the facility of a protection system, as well as a pure climbing aid. Lets suffice to say, grip cable in hand, pull and repeat with the other hand etc. In a lot of areas, the Via Ferrata routes are 'enjoyed' apparently in all weathers, which will often explain why there is a cable running across a smooth easy angled slab. When it's slightly rained and dropped in temperature to just below freezing, the 1000 metre drop only a few yards away, will ensure your tightest gripping of the cable. On a hot, sunny dry day, you would simply saunter down the slab, completely quizzical as to why anyone needs the cable there. If you're not strong enough or get tired, your hand simply uncurls on the wire and away you go. The obvious answer is to put on a climbing harness and have a sling ready to clip in, then take a rest when your hand gets tired. For experienced and strong climbers, this is quite a practical solution since all you are doing is utilising some equipment to rest if need be. If you are not experienced, or in any way at all could fall, then you need to consider two areas; how to stop - similar to a climbing fall (please read pages 203-208 first), and judgement of the strength in the actual cable attachment points.

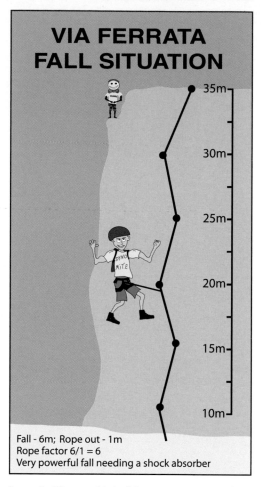

VIA FERRATA FALL SITUATION

35m
30m
25m
20m
15m
10m

Fall - 6m; Rope out - 1m
Rope factor 6/1 = 6
Very powerful fall needing a shock absorber

We know that a falling body gains energy, with increased speed of your body. Normally we use a long climbing rope as a shock absorber to slow down. If you are simply clipped into a cable with a 1 metre piece of rope, then fall 5 metres to the next attachment point to the rock, you will fall 6 metres in total. 'You' would most probably break if you instantly stopped, and could easily pull out the wire attachment point. You could of course just carry 5 metres of rope for this instance. However, the area around Via Ferrata's is pretty rocky, and there are also usually other people that you could knock or even seriously injure. Fortunately there is a much better system available. You can use a short shock absorber system. Most equipment manufacturers now make a specialist Via Ferrata system set of

lanyards. The top third of the system contain 2 lanyards with karabiners on, and are joined at the yoke. From here, a 1.5m section of climbing rope is used. The climber is attached to this at the top near the yoke with a braking device that can slide down the 1.5m section, if loaded with very high force. The two obvious factors being; the device descent rate, and a stopper at the end of the rope. By obtaining a product, designed exactly for this falling principle, you will have gone a long way to reducing your own risk factor, and to other climbers around you.

You must still seriously consider the actual substantiality of the whole Via Ferrata itself. There has been a disaster in history of a section of one pulling out

You can get special Via Ferrata karabiners for the end of each lanyard. They are spring loaded on the gate with a quick clip mechanism. Considering you may clip and unclip many hundred times, it is a balance between speed and safety.

A helmet is considered essential in Via Ferrata. This is because there will be many other people around, and you will definitely get small stones coming down from time to time. You must still be careful and aware, since even a helmet will not save you if a big lump of rock lands on your head!

Even though the force generated in a fall is big, deceleration still happens, You can get full body harnesses that spread the fall impact across the whole body. To be considered if you were also wearing a fully laden rucksac. If you are just day tripping, then you will want to be as comfortable as possible, so a normal sit harness is all that I use.

Gloves can be useful, but it is likely to be hot and you will get very sweaty, very quickly. They are worth carrying, since when you are high up in the mountains, you can go around a big buttress and into the shade. Any steel ladders or wires will then be ice cold and pretty uncomfortable. Carrying a small little sac is great for cameras, lunch, gloves, water, and ya business mobile eh! You will want spare warm clothes, and if you go to mountain areas; definitely take a guidebook in English.

This brake comes all in a special set from Petzl. The length of the lanyards are ideal, and the brake itself is very simple and effective. When attaching to a harness follow the manufacturers instructions; maillon, larks foot etc. You may fall awkwardly, and the link to your harness could be loaded in an unpredictable direction, therefore this link in principle should be the highest possible in all directions and fully locked up. (A karabiner with a low cross gate strength, would not be recommended.)

with people on it. Just like all forms of climbing, you must assess the situation. You could be somewhere, with hundreds of pasta filled tubbies, all leaping off the Via Ferrata at the same time with their non-shock absorbing systems. Simply assess the number of people on a route, examine how well the attachment points are, and make sensible judgement on the safety of the situation for yourself.

Maps are usually available locally, English guidebooks are not! Cicerone Dolomites.

INTRODUCTION

GIVE-IT-A-GO

IND/BOULDERING

OUT/BOULDERING

IMPROVEMENT

INDOOR SPORT

OUTDOOR SPORT

MULTI-PITCH

VIA FERRATA

WHERE TO GO

INDEX

To use a lanyard is simple, you clip one end (a) on the wire and the other (b) on your harness loop. Then when you get to a stanchion (fixed point), you simply attach the other end (b) to the next section of wire, and unclip (a) onto your harness for carrying. Most people leave both ends on the wire all the time, gripping together with one hand. If you have to clip it onto something after you have taken if off, then you might as well clip it onto the wire. Then you push them both on together. On steep ladders, put one arm through completely up to the armpit when clipping; this keeps you well in balance, is a powerful lever, and is strength saving.

Nearly all dodgy sections will have substantial wire cables. Some big ladders do no though. When things get hairy, you often find the gaps between the fixings down to 1 metre apart - especially on the newer 'sport Via Ferrata's.' A route like this one, is an exhausting and complete full body work out of 1000 metres, and take a 7 hour round trip.

PUNTA ANNA-GIANNI AGLIO; TOFANA MEZZO (highest grade 5-C); a wonderful position above Cortina, Dolomites, Italy

Views on G-A/Tofana; the route goes up the outrageous giant wall to the right of the huge shaded pillar! The crux section with a big drop - eeek!

INTRODUCTION

GIVE-IT-A-GO

IND/BOULDERING

OUT/BOULDERING

IMPROVEMENT

INDOOR SPORT

OUTDOOR SPORT

MULTI-PITCH

VIA FERRATA

WHERE TO GO

INDEX

North Central West:
- **Rochdale (p39)**
- **Liverpool (p175)**
- **Marple (p133)**
- Clitheroe
- Blackburn
- Burnley
- Warrington
- Salford
- Oldham
- Chester

Wales:
- Prestatyn
- Conway
- Llanwrst
- Capel Curig
- Bangor
- Llangefni
- Plas Menai
- Waenfawr
- Pwellhi
- Barmouth
- Machylleth
- Swansea
- Cardiff
- Bargoed
- Llangorse
- Brecon
- Hereford

South West:
- **Gloucester (p209)**
- Bristol
- Wells
- Street
- Taunton
- **Bude (p133)**
- Buckfastleigh
- Ivybridge
- Plymouth

- ☐ Leading facility
- ■ Bouldering facility

North West:
- **Kendal (p202)**
- Carlisle
- Cockermouth
- Penrith
- Keswick
- Ambleside
- Barrow
- Ingleton
- Lancaster
- Blackpool
- Southport

Central :
- **Nottingham (p62)**
- Wirksworth
- Shepshed
- Leicester
- Rutland
- **Birmingham (p33)**
- Stourbridge
- Coventry
- Martley

South:
- **Wimborne (p209)**
- Bournemouth
- Calshot
- Southampton
- Portsmouth
- Bognor Regis
- Basingstoke
- Oxford
- Swindon
- Towcester
- Bloxham
- Bedford

North East:
- **Newton Aycliffe (p197)**
- Newcastle
- Cramlington
- Hepburn
- Sunderland
- Hartlepool
- Billingham

North Central East:
- **Leeds (p202)**
- Guisley
- Huddersfield
- Hull
- **Sheffield Edge (p145)**
- Sheffield Foundry
- Sheffield Matrix

East:
- **Stowmarket (p62)**
- Ipswich
- Peterborough
- Kings Lynn
- Norwich
- Wymondham
- Lowestoft
- Mepal
- Cambridge

South East:
- **London Castle (I-b-cover)**
- **London Westway (p15)**
- **London Mile End (p59)**
- London Sobel
- Uxbridge Brunel
- **Amersham (p192)**
- **Crowborough (p33)**
- Hatfield
- Basildon
- Hockwell
- Upminster
- Rochester
- Canterbury
- Shoreham
- Redhill
- Guildford
- Godalming

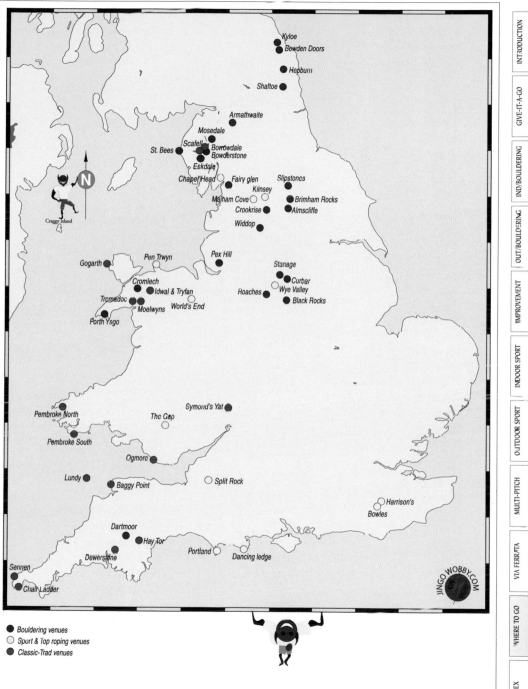

Kyloe
Bowden Doors
Hepburn
Shaftoe
Armathwaite
Mosedale
Scafell
St. Bees
Borrowdale
Bowderstone
Eskdale
Chapel Head
Fairy glen
Slipstones
Kilnsey
Malham Cove
Brimham Rocks
Crookrise
Almscliffe
Widdop
Pex Hill
Gogarth
Pen Trwyn
Stanage
Cromlech
Curbar
Tremadoc
Idwal & Tryfan
Roaches
Wye Valley
Moelwyns
World's End
Black Rocks
Porth Ysgo
Craggy Island
Pembroke North
Symond's Yat
The Gap
Pembroke South
Ogmore
Lundy
Split Rock
Baggy Point
Harrison's
Bowles
Dartmoor
Hay Tor
Sennen
Dewerstone
Portland
Dancing ledge
Chair Ladder

JINGO WOBBY.COM

● Bouldering venues
○ Sport & Top roping venues
● Classic-Trad venues

Full and comprehensive details, to every indoor wall, outdoor wall, climbing shops, bouldering areas and outside cliffs; are included in our Climber's Handbook to England and Wales.

INTRODUCTION
GIVE-IT-A-GO
IND/BOULDERING
OUT/BOULDERING
IMPROVEMENT
INDOOR SPORT
OUTDOOR SPORT
MULTI-PITCH
VIA FERRATA
WHERE TO GO
INDEX

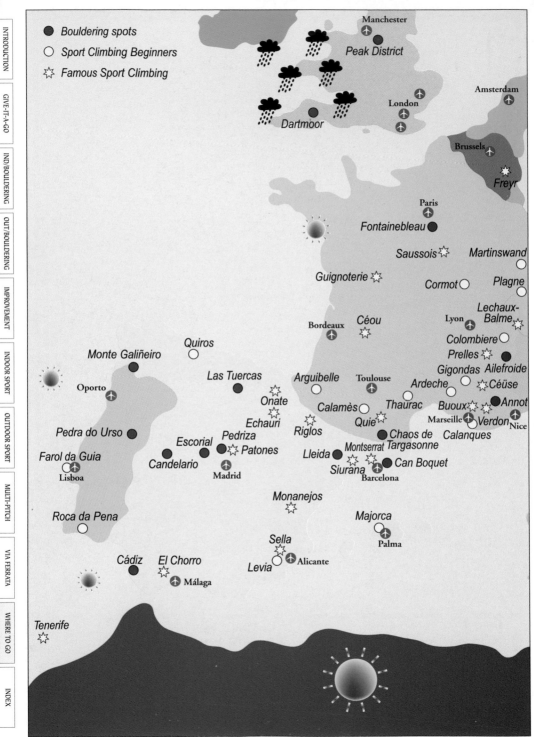

- ● Bouldering spots
- ○ Sport Climbing Beginners
- ☆ Famous Sport Climbing

Manchester
Peak District
Amsterdam
London
Brussels
Dartmoor
Freyr
Paris
Fontainebleau
Saussois
Martinswand
Guignoterie
Cormot
Plagne
Lechaux-Balme
Céou
Lyon
Bordeaux
Colombiere
Quiros
Prelles
Monte Galiñeiro
Las Tuercas
Arguibelle
Toulouse
Gigondas
Ailefroide
Oporto
Onate
Calamès
Ardeche
Céüse
Echauri
Thaurac
Buoux
Annot
Pedra do Urso
Escorial
Pedriza
Riglos
Quie
Marseille
Verdon
Nice
Farol da Guia
Patones
Lleida
Montserrat
Chaos de
Targasonne
Calanques
Candelario
Madrid
Siurana
Can Boquet
Lisboa
Barcelona
Monanejos
Roca da Pena
Majorca
Palma
Cádiz
El Chorro
Sella
Levia
Alicante
Málaga
Tenerife

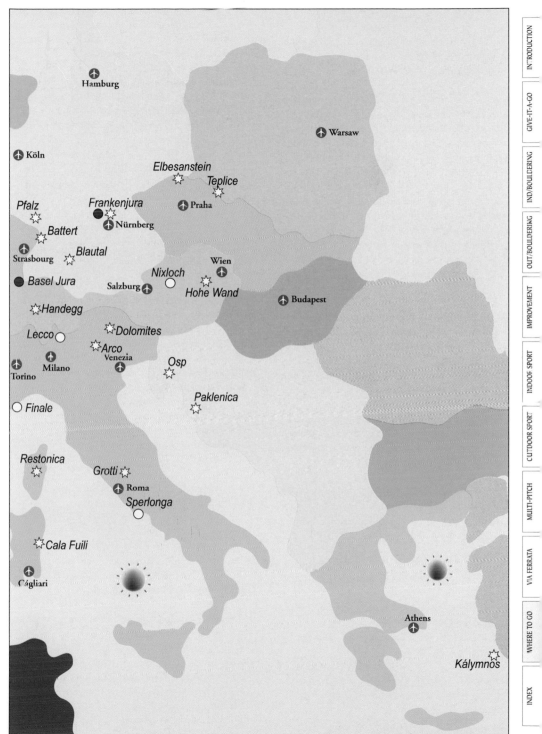

INTRODUCTION

GIVE-IT-A-GO

IND/BOULDERING

OUT/BOULDERING

IMPROVEMENT

INDOOR SPORT

OUTDOOR SPORT

MULTI-PITCH

VIA FERRATA

WHERE TO GO

INDEX

Just in case you think that the climbers photographed in this book are staged actors, here is a bit about some of them so you can see that they're not quite beginners.

Chris Cubitt: (p63) He is one of Britain's leading men climbers of today. He is a good lightweight sport climber and now ticks 8c routes in record time, alongside winning the British indoor sport climbing title; now a world superstar in ice/mixed.

Mark Edwards: (p100,167) Mark grew up in Cornwall and has dominated the scene over the past 20 years with the hardest new routes of area. He climbs mainly traditional routes, and has kept a constant output of E6-E9 adventures. His talent show through in his outrageous soloing of just about anything going.

Loïc Fossard: (p130) A super talented climber from the Alsace region in France. Has climbed many routes of 8a/b and blitzed the English Gritstone when he visited, sound talent.

Stephen Glennie: (p169) Studying medicine, when he should be climbing instead!

Neil Gresham: (p70) Neil is a top level climber dedicatied to coaching and Masterclass teaching. He writes for Climber magazine on training methods regularly.

Dave Henderson: (p111,149, 165) The elusive man from Dartmoor, yet boulderer extrodinare. Super strong fingered and very cool headed, has ticked just about everything on the moors.

Ian Hill: (p123) Self confessed bouldering addict, always to be seen crimping something or another.

Tyler Landman: (p82,121) Young Tyler is a mean climber for a shortie, cranking out font 7a, yet only 1.5metres high, should improve with age and growth.

Jeff Landman: (p111) A youngster on the scene, winning the British youth indoor bouldering champs, in 2003.

Jerry Moffatt: (p60,82) One of the greatest climbers of all time. In 1984 he did the 1st ascent of a route THE FACE, the first 8a in Germany, then following soon after with REVELATIONS, the first 8a+ in Britain. He onsighted CHIMPANZADROME 7c+, which was 2 grades harder than anything done in the world at the time. He went on to climb the all hardest routes, all over the world on every type of rock. He climbed Germany's first 8b+, and then Britain's first 8c LIQUID AMBER in 1990. He has bouldered at the top level all his life, and there is a legacy of his problems just about everywhere in Britain.

Ben Moon: (p95,125,150,162) A complete legend and incredibly strong climber. He shocked the world when he put up his first route at the age of 16, called STATEMENT OF YOUTH 8a. He then went on to literally blitz the British climbing scene with grade 8 routes. In FRANCE he climbed and jovially named the worlds first 8c, AGINCOURT. His route in 1991 HUBBLE, although the world's first 8c+, is considered by most to be 9a. His bouldering is incredible with numerous font 8b problems to his name. Winner of bouldering competitions just about everywhere.

André Neres: (p89) He won the Portuguese climbing and bouldering competition in 2003, and is now the leading young climber in both bouldering, and sport routes.

Jon Partridge: (p152) A climbing instructor often found at Amersham wall, highly talented and helpful, knows all the techniques superbly.

Simon Young: (p159) Devon bouldering addict, more often found in Fontainebleau as he has severe Sandstone withdrawl problems. Running a specialist bouldering & climbing venue at Bude.

Acknowledgements: A thank you to everyone who has helped in the production of this book. My special thanks to all the indoor walls that helped with the production and support; Wobbly for modeling, Sandy Ogilvie for some excellent photography, John Gibbons and Stow Kelner for proof reading, Wobbly for her nice T shirts; especially anyone who unfortunately didn't make it into the final edit.

INTRODUCTION · GIVE-IT-A-GO · IND/BOULDERING · OUT/BOULDERING · IMPROVEMENT · INDOOR SPORT · OUTDOOR SPORT · MULTI-PITCH · VIA FERRATA · WHERE TO GO · INDEX